Intermediate Teacher's Book

D0120550

New Headway
English Course

Liz & John Soars

Oxford University Press

Oxford University Press
Great Clarendon Street, Oxford OX2 6DP

Oxford New York
Athens Auckland Bangkok Bogota Bombay
Buenos Aires Calcutta Cape Town Dar es Salaam
Delhi Florence Hong Kong Istanbul Karachi
Kuala Lumpur Madras Madrid Melbourne
Mexico City Nairobi Paris Singapore
Taipei Tokyo Toronto Warsaw

OXFORD and OXFORD ENGLISH are trade marks of
Oxford University Press

ISBN 0 19 470224 3

© Oxford University Press 1996

First published 1996
Third impression 1997

No unauthorized photocopying

All rights reserved. No part of this publication may be
reproduced, stored in a retrieval system, or transmitted,
in any form or by any means, electronic, mechanical,
photocopying, recording or otherwise, without the prior
written permission of Oxford University Press.

This book is sold subject to the condition that it shall not,
by way of trade or otherwise, be lent, resold, hired out, or
otherwise circulated without the publisher's prior consent
in any form of binding or cover other than that in which it
is published and without a similar condition including this
condition being imposed on the subsequent purchaser.

Printed in Hong Kong

**The authors and publisher are grateful for permission
to reproduce the following copyright material:**
p 147 'An interview with Sarah Jenkins', adapted from
       'Memorable Moments' by Catherine Wrangham,
       Modern English Teacher
       (Vol 4 No 4) by permission.

Illustrations by: Gordon Hendry
Maps by: OUP Technical Graphics Department
Design by: Holdsworth Associates, Isle of Wight
Stop and checks and **Progress tests by:** Tim Falla

Contents

Introduction

The original *Headway Intermediate* was the first coursebook we wrote in the series, and inevitably we learned a lot from the writing of it. Teachers from all over the world have not only told us what they *did* like about it, but also what they *didn't* like about it. We were very keen to try again at this level because we wanted to rectify what we perceived as imbalances. Hence the *New Headway Intermediate*!

Features retained

- The basic approach and methodology are the same. We take what we see as the best of traditional approaches, and the more recent communicative approaches, and blend them.
- Grammar has a high profile. There are clear Presentations in each unit. The essential rules of form and use are given in the Language Review in the body of the unit.
- The Grammar Reference section at the back of the Student's Book provides further information about the target language. Structures are compared and contrasted, and common mistakes are listed.
- There are a lot of practice activities. These vary from being very controlled and mechanical, to semi-controlled where students have a little more freedom, to totally free.
- Activities are personalized at every opportunity. This gives the students the chance to talk about themselves, and to learn about their fellow students.
- There is a strong lexical component.
- There is at least one activity for speaking, listening, reading and writing in every unit.
- The reading and listening texts all have an authentic source (but see at New Features).
- Clear headings guide teachers and students through each unit so that everyone knows what they are doing. This makes it possible for teachers to be flexible – you can go into the book and out of it as you wish.

New features

- Nearly all the texts, in both the presentation and skills sections, are new. Not only were *we* tired of the old material, but teachers teaching it must be, too.
- The grammatical syllabus is new. The amount and the level of the grammatical input has been increased. We feel the syllabus fits more appropriately between the pre-intermediate and the upper-intermediate books.
- Most of the lexical inputs are new.
- Most of the writing syllabus is new.
- There is a *Test your grammar* section at the beginning of every unit. This short activity aims to orientate students to the language work of the unit, and allows them to show off what they already know or at least can recognize.
- There is a PostScript section at the end of each unit. This provides the teacher with an opportunity to introduce and revise some functional and situational areas.
- All the reading and listening texts have an authentic source, but many of them have been adapted to suit the intermediate level.

Organization

Student's Book

The unit structure is similar to *Headway Elementary* and *Headway Pre-Intermediate*. The Presentation and Practice sections come at the beginning of the unit. These are followed by the skills work and vocabulary work. Finally there is a PostScript section.

Test your grammar

This is a new feature. It seems to us a useful way to start a unit at this level. On the one hand, intermediate students know a lot about various areas of the language, on the other hand, they can very rarely produce a sentence which doesn't contain any mistakes.

The aim of *Test your grammar* is to orientate students to the language work that is to come. It is also an opportunity for them to show you how much they already know about the area. Intermediate students are always very keen to tell their teacher *We do this already in last year ago before*. Most of the activities in this section are for recognition rather than production.

It is essential that you do the *Test your grammar* section quickly. Unit 1 and Unit 7 are both times when you might be starting a new course with a new group of students, so the *Test your grammar* in these units also serves as an ice-breaker, get-to-know-each-other type of activity. You could allow these to go on for a bit. But in every other unit of the book, you should aim to do the *Test your grammar* in less than five minutes. If you linger too long, and ask students to analyse too deeply, there is the risk that the Presentation section is pre-empted. Students may become confused, and start to ask you all sorts of questions that you didn't want to have to answer at that stage of the lesson. So if you see seeds of doubt and furrowed brows, tell your students not to worry, and move on to the the security of the Presentation section!

PRESENTATION

There are nearly always two Presentations per unit. The target language is contextualized to illustrate the meaning, and appears in either a reading or a listening text, but usually both. Students are given a task which highlights the new grammar, and then are asked Grammar questions to draw attention to the rules of form and use.

PRACTICE

There is a variety of exercise types involving all four skills. There are repetition drills, transformation drills, pronunciation exercises, mingle activities, information

gap exercises and discussions. Students work on their own, in pairs, and in groups. There is a mixture and a balance of both pre-communicative and genuinely communicative activities, and of course, personalization runs throughout.

The Practice activities should not be done one after the other all at once. Students would become bored by too much controlled work. Break the activities up, do some in class and some for homework. You can do a Practice activity as revision at the start of the next lesson. Make sure you get a balance of controlled and free work in each lesson.

LANGUAGE REVIEW

This summarizes the input and gives students a written record of what they have learned, together with some illustrative examples.

In the Teacher's Book, we suggest when it might be appropriate for students to translate the sample sentences containing the target language. If you have a monolingual group (and you speak their language), translation can be a very powerful tool to confirm understanding. If misunderstandings ensue, it is usually because students argue about L1, not English.

There is some translation work in the *Stop and check* exercises at the back of this Teacher's Book.

SKILLS WORK

All the texts have an authentic source. The listening texts come mainly from interviews with real people, but there are also songs, radio programmes, charity appeals, poems and a lecture on the geography of Britain. The reading texts are from newspapers, magazines, biographies, short stories and literature.

We have tried to make the texts shorter and more manageable than in the original book. Where we thought it appropriate, we have graded the texts to make them more accessible for the level. There is so much for intermediate students to learn that it seems unfair to overburden them with low-frequency, obscure vocabulary.

VOCABULARY

As in all the *Headway* series, there is a very strong lexical syllabus. There are at least two vocabulary inputs per unit in the Student's Book, and at least one more in the Workbook.

Many of the vocabulary exercises have a pronunciation element.

We adopt three approaches to the teaching of vocabulary:
• We teach new words in a lexical set, for example, the weather, art, and literature.

- We encourage good vocabulary learning habits, for example, using a dictionary.
- We work on the systems of vocabulary, for example, multi-word verbs, prefixes and suffixes, synonyms, antonyms, homonyms, homophones, silent letters, compound nouns, and collocation. We do a lot of work on collocation in this book.

These approaches are integrated to varying degrees into the vocabulary sections of each unit.

Encourage your students to buy a small notebook to keep records of the words they come across. They could record the English word, the part of speech, and a translation. They could add an example sentence and the pronunciation if they were very keen! Be prepared for your students *not* to keep vocabulary records. It is too much work for the average learner, but this is not a reason for you not to encourage them to do so.

PRONUNCIATION

Pronunciation work is integrated throughout. There are always examples of the target language on tape for repetition purposes. Salient features of pronunciation are highlighted and practised when necessary.

The phonetic script is introduced in a simple manner in appropriate exercises, and the phonetic chart appears on the inside back cover of both the Student's Book and the Workbook for ease of reference.

There is also systematic pronunciation work in every unit of the Workbook.

PostScript

This is a new feature at the intermediate level, although there is a similar section called *Everyday English* in the two lower levels of *Headway*. It affords the teacher another opportunity to do some input. Functional, situational, and survival skills are presented and practised.

Workbook

The Workbook exercises reinforce the target language of the unit. They usually go from recognition to production.

There are several other features:
- An extra input of a related grammatical area
- A pronunciation exercise
- An exercise on grammatical terminology (Unit 1)
- An exercise on prepositions in every odd-numbered unit
- An exercise on multi-word verbs in every even-numbered unit

Teacher's Book

This Teacher's Book provides numerous ideas for using the course materials as well as the expected features such as answer keys and photocopiable materials. We try to show how to use the material flexibly and appropriately.

Tests

There is a *Stop and check* after every three units, and a *Progress test* after Unit 6 and Unit 12. These are at the back of the Teacher's Book for you to photocopy.

Video

There is an optional accompanying video in two parts:
- A light-hearted drama in six episodes, called *Wide Open Spaces*, about a couple who get tired of the town and try country life.
- Six short factual reports on a range of topics of general interest: seven wonders of Britain, the crime writer Agatha Christie, WOMAD (the World Organization of Music and Dance), London taxi drivers, Rugby (one of the most famous public schools in Britain), and the importance of the sea for Britain.

Finally!

Teachers are constantly making decisions, both in the preparation and execution of their lessons. We hope that *New Headway Intermediate* helps you in this process of decision-making, and that you and your students enjoy using the book.

Liz and John Soars

What a wonderful world!

Auxiliary verbs
Social expressions

Profile

Student's Book

Language
- auxiliary verbs *do, be, have*
- *have/have got*
- grammatical terms for tenses
- Present/Past Simple, Perfect, Continuous usages
- active and passive
- forming questions and negatives
- *'s = is* or *has*
- short answers

Pronunciation
- auxiliary verbs and emphasis
- intonation for *wh-* questions
- contrastive stress
- silent letters
- recognizing the phonetic alphabet

Vocabulary and everyday English
- discoveries and inventions
- useful social expressions
- silent letters

Workbook
- extra grammar – *have/have got*
- vocabulary – networks as a way of building and recording vocabulary
- pronunciation – recognizing the phonetic script
- verbs + prepositions
- grammatical terminology

Video
- Report 1 *Seven Wonders of Britain*

Photocopiable materials for this unit (TB page 119)
- This is information for the Speaking activity on SB page 9.

Photocopiable materials for this unit (TB page 119)
- This is information for the Speaking activity on SB page 9.

Introduction to the unit

As you begin *New Headway Intermediate*, you are possibly starting a new course with a new group of students. If so, your most important aim is that everyone gets to know each other and you. See if they can learn each other's names and find out a little bit about their backgrounds and interests. The *Test your grammar* section which starts the unit has a dual purpose. It is designed to help students learn a little about each other as well as testing them on their use of auxiliary verbs.

The theme of the first unit is our world, where we try to take a global view of various aspects of our lives today. The reading text is about the seven wonders of the modern world and in the listening, three people discuss their ideas about modern wonders. The first documentary on *Headway Video Intermediate* is *Seven Wonders of Britain*.

Language aims

Grammar
Auxiliary verbs

We try to take a global view of the language in Unit 1 by focusing on the auxiliary verbs which form the different tenses. This allows the teacher to assess the students' knowledge of verb forms they should be familiar with, but which they may have difficulty in using correctly, for example Present Simple and Continuous, Past Simple and Continuous, Present Perfect Simple and Continuous, future forms, active and passive, and short answers. Expect students to make mistakes in all these areas at this level!

The emphasis in Unit 1 is on the *formation* of the tenses. All of them are revisited in later units and examined in greater depth to explore similarities and differences of *meaning,* and to provide extensive discriminatory practice.

Obviously there is some focus on meaning as well as form in Unit 1 because students are using language in context. But remember that you are reminding learners of what they (should/might) know, so when mistakes occur don't try to teach the whole of the English language in the first few lessons.

Note that the passive voice is not dealt with in its own unit. It is presented along with the active equivalent in Units 2, 3 and 7. There is an introduction to the passive on page 144 of the Grammar Reference section.

Question forms

Learners have perennial problems forming questions in English. They need to use an auxiliary verb, and if there isn't one in the statement, they need to use *do/does/did*. In many languages questions can be formed simply with a rising intonation, but in nearly all questions in English the subject and verb are inverted. There are at least five activities in Unit 1 that practise question formation.

have/have got

Have/have got are also forms that present endless difficulties for obvious reasons.

PROBLEMS

- *Have got* is present perfect in form, but present in meaning.
- *have got* doesn't require *do/does* to form the question and negative.
- The full verb *have* with *did* is the favoured form to refer to the past, and must be used in the present to express habitual activities: *I have a meeting every Monday*; *What time do you have lunch?*
- People say that *have* as a full verb is more common in American English, but it is becoming more frequent in British English, too.

This area is presented formally in *Headway Elementary* and *Headway Pre-Intermediate*. In this book it does not have its own Presentation. It is practised frequently, especially in the first three units, so be ready to sort out problems which are bound to occur. There is an explanation on page 143 of the Grammar Reference section, and further explanation and a practice exercise on page 8 of the Workbook.

Vocabulary

In the vocabulary section, there are two exercises on the relationship between sounds and spelling in English. Students are encouraged to refer to the phonetic symbols on the inside back cover of the Intermediate Student's Book and Workbook of *New Headway English Course*, and they will become familiar with this chart as they work through the course.

PostScript

Various social expressions, some informal and some not, are introduced and practised. They have been selected in the hope that they will be used during the rest of the course, as normal day-to-day interactions take place between all the people in the class. Encourage students to use some of them: *'Sorry I'm late. I got held up.' 'I'm fed up with this weather.' 'Let me buy you a drink.' 'I'm just going to the loo.'*

Remember that the PostScript can be used at any point in Unit 1. It doesn't have to be done last.

Workbook

- Extra grammar – *have/have got*
- Vocabulary – vocabulary networks as a way of building and recording vocabulary
- Pronunciation – recognizing the phonetic script
- Verbs + prepositions
- An exercise on grammatical terminology

Notes on the unit

Test your grammar (SB page 6)

This particular *Test your grammar* section has several aims and will therefore take longer than usual. It should involve students from the very beginning, and give them an opportunity to get to know each other as they ask their partner the questions and talk about themselves; it will challenge students to form questions, which they often find difficult; and it will test students in their understanding and use of basic tenses such as Present Simple and Continuous, Present Perfect Simple and Continuous, and Past Simple.

PROBLEMS

- Students could still be very uncertain in their use of these tenses. Reassure the student who says 'I no understand present, past ...' by saying 'Don't worry. That's why we're studying this book.'
- Students often say **I born in ...*, rather than the passive *I was born in ...*
- There will undoubtedly be problems with *have/have got*, as referred to above. If this is a big problem for most of the students, you will need to provide a quick explanation. If most of them seem to know it in theory but make mistakes in practice, just correct the mistakes – but continue to correct the mistakes vigilantly for weeks to come! Remember the explanation in the Grammar Reference section, and further explanation and an exercise in Unit 1 of the Workbook.

There are examples of *have/have got* in the Presentation and all the Practice exercises, so monitor students' production very carefully.

1 Students work alone to form the questions. When they have finished, ask various students to ask you the questions so you can check that they have formed them correctly. Answer questions about *you*, and so tell your new students about their teacher.

Answers
a Where do you live?
b How many languages do you speak?
c Why are you learning English?
d Which countries have you been to?
e Where/When were you born?
f How long have you been learning English (for)?
g How many brothers and sisters do you have/have you got?
h How much money have you got/do you have in your pocket?
i Where did you go last night?
j What are you wearing?

Correct mistakes carefully, including pronunciation mistakes. Remember that *wh-* questions must start high, and then fall.

A quick explanation of Present Simple and Present Continuous should be enough. Don't be tempted into a lengthy explanation of Present Perfect Continuous. The sentence *I've been learning English for three years* is almost idiomatic for learners.

Students work in pairs to ask and answer the questions. Let this go on for a while. It should allow students to get to know each other if they don't already. Go round the pairs and monitor.

Ask one student to tell the class about his/her partner. Note that we are now using the third person – *he* and *she* – and you might want to tell the class this. Correct, but don't overcorrect. You don't want to spoil the flow. Students should be quite keen to learn about each other.

Ask a few other students to do the same. If you have a large class, you won't be able to get round everyone. Try to remember who you haven't asked so that you can remember to include those people when you next ask students to contribute in front of the whole class.

2 Students work in pairs to make the statements negative. If they want to argue that the information is factually incorrect, for example, it really *is* raining, then use a different sentence, for example *It's snowing*.

Answers
a My mother **doesn't work** in a bank.
b It **isn't raining**.
c I **didn't go** out last night.
d I**'m not learning** Russian.
e We **haven't got** a dog.
f I **didn't have** a shower this morning.
g English **isn't spoken** in every country in the world.

SUGGESTION
There is no overt focus on auxiliaries in this *Test your grammar* section. They are practised implicitly in positive, question and negative forms. You could, if you wanted, ask students to identify some auxiliary verbs in Exercises 1 and 2 of the *Test your grammar* now that they have finished doing them.

PRESENTATION (SB page 6)

1 Students work in pairs or small groups to do the quiz. Encourage them to use dictionaries if there are unknown words. If you prefer, you could check words such as *ray, leap, worship* before they start.

When you think everyone is ready, ask one student to read out a question, and another student the answer. Invite the rest of the class to say if they agree or not. Continue like this for the rest of the quiz.

2 **T.1**   Play the tape and check the answers.

Answers
1 1896	8 *Thriller* by Michael Jackson
2 8 minutes	9 Very Important Person
3 stepping onto the moon	10 He failed a drug test.
4 animal products	11 watching a play in the theatre
5 India	12 four times
6 Germany	13 four wings
7 Hinduism	14 raw fish and rice

3 Ask students to find examples of the tenses. The aim is diagnostic – how much does this class know? Some will know them all, some might know very few.

Answers
The number in the brackets refers to the question in the Quiz.

Present Simple – *does take* (2), *doesn't eat* (4), *does stand for* (9), *does have* (13)
Present Continuous – *are buying* (5), *are eating* (14)
Present Simple passive – *are worshipped* (7)
Present Perfect Simple – *has sold* (8), *has won* (12)
Past Simple – *did start* (1), *said* (3), *didn't get* (10)
Past Continuous – *was doing* (3, 11)
Past Simple passive – *were printed* (6), *was assassinated* (11)

● Grammar question

Ask students to identify some of the auxiliary verbs from the quiz.

Read aloud the Grammar question. Don't expect a precise and comprehensive explanation – something along the lines of *to form tenses like Present Perfect and Present Continuous and passive, to form questions and negatives in the Present Simple* will be enough.

SUGGESTION

Unless you drew students' attention to auxiliary verbs at the end of the *Test your grammar* section, there will have been no overt focus on them at all so far. Before doing the Grammar question, you might like to do the following.

Write seven sentences on the board.

We are learning English.
English is spoken all over the world.
I don't like maths.
Do you smoke?
Why didn't you come to the party?
I haven't had anything to eat today.
What does your father do?

Ask students what is special about the words underlined. Ask if they mean anything. Elicit the fact that they are all auxiliary verbs. Ask *What do auxiliary verbs do?* The best you can expect is *They help other verbs*. If you have a multi-lingual class and you suspect they don't know what an auxiliary verb is, ask them to check in their dictionaries.

Draw students' attention to *had* and *do* in the last two sentences. Ask *Are they auxiliary verbs?* Students might answer correctly, or you might have to explain that they're not, they are full verbs.

4 Students work in pairs or small groups to think of some general knowledge questions. You could put some categories on the board to help them. They then ask the rest of the class.

History   Different countries   The natural world
Famous people   Sport   Food and drink

They then ask the rest of the class.

PRACTICE   (SB page 7)

1 Grammar and pronunciation

1 **T.2a** Read the instructions and play the example on tape. This exercise practises forming the negative, but also contrastive stress. Ask three or four students to repeat the sentence *It doesn't rise in the west! It rises in the east!* Really exaggerate the intonation yourself, and get students to copy you.

NB *Question k is a slightly different pattern from the other sentences.*

Go round the groups, monitoring and correcting. You will really need to push students to get the intonation correct!

T.2b Listen and check. Go over the exercise again as a class.

2 Students work in pairs to write the questions. When they have finished, get the answers as a class. Insist on good pronunciation. Having established a question, ask someone to direct that question at another student in the class, and get that student to answer with the real information.

NB *The question 'How long does it take you to ...?' often causes problems.*

Answers
a What did you do last night?
b What sort of books do you like reading?
c Have you (ever) been to America?
d What's the teacher doing?
e What does your father do?
f Why didn't you do your homework last night?
g How long does it take you to come to school?
h What are you doing next weekend?
i Have you got/Do you have a CD player at home?

Students work in pairs to ask and answer the questions. Correct carefully.

2 *is* or *has*?

T.3 This activity would make a nice little warmer done at the beginning of a class.

It is more difficult than it might at first appear. Give students time to think, possibly pausing the tape recorder in between sentences.

Answers

1 is	5 is	9 is
2 is	6 has	10 has
3 has	7 is	
4 has	8 is	

3 Short answers

Students will undoubtedly have come across short answers before. Your students probably don't use them because they are too complicated. They require too much analytical thought to use correctly, by which time the moment has passed. Students won't be using them at the end of this lesson either! They need to come from a spontaneous, instinctive source, and this will only come at a much later stage of language learning.

However, this is not to prevent the process of consciousness raising. Most items of language are recognized long before they are produced. Short answers (along with reply questions and question tags) are a very important part of the language, especially the spoken language, and mastery will only come through extensive exposure.

1 **T.4a** Students read and listen to the conversation. Ask one or two comprehension questions.

Who are the people?
What time is it?
Is the girl nice to her father?

2 **T.4b** Play the second conversation. Students identify the difference.

> **Answer**
> Of course, the girl sounds a lot nicer with her voice, but she also uses short answers to sound more friendly or polite, rather than just saying *yes* and *no*.

Read the explanation as a class. Students practise the dialogue using short answers. They should be able to do this by looking at the dialogue in the Student's Book and adding the short answers. Ask one or two pairs to say the dialogue to the class.

3 **T.5** Students listen to the questions and answer them with a short answer. Pause the tape after each one, and ask two or three students the same question.

4 This is a mingling activity. Read the instructions and ask students to think of two more *yes/no* questions. Ask them to stand up and ask three other students the questions. Go round monitoring and correcting.

4 Reading and tenses

NB *Remember that these practice activities are not meant to be done one after the other as a block. You decide when you want to do them. Intersperse controlled activities with freer ones, so you end up with a balanced timetable.*

The aim of this activity is tense practice rather than auxiliaries. Some students will find it easy, others will have problems. Ask students to do it in pairs.

> **Answers**
> | | |
> |---|---|
> | a began | f is published |
> | b was started | g has |
> | c cost | h has had |
> | d developed | i has worked/has been working |
> | e sells | j are trying |

5 Speaking

You will need to photocopy the Student **A** and Student **B** information on page 119 of this Teacher's Book. They are doubled to save you paper, so you need to cut them.

Students should be familiar with the principles of an information gap activity by now, but it can appear strange to people who have never come across them before. Make sure students know what they have to do.

Read the instructions as a class and look at the example. Explain carefully that Student **A** will have different information from Student **B**.

Give out the pieces of paper. Ask students to spend two or three minutes looking at their information about Charles Hendrickson and preparing their questions. Then they can ask and answer questions.

When students have finished, ask for the questions again and correct any mistakes. Make sure the questions start with a high intonation.

LANGUAGE REVIEW (SB page 9)
Auxiliary verbs

Read the Language Review together in class, and/or ask students to read it at home. If you have a monolingual class, you could use L1 and ask students to translate some of the sentences.

Ask students to read the Grammar Reference section at home.

ADDITIONAL MATERIAL

Workbook Unit 1
Exercises 1–6 All of these practise the input of this unit.
Exercise 7 Explanation and an exercise on *have/have got*

● READING AND LISTENING (SB page 10)
Pre-reading task

1 Read the introduction as a class. Students match the pictures with the drawings. Don't be surprised if your class can't do very many! The last part of the task could invite an interesting group discussion, and draws the students together as a class.

> **Answers**
> a The Pyramids
> b The Temple of Diana
> c The Colossus of Rhodes
> d The Pharos
> e The Tomb of Mausolus
> f The Statue of Zeus
> g The Hanging Gardens of Babylon
>
> Only the Pyramids can still be seen, but remains of the Pharos lighthouse were discovered in 1995.

2 The aim of this second pre-reading task is to move students away from the idea of wonders being only buildings in preparation for the reading text.

Read the instruction as a class. Offer some suggestions yourself, e.g. rockets, television, computers. Don't be surprised if students are not very creative. It doesn't matter if this discussion doesn't last very long.

Reading

1 Students read the newspaper article to themselves. Allow enough time for this.

2 Read out the first part of this question.

> **Answer**
> She says that modern wonders aren't buildings, as the ancient wonders were, because science and technology have produced such amazing advances.

Students work alone to put the wonders in order of importance for themselves. They could discuss this in pairs, before having a class discussion. Ask students *Why do you think that is so important?*

Before the Comprehension check, you could go through the article again, with either you reading it aloud or students taking it in turns. Reading aloud can be fun as long as the students' pronunciation isn't too bad!

Comprehension check

Students discuss their answers in pairs.

> **Answers**
> a medical science   e holidays
> b Olympic Games   f agriculture
> c computers   g space travel
> d we are still here

Language work

Students work in pairs to write in the correct auxiliary.

> **Answers**
> 1 have   3 were   5 didn't
> 2 don't are   4 has   6 are

> **SUGGESTION**
> Here is an idea for more vocabulary work.
>
> Write the following words on the board. Students must decide which topics of the newspaper article they go with, e.g. *tractor* goes with *Agriculture*.
>
> There are four words for each category.
>
> | | | | |
> |---|---|---|---|
> | *tractor* | *rocket* | *screen* | *operation* |
> | *medal* | *beach* | *bomb* | *corn* |
> | *marathon* | *towel* | *missile* | *farm* |
> | *surgeon* | *explosion* | *combine harvester* | |
> | *leisure* | *moon* | *mouse* | *CD rom* |
> | *sprinter* | *antibiotic* | *astronaut* | *nurse* |
> | *nuclear power* | *stadium* | *relax* | |
> | *planets* | *program* | | |
>
> This could serve to introduce the exercise on pages 8–9 of the Workbook on vocabulary networks.

Listening

T.6 Students listen to three people giving their ideas of the wonders of the modern world. Then you could suggest that they listen again whilst reading the tapescript.

> **Answers**
> *The washing machine*
> It's good because it gives people more free time, but do we wash our clothes more than is necessary?
>
> *The fax machine*
> It's good because it helps with communication across the world, but it never leaves you alone, it can always get you.
>
> *Planes*
> You can go almost anywhere in the world in less than twenty-four hours.
>
> *The microchip/computer*
> There is something new very often.
>
> *The phone*
>
> *Free time*
> We get more free time with machines, but do we just fill it again with some other activity?

If students appear interested, you could pick up on a previous idea and ask students to suggest their wonders of the modern world. Now that they see that the wonders can be things or ideas, they might have more to offer.

ADDITIONAL MATERIAL

Workbook Unit 1
Exercise 8 Vocabulary of holidays and medicine
Video Report 1 *Seven Wonders of Britain*

● SPEAKING (SB page 12)

Discussion

1 Students work in pairs to decide the order of importance.

2 Pairs now work together to persuade the others that their order is best. This is called a 'pyramid discussion'. It doesn't matter if one pair convinces the other pair or not as long as it generates discussion.

3 Ask students to add to the list of machines. Don't let this drag on too long. Students might be fed up with talking about machines by now.

● VOCABULARY AND PRONUNCIATION

Sounds and spelling

Your students probably know that English spelling isn't phonetic. They will have come across words like *women, meat/bread, Wednesday* and *food/good* and know that English pronunciation isn't regular.

1 Read the introduction as a class. Your students are only ever required to recognize phonetic symbols, not produce them.

2 Read the instructions as a class. Students work in pairs to decide which word doesn't rhyme.

T.7 Play the tape to check the answers.

> **Answers**
> a read (present) d said   g pear
> b work   e food   h cows
> c phone   f weak

Ask two students to read aloud the words in this exercise.

Silent letters

1 Read the instructions as a class. Students work in pairs to cross out the silent letters.

> **Answers**
> a sig̸n   e receip̸t   i sa̸lmon
> b h̸onest   f k̸nee   j cup̸board
> c ha̸lf   g i̸ron   k whis̸tle
> d com̸b   h lam̸b   l answ̸er

2 This is an exercise to practise recognition of phonetic symbols. Students work in pairs to write the words.

T.8 Play the tape to check the answers.

> **Answers**
> a castle   e knock   i psychology
> b bomb   f foreign   j grandma
> c sandwich   g heart
> d island   h knowledge

A love poem!

Ask students to work out the poem. When they are ready, they can read it out aloud as a class. The chorus should be fun!

> **Answer**
> Roses are red
> The sky is blue
> The world is wonderful
> And so are you

ADDITIONAL MATERIAL

Workbook Unit 1
Exercise 9 Recognizing the phonetic symbols

● WRITING   (SB page 13)

Correcting mistakes

It is obviously important for students to be able to find their mistakes in their own written work. Unfortunately, it is easier to find mistakes in other people's work because your own work is the product of what you think is correct! Nevertheless, it is worth practising.

1 Ask students to work in pairs to find and correct the mistakes. Check their answers.

> **Answers**
>
> 18 Greencroft Gardens
> London NW 6
> Tuesday 10 May
>
> Dear Stephanie
>
> How are you? I'm very well. I came **to** London two weeks ago **to** study at a language school. I want **to** learn English because **it** is a very important language. I'm **staying** with **an** English family called Bennett. They have two **sons** and a daughter. Mr Bennett is **a** teacher, and Mrs Bennett **works** in a hospital. English people **are** very kind, but they speak very quickly!
>
> I study in the morning. My **teacher's** name is Ann. She **told** me my English is OK, but I **make** a lot of mistakes. Ann **doesn't** give us too much homework, so in the afternoons I **always go** sightseeing. London is much **bigger** than my town. I like **painting very much** , and I'm very **interested in** modern art, so I visit galleries and museums. I have met a girl called Christina. She **comes** from Greece, and she **has** a lovely flat near Regent's Park. Last night we **went** to the cinema, but the film wasn't very **exciting** .
>
> **Would** you like to visit me in London? Why don't you come for a weekend?
>
> Write to me soon. I'd love to see you.
>
> Love
>
> Kati

2 Students write a similar letter for homework.

> **SUGGESTION**
> Sometimes, before students hand in future pieces of homework, ask them in pairs to swap their work. They should try and find mistakes in their partner's work. Ask them to write the corrections in pencil rather than pen, as they might make another mistake!

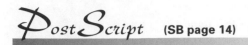 **(SB page 14)**

Social expressions

The aim of this exercise is to introduce students to useful expressions for actual classroom use for the rest of the course. Students will sometimes be late, buy new clothes, arrange to meet outside class, etc. With a bit of nudging from you, these expressions could be used naturally and appropriately on many occasions in day-to-day interactions.

1 Read the introduction as a class. Explain that *Hang on a sec. I'm just going to the loo* means *Wait a second. I'm just going to the toilet. Loo* isn't rude; it's informal and familiar. Explain that if a student is in a situation and he/she doesn't know whether to use the word *loo* or not, the best advice is 'Don't. Say *toilet.*'

Students work in pairs to match a line in **A** with a line in **B**. This is more difficult than it seems. Some students will think that this is an easy exercise and race through it. Quietly go and check their answers. If there are mistakes, tell them *how many* there are without saying *what* they are.

2 **T.9a** Students listen and check their answers. Go over any problems. Ask students to memorize some of the dialogues, then in pairs they can practise some with their books shut.

3 **T.9b** Students listen to the sentences and reply, using one of the lines in column **B**.

Sample answers

1 **A** I'm having Friday off . We're going away.
  B That's a good idea. The break will do you good.

2 **A** I'll see you at about 7.
  B Sorry. I can't make it then. What about a bit earlier? later

3 **A** This weather's depressing, isn't it?
  B I know, it's terrible. I'm longing for some sun.

4 **A** Hey! Nice jeans!
  B Thanks. They cost an absolute fortune.

5 **A** Sorry I'm late. I overslept.
  B Never mind. You're here now. Come and sit down.

6 **A** Alan's going to invite Suzie to the party next week.
  B Really? I don't know what he sees in her.

7 **A** For homework learn one hundred new words.
  B You must be joking!

4 Students choose one or two of the dialogues and continue them. Read the example as a class.

Don't forget!

Workbook Unit 1

Exercise 7 Explanation and practice of *have/have got*

Exercise 10 Verbs + preposition

Exercise 11 Grammar terminology (This is best done in class.)

Wordlist This is on page 155 of this Teacher's Book for you to photocopy and give to your students.

Video Report 1: *Seven Wonders of Britain*: some of Britain's wonders.

Happiness!

Present states and actions
Active and passive
Numbers

Profile

Student's Book

Language
- Present Simple/Continuous
- state/action verbs
- active/passive in the present
- *not very* + opposite adjective
- *you* meaning 'people in general'

Pronunciation
- final *-s*
- numbers

Vocabulary and everyday English
- adverbs of frequency
- sport and leisure
- describing a person
- numbers, prices, dates, phone numbers, fractions, decimals, percentages

Workbook
- extra grammar – Present Continuous + *always*
- pronunciation – final *-s*
- vocabulary – synonyms and antonyms
- *look* and *be* as multi word verbs

Video
- *Wide Open Spaces* Episode 1

Photocopiable materials for this unit (TB page 120)
- This is an extra vocabulary exercise for the reading text on SB page 20.

Introduction to the unit

The theme of this unit is *Happiness*. Men and women who find happiness in a variety of ways feature in the different sections of the unit. The topic provides suitable contexts for much practice of the main linguistic aims of the unit, the present tenses. At the intermediate level we do not just concentrate on the differences between the Present Simple and Continuous tenses, but we focus on state verbs which cannot be used in the continuous, and we also practise Present active versus Present passive.

The skills work includes a reading text about a very unusual nun, a listening activity where three people briefly describe why they like their favourite sport, and a parallel writing activity describing a person. There are many opportunities for both controlled and free speaking practice throughout the unit.

Students can watch the first episode of the drama, *Wide Open Spaces*, on *Headway Video Intermediate*. This will be particularly appropriate after the Presentation sections.

Language aims

Grammar
Present states and actions

At this level students will of course be familiar with the forms and some of the uses of the Present Simple and the Present Continuous tenses. Our assumption in the Presentation sections is that work on these tenses will be revision for students. Therefore the tasks are quite challenging, and there are many opportunities for the students themselves to offer explanations of form and use. Both Presentations focus on the different uses of the Present Simple and the Present Continuous, but Presentation 2 explores and practises further aspects of the language. State verbs, such as *understand* and *like* are highlighted and practised; similarly the Present passive is checked.

PROBLEMS

Intermediate students can sometimes resist work on the Present Simple and the Present Continuous because they feel that they 'know' them already. In practice this invariably means that they still make frequent mistakes when trying to use them, particularly with -s in the third person, when forming questions and negatives, and of course when trying to choose which of the two tenses to use. To overcome this resistance, we have challenging tasks and additional related language areas included in the unit. Students should benefit from the practice, especially the discriminatory activities, and enjoy the opportunity to 'show off' their knowledge before exploring new language (state versus active verbs, and the passive voice).

Vocabulary

The main lexical area is that of sports and leisure. The task encourages students to use their dictionaries to extend their vocabulary in their chosen sports.

NB *Many of the vocabulary tasks in 'New Headway Intermediate' are designed to help students use their dictionaries intelligently and keep vocabulary records for themselves. Do encourage your students to start a vocabulary notebook, but don't get disheartened if only a few very keen ones take up the idea!*

PostScript

Students always make mistakes with numbers, so the recognition and production of a variety of these is revised in the PostScript.

Workbook

- Extra grammar – Present Continuous with *always* to express some degree of irritation as in *I'm always losing my glasses.*
- Pronunciation – -s at the ends of words, /s/, /z/, /ɪz/
- Vocabulary – synonyms and antonyms
- Multi-word verbs – *look* and *be*

Notes on the unit

Test your grammar (SB page 15)

This activity should only take a few minutes of class time. It is designed to focus on the linguistic aims of the unit, and to allow students to show off what they can *recognize* about the uses of the Present Simple and the Present Continuous before they are asked to produce them.

Ask your students to work in pairs. Emphasize that you want them to do the exercise quickly. Then go through the activity again with the whole class, asking for the correct answer and a *very* brief explanation.

NB *Do not be tempted to give lengthy explanations as to why the sentences are correct or incorrect. If students have lots of questions, tell them that you are going to be studying the area later in the lesson. Also, don't worry about how your students give their explanations as long as they're on the right track. In a monolingual class they could even use L1.*

Answers

1 She speaks five languages.
(*She's speaking five languages* is impossible!)

2 Look at that man! He's wearing such a funny hat.
(The man is wearing the funny hat now, I can see him. Only a habit can be expressed in the Present Simple *He always wears funny hats.*)

3 Don't take that book back to the library. I'm reading it.
(I'm reading this particular book, not necessarily now at this moment, but now in this period of time. Different from a more general habit *I usually read for a bit before I go to sleep.*)

4 They have two daughters and two sons.
(*Have* [possession] cannot be used in the Continuous.)
They're having two daughters and two sons.
Not very likely unless the doctor's told them that they're expecting quads!)

5 Do you understand Spanish?
(*Understand* cannot be used in the Continuous.)

6 We think opera is boring.
(*Think* [opinion] cannot be used in the Continuous. Ask your students why the cartoon is funny.)

7 English is spoken all over the world.
(Must be passive. *People speak English/English is spoken.*)

NB *Number 7 is the only example of a passive sentence in this exercise.*

PRESENTATION (1)   (SB page 15)

Present Simple

Presentation (1) illustrates the use of the Present Simple tense, and practises all its forms. The aim of the first two exercises is to set the scene via a class discussion for the presentation text in exercise 3 on the next page. It is not intended that the discussion should go on too long, as it is a means to an end, but if your class takes off on the subject only *you* can be the judge of what is best for your particular students in the time available.

Remember the discussion is fluency work and as long as students get their message across in English don't worry too much about the language mistakes. Try to encourage free speaking. In some classes this is very difficult – it depends on the personality of the individual student. Do try, but don't be too downhearted if they are not very forthcoming. Just move on.

1 First ask your students for comments on the people in the pictures, such as *Who looks happiest?*

Now ask what they think is the happiest time of a person's life. Encourage ideas with more specific prompts.

Do you think your teens are the best years? Forties? What's good/bad about being a teenager? etc.
What about your parents/grandparents? etc.

2 Read aloud the introduction to the graph showing the results of a survey about who are the happiest people in Britain.

Ask students to look at the graph in pairs and answer the questions above it. Get feedback from the class.

Answers
At what time in their lives are British people happiest?
Between the ages of 35 and 54. When they're middle-aged.

When are they least happy?
Between 15 and 19, when they are teenagers but particularly when they are over the age of 65.

Why do you think this is?
(There could be a variety of suggestions here)
• Perhaps middle-aged people are happiest because they're at the peak of their careers and earning more money than when they were younger.
• Perhaps they're happiest because their children are no longer very young, and they have more freedom again.
• Perhaps they have learnt to be content with life, and those 45 to 54 are over their 'mid-life crisis'!
• Teenage years can be difficult because they are between childhood and adulthood, and teenagers are often self-conscious, moody and spotty!
• Teenagers often have to take a lot of exams and may be worried about their futures.
• Perhaps people over 65 are less happy because they are not as active as they once were. They may have health problems or money problems if they are trying to live on a small pension, etc.

Ask if any results are surprising, and why.

3 This activity moves to the *main* aim of this Presentation section: revision and practice of the Present Simple tense. You should make this clear to your students.

Ask them to look at the picture of John Smith on page 16. John Smith is the most common man's name in Britain, and he is a typical example of a middle-aged Mr Happy as referred to in the graph. Ask students what they can predict about his lifestyle from the picture.

T.10 Play the tape and ask students to read the text as they listen.

SUGGESTIONS
• We often suggest that students should read and listen at the same time to presentation texts because many of them appreciate the reinforcement that each skill gives to the other. However, you know your students best and you must feel free to vary the procedure to suit their particular abilities. Here, for example, you might want your students to listen first, then read, or simply to read without listening at all. It is up to you.
• You might want to pre-teach the adjective *steady* /'stedi/ as in *a steady job* = an unchanging, dependable job.
• The verb *to potter* (to work in a slow, contented manner) will undoubtedly be new to your students. It is probably best taught in the context of the story of John Smith. It is a verb which seems to fit his personality and lifestyle!

● Grammar questions

These questions should not prove difficult for intermediate students. This should be an opportunity for them to show off some grammatical knowledge. You could ask them to work on the questions with a partner first and then conduct a full class feedback. You could perhaps write the answers on the board, with some examples provided by the students.

Answers
• The Present Simple tense. The verbs are all in this tense because the general lifestyle and daily habits of John Smith are being described.
• They end in *-s* because they are all in the third person singular, *he* and *she*.
He lives, he owns, she runs
• The auxiliary verbs *do* and *does*, *don't* and *doesn't* form the questions and negatives.
(This is revision from Unit 1)
Does he go out every evening? No, he doesn't.

PRACTICE (SB page 16)

NB There is only one practice activity in Presentation (1) , and it focuses on the forms of the Present Simple. There is further practice in Presentation (2) in discriminatory exercises with the Present Continuous.

Speaking

1 Do this activity as a class. Correct any problems they might have with the questions and negatives and the -s on the third person singular. One student asks and another answers the questions about John Smith across the class in open pairs. Try to ensure that most students get a turn, and encourage student-to-student correction as well as correcting yourself. You can accept short answers, but encourage longer answers to maximize controlled language practice. You can point out to your students that shorter answers are more natural.

> **Answers**
>
> a Where **does he** live?
> (He lives) in a detached house in the South of England. (He doesn't live in London.)
>
> b What **does he** do?
> He's an accountant. (He has a steady job in an office in London/He works in an office in London.)
>
> c How many children **does he have**? (or How many children **has he got**?)
> Two. (**He has** two children/He's **got** two children.)
>
> d How **does he** relax after work?
> He watches TV or a video, and two evenings a week/sometimes he meets friends for a drink in the pub. (He doesn't go out every evening.)
>
> e How much **does he spend** per week?
> £120 on average. (He spends £120 on average.)
>
> f What **does he** do at the weekend/at weekends?
> He (regularly/often) eats in restaurants. goes to see shows, or plays golf. Most weekends he (puts on a pair of/some old blue jeans and) potters in the garden.
>
> g How often **does he** go on holiday abroad?
> More than once a year.

T.11 Play the tape if you feel your students will benefit from it, but tell them that their answers might not be exactly the same as the tape but may still be correct. The tape has the more natural short answers.

2 The activity now changes from practice of the third person to first and second persons. Students work in pairs. Make sure that they realize that the activity is now personalized and that they are to ask and answer *real* questions about each other.

> **Answers**
> Are you married?
> Where do you live?
> What do you do?
> Do you have any children? How many do you have?
> How do you relax after work/school?
> How much do you spend per week? (You could revise *Mind your own business!* in response to this! It appeared in the PostScript of Unit 1.)
> What do you do at the weekend/at weekends?
> How often do you go on holiday abroad?

Go round the pairs helping and correcting. Listen for the more interesting examples so that you can choose them for the feedback.

Round off the activity by asking one or two students to report back on their partners, thereby practising the third person again.
Maria isn't married. She lives in a houseboat … etc.

3 This task is meant to be a short concluding discussion, as it is often a good idea to follow controlled speaking practice with some freer speaking.

Your students may well have told you by now how boring they think John Smith's life is. Encourage some more talk about this and how such a boring man can be so happy! His wife is presumably less happy because she does more in the home and earns less at work than her husband (or maybe she just finds her husband very boring and predictable to live with!) Try to lead this to some further discussion of the roles of men and women in the students' countries. Who works harder? Men or women? Who is happier? Why?

ADDITIONAL MATERIAL

Workbook Unit 2
These additional exercises can be done in class to supplement the coursebook or set as homework.
Exercises 1–4 Further practice of all forms of the Present Simple
Exercise 5 Pronunciation exercise on -s at the end of words. The different endings /s/ /z/ /ɪz/ are practised.

PRESENTATION (2) (SB page 17)

Present Simple and Present Continuous
Active and passive

The aim of the first part of Presentation (2) is to compare and contrast the uses of the Present Simple and Present Continuous tenses.

1 **T.12** Before you play the tape, ask your students to compare the picture of Roger with that of John Smith on the previous page. They are exactly the same age. Do they look similar? Do they have the same jobs? What is Roger's job?

Now ask them to listen and say afterwards if they think that Roger is as happy as John. Is his life is more or less interesting than John's life?

Go through the questions about Roger quite quickly, with you (or a student) reading them aloud.

Answers

- He lost his job.
- He worked with computers. Now he's a gardener.
- He lives in a flat in London.
- No, he's not married, but he has a girlfriend called Fiona.
- Fiona's a graphic designer, and she earns more than Roger.
- Roger collects old radios, and Fiona collects old cookery books.
- No, he doesn't. (He only takes his dog for walks.)
- Yes, there's one problem. His job's seasonal, so he doesn't earn much in autumn and winter.
- No, he doesn't.
- No, it isn't. But he's also a very happy man.

2 Play the tape again. Tell your students to listen carefully because they have to complete the sentences **a–l** with the *exact* words that Roger uses.

Ask them to compare their answers with a partner before you go through it as a class.

Answers

a In summer I *usually* **leave** home at about 5.30 in the morning.

b I **have** a small van, and I **carry** all my tools and equipment in that.

c It's autumn now so I**'m tidying** the gardens and I**'m picking up** leaves.

d I**'m planting** lots of daffodils and tulips.

e After work I *always* **go** home and **relax** in a hot bath.

f I *usually* **cook** our evening meal because she **gets** home from work after me.

g At weekends we *often* **drive** into the country and **go** to antique shops and antique sales.

h We **don't have** a television! Everybody **has** one these days but we **don't**.

i I **collect** old radios and Fiona **collects** old cookery books.

j I've just bought two 1930s radios and I**'m cleaning** them and **mending** them.

k I *never* **play** any sports.

l I **don't earn** much in autumn and winter so I**'m not earning** much at the moment.

Follow the feedback with the grammar questions.

● Grammar questions

Go through these with the whole class, reading the questions aloud. Put a few examples on the board as you go through.

SUGGESTION

It is a nice idea to vary this procedure sometimes and invite individual students to write the examples on the board whilst the others comment.

Answers

– The verbs in **a** and **b** are in the Present Simple – *leave* in **a** because it is a present habit, and *carry* in **b** because it is always true. Also, *have* for possession can only be used in the simple forms.

Other examples:
I always go home and relax in a hot bath.
I usually cook ... because Fiona gets home ...
... we often drive ... and go to antique shops.
We don't have a television ... Everybody has ... we don't ...
I collect ... Fiona collects ...
I never play...

– The verbs in **c** are in the Present Continuous because autumn is the period of time now, and Roger is describing what he is doing now: *tidying gardens* and *picking up leaves.*

Other examples
I'm planting lots of ...
I'm cleaning and mending ...

– The words in italics are adverbs of frequency and they nearly always go with the Present Simple tense.

NB *'Always' is an exception to the rule. It can be used with both Simple and Continuous tenses but there is a subtle difference in meaning. It can be used to express an attitude of irritation on the part of the speaker.*

Examples:
I'm always losing my glasses.
They're always arguing.

The use of 'always' with the Present Continuous is introduced and practised in Unit 2, exercise 8 of the Workbook (page 14).

3 This is to provide some quick and simple practice of the Present Continuous. Students could describe what Roger is doing in pairs, or you could have student-to-student questions and answers across the class.

What's he doing?/What's he wearing?/What's happening in picture 1? etc.

Answers

Picture a He's cutting the grass. He's wearing a hat and shorts. He's whistling.

Picture b He's driving his van. He's listening to the radio. The sun's shining.

Picture c He's cooking the dinner. He's wearing an apron and drinking a glass of wine. Fiona's arriving home.

Picture d Roger and Fiona are driving in the countryside. They're wearing sunglasses. Fiona's reading a map. The dog is sitting in the back.

Picture e He's mending a radio. Fiona's reading a book. The dog is sleeping.

PRACTICE (SB page 18)

1 Note-taking and speaking

This activity is to round off the stories of John Smith and Roger.

Ask students to work in pairs without looking back at the texts and see what they can remember about the two men. Direct them by indicating two columns on the board, one headed SIMILARITIES, the other DIFFERENCES. Ask them to do the same in their notebooks and work together pooling ideas to fill them in.

> **SUGGESTION**
>
> An alternative is to have a student up at the board making notes in each column according to ideas offered by the other students in the class.

Answers

Similarities
(There are only a few similarities, but they are both happy with their lives.)
They're both 45.
They both have a dog.
They're both happy.

Differences
(There are a lot of differences. Here are some examples, but you and your students may well find more.)

  John
• is married, has children.
• lives in a house, near London.
• has a steady job in an office in London.
• has a wife who earns less than him.
• watches TV, plays golf, goes to restaurants and shows.

  Roger
• isn't married. No children.
• lives in a flat, in London, but doesn't work there.
• doesn't have a steady job – it's seasonal.
• works in the open air, not in an office.

• has a girlfriend who earns more than him.
• doesn't have a television.
• doesn't play any sport, collects old radios.
• doesn't often eat in restaurants or go to shows.

Encourage as much speaking as possible in the feedback. With luck there should be some freer production of the Present Simple!

2 Dialogues

This activity is designed to provide some controlled speaking practice where the Present Simple and the Present Continuous are clearly contrasted.

1 **T.13** You could play the dialogue first and ask a few questions about it, before asking your students to read and listen at the same time.

What does he do?
What's he doing at the moment?

It can be both challenging and satisfying for students to memorize occasionally, especially for stress and intonation practice. Go round and monitor the pairs as they practise it.

2 This section is a semi-controlled role-play. Check that your students know all the jobs in the pictures. Ask them in their pairs to choose two or three that interest them and make up similar dialogues to exercise 1. Go round and listen to check. Make a note of any interesting ones, then you can ask selected pairs to act out their dialogues. Acting out can have a very beneficial effect on students' stress and intonation.

3 This personalized activity can be very short. Do it in open pairs across the class with a few students. Suggest that students write some of the dialogues for homework.

3 Discussing grammar

see p144

NB *This is the first Discussing grammar activity in New Headway Intermediate. In these activities we want to encourage students to work things out for themselves and revise what they already know.*

This is where we start to explore some of the verbs that cannot be used in the Continuous.

> ⚠ Read the caution box aloud. You could ask them if they know any more state verbs and write them on the board.

1 Students discuss the box of verbs in pairs and underline the ten state verbs. Go round and monitor their discussion.

Answers

go   <u>understand</u>   believe   <u>like</u>   <u>agree</u>   enjoy
cost   <u>want</u>   listen to   <u>think</u> (= opinion)
<u>mean</u>   <u>know</u>   play   <u>love</u>   tell

<u>NB</u> *'Agree' might cause a problem because 'I'm agree' or 'I'm agreeing' are common mistakes. Also 'enjoy' being an action verb can seem strange, especially as 'like' is not. You may need to point out that 'like' expresses an opinion ('I like parties'), but with 'enjoy' you can be active in an experience. ('I enjoy parties and I'm enjoying this party very much.')*

2 Go through the instructions and example. Then monitor your students doing of the exercise.

Answers

a Jim isn't wanting an ice-cream. He doesn't like it. (✗)
Jim **doesn't want** an ice-cream. He doesn't like it.

b We're enjoying the course very much. We're learning a lot. (✔)

c I'm understanding you but I'm not agreeing with you. (✗)
I **understand** you but I **don't agree** with you.

d Do you think that Vanessa plays golf well? (✔)

e I'm sorry. I'm not knowing the answer. (✗)
I'm sorry. I **don't know** the answer.

f I'm not believing you. You're telling lies. (✗)
I **don't believe** you. You're telling lies.

g They know the car costs a lot of money but they want to buy it. (✔)

h She listens to a French song but she doesn't understand what it is meaning. (✗)
She **'s listening** to a French song but she doesn't understand what it **means**.

Ask your students to read the Grammar Reference section on pages 143–4 about action and state verbs. They could do this in class or as homework.

3 Do this exercise as a full class activity. Give the students a few seconds to look at each pair of sentences and then ask for answers. This exercise could also be set as homework and discussed in class later.

Answers

a Alec and Mary are Scottish. They **come** from Glasgow. They'll be here very soon. They**'re coming** by car.

b Lisa can't answer the phone. She**'s having** a bath. She **has** (= possession) two new pairs of jeans.

c I **think** (= opinion) that all politicians tell lies. I**'m thinking** about my girlfriend. She's in New York at the moment.

d We**'re not enjoying** this party at all. The music is too loud.
We **don't enjoy** going to big parties.

e Be quiet! I**'m watching** my favourite programme. I always **watch** it on Thursday evenings.

f John's not at home. He**'s seeing** (= visiting) the doctor about his sore throat.
I **see** (= understand) the problem but I can't help you. Sorry.

g Mmmmm! Dinner **smells** good. What is it?
Why **are** you **smelling** those roses? They're plastic!

h (Careful! This is a passive example, a prelude to the exercise on the passives which follows this one.)
This room **is** usually **used** for big meetings.
But today it**'s being used** for a party.

ADDITIONAL MATERIAL

Workbook Unit 2

Exercises 6–8 Present state and action verbs. These could be done in class but, given time restrictions, it is more likely that you will set them as homework.

4 Present Simple active or passive?

1 This is a recognition exercise designed to remind students of the difference between active and passive. Do it quickly with the whole class.

Answers

a and **c** are active.
b and **d** are passive.

2 Before you do the next activity do a little bit of arithmetic with the class! Ask them how many minutes there are in an hour, and then how many seconds there are (3,600). Now read to them the title of the newspaper article which is about what can happen round the world in just one short hour. Illustrate via the example that your students have to choose between Present Simple active or passive.

Put students into pairs to do it, or ask them to try it alone and then compare their answers with a partner. As you go through the answers with the class, ask them if any of the information surprises them.

SUGGESTION

Turn the activity into a kind of a quick quiz. Before you ask your students to look at the exercise in their books, ask them questions about each piece of information given, for example, *How many babies do you think are born in an hour?*

Encourage them to *guess* the answers, and write their suggestions on the board. Then put them into pairs to do the exercise. In this way they become more motivated to find out whose ideas were closest to the real answer. This approach takes longer to do but creates more interest in the activity.

Answers
1 The world's population **grows** by 9,300.
2 £75 million **is spent** on all kinds of weapons.
3 Your heart **beats** 4,800 times.
4 Your hair **grows** 0.18796mm.
5 12,540,000 Coca-Colas **are drunk**.
6 916,500 McDonald's hamburgers **are eaten**.
7 17,465 bottles of whisky **are produced** in Scotland.
8 1,426,940 letters **are sent**.
9 The Pentagon in Washington **receives** 8,300 telephone calls.
10 £558,000 worth of goods **are sold** in Harrods department store.
11 12,000 passengers **pass** through Heathrow airport.
12 166 Volkswagen cars **are made** in Germany.

ADDITIONAL MATERIAL

Workbook Unit 2

Exercises 9–11 The present passive. These could be done in class but, given time restrictions, it is more likely that you will set them as homework. However, the poem in Exercise 11 is good to do in class.

LANGUAGE REVIEW   (SB page 20)

Present Simple
Present Continuous
State Verbs
Passive

Read the Language Review together in class, and/or ask students to read it at home. If you have a monolingual class, you could use L1 and ask students to translate some of the sample sentences.

Ask students to read the Grammar Reference section at home.

● READING AND SPEAKING   (SB page 20)

Sister Wendy, TV Star!

The article about Sister Wendy comes from a newspaper.

Pre-reading task

This is to set the scene, and to try and create interest in the topic of the text by thinking about the lives of nuns or others in religious orders. Students' ideas on this may well vary according their cultural background.

1   Put the students into small groups and give them a few moments to consider the questions. Ask them to make notes and choose a group leader to give the feedback. Here are some possible answers, but there could be many more depending on the students' own experience. Sometimes quite a lively discussion can result.

Nuns always get up early, pray a lot, go to church a lot, work hard, wear a uniform called a 'habit'.

They sometimes teach children, help the poor and sick, sing a lot, grow their own vegetables. Some live in silence and don't speak at all.

They never get married, have their own children, or have a lot of money.

2   Students should remain in their groups for this activity. Again, there might well be different opinions about which items might be important to nuns. Don't let the group discussion go on too long – remember that this activity is just to stimulate interest.

NB *The point of this list is that many of the items which one would not normally associate with a nun's life, do, in fact, play a part in Sister Wendy's life, for example, food and drink, hotels, travel, television, and money.*

Reading

1   Use the photographs to focus students' attention on Sister Wendy. Prompt comments with further questions if necessary, such as

Does she look like a typical nun?   Where is she? What's she wearing? etc.

Also take the opportunity via the photographs to pre-teach the vocabulary: *spectacles* and *buck teeth*, as *bespectacled* (someone who wears spectacles) appears in the article.

2   Ask students to read the text fairly quickly and at the same time check which things in the box above she mentions. You should set them a time limit of about three minutes and inform them that they can read it in more detail soon. You could ask them to discuss in pairs which items in the box are mentioned before conducting a full class feedback. Ask which of the things she mentions are surprising for a nun's life.

Answer
The article mentions Sister Wendy's love of **prayer** and **solitude**, she loves praying silently and alone. This is unsurprising. However, the article also mentions how much she loves good **food** and **wine** and eats in famous restaurants; how she **travels** round Europe staying in international **hotels**; how she appears on **television** because she makes programmes about the art treasures of Europe, and how she earns quite a lot of **money**. These things are more surprising for a nun.

Comprehension check

Ask students to do this in pairs and read the article again as they work through the questions with their partner.

1 Tell your students that they have to find out what each of the numbers refer to. Get feedback from this exercise before they go on to the next.

Answers

16	She became a nun when she was 16.
22	She often doesn't speak to anyone for 22 hours a day.
20	She has lived in solitude for over 20 years.
95%	She is alone for 95% of the time.
50	She has been a nun for nearly 50 years.
1,200	She earned £1,200 for her first television series.

2 Ask students to work together. Monitor them, then go through the answers as a class. Get students to correct the wrong answers, but sometimes you can ask for further information when the answer is correct.

Answers

a Sister Wendy spends a lot of time alone. (✔)

b She travels to art capitals all over the world. (✘) (She only travels in Europe.)

c Her television programmes are popular because she meets famous art historians and interviews them. (✘) (They're popular because she speaks clearly and plainly, and not in the language of an art historian.)

d She believes that God wants her to lead this double life. (✔)

e She doesn't enjoy being alone in her caravan any more. (✘) (This is what she enjoys most of all.)

f She only eats plain food and she doesn't drink alcohol. (✘) (She loves good food and wine.)

g Some of her teeth are missing. (✔)

h She loves watching herself on television. (✘) (She hates/can't bear watching herself. She thinks she looks silly.)

i The other nuns at the monastery always watch her programmes on television. (✘) (There is no television in the monastery, so they don't watch.)

j Sister Wendy is using the money she has earned to improve the monastery. (✔)

Language work

1 The aim of this exercise is to provide students with practice in forming questions mainly in the Present tenses. They could work in pairs or small groups to do it.

Answers

I (a) **When did you become a nun, Sister Wendy?**

SW When I was sixteen. Goodness, that's nearly fifty years ago!

I (b) **And where do you live?**

SW In Norfolk. In a Carmelite monastery. Well, not actually in the monastery but in the grounds. I have a caravan.

I (c) **Do you travel all around the world?**

SW No, I don't. Just in Europe — that's far enough!

I (d) **Why do you think your art programmes are so popular?**

SW I don't really know. I'm not sure why they're popular. I feel that I look so silly, but perhaps people find it funny to watch a silly old nun!

I (e) **Do you enjoy going on tour?**

SW Yes, I do. Of course I do. The tours are really interesting and everybody enjoys a life of luxury now and then. I love good food and drink, but you know, I'm happiest on my own in my caravan.

I (f) **Do you watch yourself on television?**

SW No, I don't! I look ridiculous. I never watch if I can help it!

I (g) **What are you doing with all the money you're earning?**

SW I'm using it to help the monastery. Some new shower rooms are being built. That's good, isn't it?

2 **T.14** The full interview is on tape so that students can develop their listening skills whilst checking their answers. Ask them to listen and find out if their questions are exactly the same as on the tape. There may be some minor differences. You will need to answer their queries.

SUGGESTION

There is an extra vocabulary exercise on page 120 of this Teacher's Book for you to photocopy and use to supplement work on the reading text.

Answers

a She lives in solitary confinement. (line 4)

b She ... gives her personal opinions on some of the world's most famous works of art. (lines 15–17)

c She speaks clearly and plainly, with none of the academic verbosity of art historians. (lines 24–25)

d I am a disaster as a person. (line 35)

e I'm not good at being with other people. (lines 36–37)

f She takes delight in poring over menus ... (lines 45–46)

g I can't bear to watch myself on television. (line 51)

SUGGESTION
You could round off the lesson on Sister Wendy with a discussion on loneliness. Write the adjecitves *lonely* and *alone* on the board. Ask the class the difference in meaning between the two words.

Ask if they would like a life of solitude. Do they need other people to make them happy? How often are they alone? Have they ever been lonely in their lives? Do they enjoy their own company?

● VOCABULARY AND LISTENING
(SB page 22)

Sport

Sport is something that makes a lot of people happy. You could start the lesson by generally brainstorming all the sports your students can think of, or you could ask which sports your students play. This could take the form of a mingle activity where students stand up and circulate, asking as many others as possible which sports they play or watch. They could start a list of sports, and all of these could be pooled in a class feedback session.

1   Now turn to the book and look at the pictures of the sports. Are there any not mentioned already? Ask students to add to their lists.

2   Ask students to work in pairs to do this. Check answers with the whole class.

Answers
The rules are in brackets.

play tennis, volleyball, football.
        (A game with a ball, often in teams.)

go   jogging, fishing, skiing.
        (A sporting activity, ending in *-ing*.)

do   exercises, athletics, aerobics.
        (A sporting activity, often an exercise activity, *not* ending in *-ing*.)

3   Ask your students to copy the columns from the book. When filling in the columns encourage the students to choose sports that most interest them. You may need to go round and help them use their dictionaries and sometimes for speed give them the words yourself. Be careful with the timing of this activity. If it goes on too long your students may become overloaded with new vocabulary. It is a good idea to leave enough time for them to be able to tell you and each other a bit about their chosen sports.

4   **T.15**   These are original recordings. Introduce them by focusing on the drawings and asking what they are and which sports they go with (to teach the vocabulary for the tape). Students may recognize that

goggles and *mittens* (often shortened to *mitts*) are for skiing, and the *leotard* is for exercises and keep-fit. The *knee pads* could be for many sports, they are in fact for volleyball. Let students guess, and then they can listen and find out. Ask students to draw three columns and take notes about Suzanne, Dorothy and Martin.

ALTERNATIVE APPROACH
If you have three tape recorders and enough room, you can do this as a jigsaw activity. Divide the class into three groups and ask each group to listen to one person, answer the questions and then swap information with the other groups. Round off the activity by playing all three to the whole class.

Answers
Suzanne (She is Canadian, but now lives in England.)
• She's talking about skiing.
• It seems she goes every winter, to the French Alps (when she was a child she skied in Canada).
• The equipment she mentions: skis, boots, poles, ski-suit, hat, goggles, mittens, socks, and rucksack.
• She likes it because winters in England aren't very sunny, and she loves the brilliant sunshine high up in the mountains. She also likes the social life.
• She says she's not the greatest/best skier in the world but she's quite good (respectable) and safe.

Dorothy (She is an English lady of 83)
• She's talking about going to a keep-fit class and doing exercises.
• She goes once a week, on a Thursday, to a Salvation Army Hall in Branksome.
• She only mentions a yellow leotard.
• She likes it because she likes moving to music and she has made a lot of much younger friends. She is the eldest.
• She says that she thinks she's good at it and the instructress tells the others that she an example to them all.

Martin
• He's talking about volleyball.
• He plays it in winter in sports centres twice a week, and in summer on the beach once a week.
• The equipment he mentions: a ball, a net and knee pads (because you fall a lot.)
• He likes it because it's a team game with friends and it's a fast game.
• Yes. He seems to be good because his team have won a few tournaments.

Students could check their notes in pairs or small groups before you go through the answers in a full class feedback.

5 This is a short personalized activity, picking up from exercise 1 where the students may have said which sports they like. They could stay in their pairs or groups and find out a little more about each other's favourite sports. Alternatively, they could ask you these questions and find out about your sporting activities.

● WRITING (SB page 22)

This is the first descriptive writing task.

1 and 2 These are to create interest in the writing activity to follow via some personalization about members of the students' families. It can be quite interesting when students read their sentences aloud and explain why they chose him or her.

3 Encourage some comment about the photo of Aunt Emily. Ask what she looks like and what her personality is like. Does she look kind? What about her daily life? What does she do? Now ask students to read the text.

4 This exercise requires the students to begin some detailed study of the text. Ask students to do it and perhaps check with a partner before you go through it as a class.

> **Answers**
> Of all my relatives, I like my Aunt Emily the best. She's my mother's youngest sister. She has never married, and she lives alone in a small village near Bath. She's in her late fifties, but she's still quite young in spirit. She has a fair complexion, thick brown hair which she wears in a bun, and dark brown eyes. She has a kind face, and when you meet her, the first thing you notice is her lovely, warm smile. Her face is a little wrinkled now, but I think she is still rather attractive. She is the sort of person you can always go to if you have a problem.
> She likes reading and gardening, and she goes for long walks over the hills with her dog, Buster. She's a very active person. Either she's making something, or mending something or doing something to help others. She does the shopping for some of the old people in the village. She's extremely generous, but not very tolerant with people who don't agree with her. I hope that I am as happy and contented as she is when I'm her age.

5 Do this with the whole class.

> **Answers**
>
> | | |
> |---|---|
> | quite young (lines 3–4) | = fairly young, more young than old. |
> | a little wrinkled (line 7) | = a bit wrinkled, not a lot. |
> | rather attractive (line 7) | = quite attractive, more than just attractive. |
> | very active (line 10) | = often active |
> | extremely generous (line 13) | = very, very generous. |

6 Ask students to find 'She's … not very tolerant' (line 13) and read aloud the explanation. Do the first adjective with the class to give them the idea and then ask them to do the others in pairs. The adjectives should be familiar to them.

> **Answers**
> rude   – not very polite
> boring – not very interesting
> mean   – not very generous/kind
> ugly   – not very pretty/handsome/beautiful/ attractive/good-looking
> cruel – not very kind
> stupid – not very clever/intelligent

7 Do this very quickly with the whole class. Ask them to find 'you' (lines 6, 8) and ask your students what it means.

> **Answer**
> It is the general 'you' meaning 'people in general', translated into many languages as 'one', as in *on* (French), *man* (German). 'One' is only used very formally in English.

8 This could be started in class and completed for homework. Encourage students to read and sometimes check each other's written work when they bring it back to class. Always give sufficient time in class to go over pieces of extended writing. Students can get a feeling of satisfaction from having a correct and well-expressed version. You could start a classroom notice-board for the best and most interesting pieces.

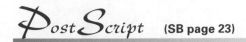

(SB page 23)

Remember that this section is very much movable. You could insert these exercises anywhere in the unit, possibly using them as a warmer at the beginning of a lesson.

Numbers

The exercises should all be revision, and therefore should be covered quite speedily.

1 and 2 Ask students to read the numbers aloud quickly round the class. check as they do this that they are putting *and* in correctly.

> **Answers**
>
> 1 fifteen, fifty, four hundred and six, seventy-two, one hundred and twenty-eight, ninety, nineteen, eight hundred and fifty, one thousand five hundred and twenty, thirty-six, two hundred and forty-seven, five thousand, one hundred thousand, two million
>
> *And* is used with the last figure after hundreds, thousands and millions.
>
> 2 a/one hundred pounds, fifty p /piː/ (or pence), nine pounds forty, forty-seven pounds ninety-nine pence (or, forty-seven ninety-nine), four hundred dollars, five thousand French francs, one thousand deutsch marks
>
> a/one quarter, three quarters, two thirds, twelve and a half
>
> six point two, seventeen point two five,
> fifty percent, seventy-five point seven percent, one hundred percent
>
> nineteen ninety-five, nineteen thirty-nine, seventeen eighty-nine,
> the fifteenth of July nineteen ninety-four,
> the thirtieth of October nineteen sixty-seven
>
> oh one eight six five eight seven six seven six, oh one seven one five eight six double-four three one, double-oh double-four nine two five two seven oh double-nine two

3 **T.16a** Students listen, check and practise.

4 **T.16b** This exercise is to practise hearing numbers in context. Get feedback after each conversation or at the end of all five. Ask what the number refers to.

> **Answers**
>
> 1 the fifteenth, the twenty-fourth (dates)
> nine and a half hours (the length of a flight)
>
> 2 1.5%, 9% (inflation figures)
> two and three quarter million (people out of work)
>
> 3 six pounds   (the price of a cinema ticket)
> 4929 502 428 508 (Visa card number)
> 04/99 (date)
> 7.45 (time)
>
> 4 £39.99 (the price of some shoes)
> half (everything is half price in the sale)
>
> 5 4887621 (telephone number)
> hundredth (a hundredth birthday party)
> eighteenth (date)
> three o'clock (time)

Don't forget!

Workbook Unit 2

Exercise 12 Vocabulary – synonyms and antonyms

Exercise 13 Multi-word verbs with *look* and *be*

Wordlist This is on page 156 of this Teacher's Book for you to photocopy and give your students.

Video *Wide Open Spaces*: Nick and Maddy, a young couple living in London, try to sell their flat.

Telling tales

Past tenses
Active and passive
Giving opinions

Profile

Student's Book

Language
- Past Simple/Continuous
- Past Perfect
- Past active/passive

Pronunciation
- *-d* or *-ed*
- *was*/*were* weak forms

Vocabulary and everyday English
- art, music, literature
- giving opinions
- verb + noun collocations

Workbook

- *'d = had/would*
- extra grammar – *while, during, for*
- vocabulary – position of adverbs
- pronunciation – verbs that sound the same

Video

- Report 2 *Agatha Christie*

Photocopiable materials for this unit (TB page 120)
- This is an extra vocabulary exercise suggested for the reading passages on SB pages 30–31.

Introduction to the unit

The theme of this unit is telling stories, both fictional and factual. This provides the means of illustrating and practising the narrative tenses – the Past Simple, the Past Continuous and the Past Perfect.

The skills work includes biographies of three famous people from the arts, and the main vocabulary work is linked to this arts theme. The writing and listening skills are combined in this unit and are based upon a frightening holiday story.

Report 2 of the *Headway Video Intermediate* is about the life of Agatha Christie, the world famous detective story writer.

Language aims

Grammar

Past tenses

We assume that your students will have some familiarity with narrative tenses, but will nevertheless benefit from revising them, particularly in activities where they are required to discriminate between them. The unit is therefore constructed as follows:

Presentation (1) compares and contrasts the Past Simple and the Past Continuous. Presentation (2) focuses on the Past Perfect, and compares and contrasts it with the uses of the Past Simple and the Past Continuous.

The Past Simple passive is featured in the reading texts and is practised in the language work which follows these.

Vocabulary

The vocabulary section is a word-sort on art, music and literature, which sets the scene and introduces some necessary vocabulary for the reading texts.

The presentation texts, which are two of Aesop's fables, contain a few rather difficult items of vocabulary. However, the pictures can been used to pre-teach these.

PROBLEMS

- The Past Simple has to be used in English for completed actions in the past when other languages can employ the Present Perfect.

  *I bought it last year. *I ~~have bought~~ it last year.*

  We deal with the Present Perfect in depth in Unit 7. Until then just remind students, if they make this mistake, that specific past time must be expressed by the Past Simple.

- Many common verbs are irregular. These are highlighted in Presentation (1), and there is an irregular verb list in the Student's Book on page 157. They are also practised in an exercise in the Workbook.

- There are three pronunciations of *-ed* at the end of regular Past Simple verbs and past participles.

  /t/ *washed*   /d/ *lived*   /ɪd/ *wanted*

  These are practised in Presentation (1).

- As in the Present Simple with the use of *do*, *does*, *don't* and *doesn't* in the questions and negatives, students can wonder about the use of *did* and *didn't* in the Past Simple. The connection between these should be pointed out.

  Common mistakes

  **I ~~did see~~   *I didn't ~~went~~   *When you ~~saw~~ him?*
  She ~~no come~~ yesterday

- The use of the Past Continuous for interrupted past actions is usually quite clear when contrasted with the Past Simple.

  I was having a bath when the phone rang.

  However, the use of the Past Continuous as a descriptive, scene-setting tense can be more difficult to explain. It is best illustrated in context.

  The sun was shining, the birds were singing – and then something terrible happened!

- Over-stressing the pronunciation of *was* and *were* can sound very unnatural in the Past Continuous as they are normally weak in context.

  /wəz/ *He was coming.*   /wə/ *They were sitting.*

- The Past Perfect tense has the problem of the contracted form *'d* because it is also the contracted form of *would*. It can be difficult for students to recognize the difference.

  He'd (had) said he'd (would) come.

  There is an exercise on this in the Workbook.

PostScript

Giving opinions was chosen so that students can give opinions about books, music, films, etc.

Workbook

The conjunction *while* and the prepositions *during* and *for* are practised in the Workbook. There is an exercise on the position of different adverbs in sentences to supplement the Writing section.

Notes on the unit

Test your grammar   (SB page 24)

1   Ask students to discuss the sentences in pairs. They should be able to work out the different meanings quite quickly, but **a** might be a problem. Get class feedback, take care to keep your explanations brief.

Answers
a When Sylvia arrived home, Tim *began to cook* the dinner.
b When Sylvia arrived home, Tim was *in the middle of cooking* the dinner.
c When Sylvia arrived home, the dinner was ready. *Tim cooked it before she arrived.*

2   Ask students to describe what they can see in the pictures. Tim is wearing an *apron*. This will probably be a new word and perhaps worth teaching.

Answers
1–c (The dinner is on the table.)
2–a (Tim is putting on his apron, ready to start cooking.)
3–b (Tim is at the cooker, cooking.)

PRESENTATION (1)   (SB page 24)

Past Simple and Past Continuous

The ancient stories of Aesop seem to fascinate many students. Set the scene before you start the Presentation. Write *Aesop's Fables* on the board. Ask students what a fable is. Ask if students know of Aesop and can tell you any of his stories.

NB A 'fable' is a short story that teaches a lesson.

Aesop was a Greek slave who lived in the 6th century BC. He wrote down over a hundred fables; he was not the author of all the fables; he collected them from many countries. His most famous ones are 'The Hare and the Tortoise', 'The Lion and the Mouse', 'The Wolf in Sheep's clothing'. Many fables have animals as their main characters. However, 'people' are the main characters in the two fables used in Unit 3.

1 Students look at the pictures of the bald knight. Encourage them to guess what the story is about. Ask them a few questions: *Who/What is it about? When do you think it happened?* Use the pictures to pre-teach the following vocabulary: *bald, knight, wig, curly, go hunting,* and *branch* (of a tree).

2 Students should be familiar with the irregular verbs in the story, but check the list on page 157 if they are unsure. Ask them to work on their own and then check with a partner. Check the answers with the whole class.

Answers
The Bald Knight
Once upon a time, a long time ago, there was a knight who, as he **grew** older, **lost** all his hair. He **became** as bald as an egg. He didn't want anyone to see his bald head, so he **bought** a beautiful, black, curly wig.

One day some lords and ladies from the castle invited him to go hunting with them, so of course he **put** on his beautiful wig. ' How handsome I look!' he **thought** to himself. Then he **set** off happily for the forest.

However, a terrible thing happened. His wig **caught** on a branch and **fell** off in full view of everyone. How they all laughed at him! At first the poor knight **felt** very foolish but then he **saw** the funny side of the situation and he started laughing, too.

The knight never **wore** his wig again.

THE MORAL OF THIS STORY IS: WHEN PEOPLE LAUGH AT US, IT IS BEST TO LAUGH WITH THEM.

Discuss their ideas for completing the moral.

3 Now the focus moves from the Past Simple to the Past Continuous. Ask students to work in pairs to discuss where they think the sentences fit. Ask them just to mark the text in three places.

Answers
a 'How handsome I look!' he thought to himself, as he <u>was dressing</u> in front of his mirror. (line 13)
b He <u>was riding</u> along, singing merrily to himself, when he passed under an oak tree and his wig caught on a branch and fell off in full view of everyone. (line 15)
c … and he started laughing, too. They <u>were</u> all still <u>laughing</u> when they arrived back at the castle. (line 20)

4 **T.17** Get quick feedback on their ideas. However, don't give the correct answer yourself – play the tape for the students to listen and check for themselves.

● Grammar questions

Go through these with the whole class, reading the questions aloud.

Answers
– The <u>underlined</u> verbs in exercise 3 are all in the Past Continuous.
– The first sentence means that he fell off his horse and then he started to laugh. The second sentence means that first he started to laugh and fell off in the middle of laughing. We don't know if he continued to laugh afterwards! This is an example of the interrupted Past Continuous.

SUGGESTION
You could draw time lines on the board.

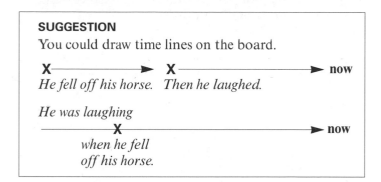

PRACTICE (SB page 25)

1 Grammar

This exercise could be set for homework, but it is better done in class as it provides immediate reinforcement of the grammar questions. Students work alone and then discuss their answers in pairs or small groups. Check through with the whole class.

Answers
a While he <u>was riding</u> in the forest he <u>lost</u> his wig.
b When I <u>arrived</u> the party was in full swing. Paul <u>was dancing</u> with Mary, and Pat and Peter <u>were drinking</u> champagne.
c When I <u>finished</u> the ironing, I <u>cooked</u> dinner.
d How fast <u>were they travelling</u> when their car <u>had</u> a puncture?
e A police car <u>passed</u> us on the motorway when we <u>were doing</u> 80 miles per hour.
f I <u>took</u> a photograph of him while he <u>was eating</u> an ice-cream.
g He <u>didn't like</u> the photo when he <u>saw</u> it.
h I'm sorry I <u>woke</u> you. What <u>were you dreaming</u> about?

2 Pronunciation

T.18 This a short exercise to help in production of regular past tense endings. It is movable, for example it could be used as a warmer to the lesson on the Past Perfect because it is also relevant to past participle endings.

Answers

/t/	/d/	/ɪd/
cooked	arrived	wanted
finished	lived	started
laughed	travelled	visited
danced	listened	invited

3 Speaking

1 This activity provides controlled oral practice of the third person of the Past Continuous.

2 Students work in pairs and ask and answer the questions. Monitor them, paying particular attention to the weak forms of *was* /wəz/ and *were* /wə/.

Answers

What was she doing at 7 o'clock (in the morning)?
She was packing her suitcase.

What was she doing at 8 o'clock?
She was driving to the airport.

What was she doing at quarter to ten?
She was flying to Edinburgh /ˈedɪnbrə/.

What was she doing at half past eleven?
She was having a meeting.

What was she doing at half past one?
She was having lunch.

What was she doing at 3 o'clock?
She was visiting a school.

What was she doing at half past six?
She was writing a report on the plane.

What was she doing at quarter to nine?
She was cooking a meal.

What was she doing at ten o'clock?
She was listening to music.

3 This is the same activity as above but personalized and therefore giving practice of *you* and *I*.

After students have written their lists, you could do it as a mingle activity to change the pace and focus of the lesson. Join in yourself and make a note of anything interesting to refer to in feedback.

End the lesson with students asking *you* what *you* were doing at different times yesterday.

4 Life stories

T.19 This is the true story of Sylvia's grandparents, Victor and Aileen Gibbs. Ask students to look at their photograph, and guess when and where it was taken.

There might be variation in the students' versions but they should compare theirs with the real story on the tape. Sylvia is speaking.

NB *There is an exercise on 'while', 'for' and 'during' in Unit 3 of the Workbook and it is a good idea to do this before doing this one.*

Answers

They met and fell in love while they were working together in Malaysia.

They got married during the Second World War.

They had their first son while they were living in Hong Kong.

They lived in Hong Kong for five years.

They had five more sons when they returned to Britain.

They sent their sons to boarding school while they were working abroad.

They lived in six different countries during their marriage.

They were happily married for over forty-five years.

My grandfather died during the summer of 1991.

ADDITIONAL MATERIAL

Workbook Unit 3

Exercises 1–5 These exercises give further practice of the Past Simple and the Past Continuous.

Exercise 12 This practises *while*, *for* and *during*.

PRESENTATION (2)   (SB page 26)

Past Simple and Past Perfect

1 This is another of Aesop's fables. This time the students hear it before they read it.

First, ask students to look at the pictures and try to guess what the story is about. Again, you need to use the pictures to pre-teach some vocabulary before your students listen to the story. Teach them:

vineyard /ˈvɪnjəd/, *grapes*, *treasure* /ˈtreʒə/, *bury* /ˈberi/, *coins*, *necklace* /ˈnekləs/

2 **T.20** Ask them to close their book and listen to the story. Were their ideas correct?

3 Students read and then work with a partner to try and complete the moral.

Answer
The moral is:
HARD WORK BRINGS ITS OWN REWARD.
(Accept other versions that mean the same. For example:
Hard work brings success, wealth and happiness.)

4 Ask students to work in pairs.

Answers

| a | 2 | c | 6 | e | 5 |
| b | 1 | d | 3 | f | 4 |

5 Play the tape again, and ask students to listen and check their answers. You could ask individuals to read aloud sections of the completed story round the class.

● Grammar questions

Read aloud the grammar questions to the whole class and ask for answers.

> **Answers**
> – The verb forms are all in the Past Perfect tense.
> – **b** is true.
> – **a** means they began looking while he was still alive.
>   **b** means he died before they started looking.

SUGGESTION

You could draw time lines on the board.

Their father was dying.

a ——————**X**————————————▶ **now**

They started looking for the treasure.

b **X**————————▶———————**X**————————▶ **now**

Their father died.   *They started looking.*

You could at this point read through the Language Review on page 28. This explains the differences.

PRACTICE   (SB page 27)

1 Discussing grammar

1 This is discrimination practice between the three past tenses. Students are asked to recognize differences in meaning and build their grammatical awareness as a step towards consistently correct production.

NB It can be as good for oral fluency to discuss grammar in pairs as it is to discuss other topics! If L1 is at times used in a monolingual class, don't be too harsh! Circulate as they discuss.

> **Answers**
> a *were drinking* = I arrived in the middle of the party, i.e. there was still champagne left for me!
>
>   *'d (had) drunk* = The champagne was finished when I arrived, i.e. there was none left for me!
>
> b *went* = The children didn't go to bed until I arrived home.
>
>   *had gone* = The children were already in bed when I arrived home.
>
> c *was doing* = They haven't taken the exam yet.
>
>   *'d (had) done* = They have taken the exam and passed it.
>
> d *were staying* = They are staying at the Ritz now.
>
>   *had stayed* = They stayed in the Ritz at some time in the past.
>
> (These are examples of Reported Speech.)

2 Use the example to show students how they need work out what happened first before they try to join the ideas using the Past Perfect.

> **Answers**
> a My headache disappeared when I'd taken the aspirin. (*My headache disappeared when I took the aspirin.* This is also possible.)
> b He stopped for a break after he'd driven 200 miles.
> c I couldn't pay for my ticket because a thief had stolen my wallet.
> d As soon as she'd passed her driving test, she bought a car.
> e I didn't go to Italy until I'd learnt Italian. (Take care with this one, the use of *until* can cause problems.)
> f He didn't tell the policeman that he'd taken the money.
> g We didn't tell Anna that George had rung.

NB The last two sentences, f and g, are both examples of Reported Speech. This follows the Past Perfect rule of one action happening before another in the past. The event happened before the 'telling'.

2 Dictation and questions

This is not a full dictation. Students are required to write down only the teacher's answers to their questions.

NB Occasional dictations can be useful for developing listening skills. Students sometimes need to listen for exact words, not just for overall meaning.

Demonstrate the procedure with the example.

Answers Students' questions	Teacher's answers
1 Where did they go on holiday?	To a Greek island.
2 What did they do everyday?	They went swimming and lay in the sun.
3 Where were they swimming?	In the sea near the hotel.
4 What did the huge wave do?	It knocked Wanda's sunglasses into the water.
5 Why was Wanda very upset?	Because Roy had given her the sunglasses for her birthday.
6 Where were they sunbathing?	On another beach.
7 What was Wanda wearing?	A cheap pair of sunglasses which she had just bought.
8 What did the wave do (this time)?	It covered poor Wanda from top to bottom.
9 What did she see?	The sunglasses which Roy had bought her.

Completed text

Last summer Wanda and Roy went on holiday to **a Greek island**. Every day they **went swimming** and **lay in the sun**. One morning they were swimming **in the sea near the hotel** when a huge wave **knocked Wanda's sunglasses into the water**. Wanda was very upset because **Roy had given her the sunglasses for her birthday**.

The next day they were sunbathing **on another beach** and Wanda was wearing **a cheap pair of sunglasses which she had just bought** when suddenly there was another huge wave, which **covered poor Wanda from top to bottom**. She was furious, but then she looked down and to her amazement she saw **the sunglasses which Roy had bought her**.

You could ask individual students to read aloud parts of the completed text round the class.

3 Stress and intonation

1 Do this first in open pairs across the class, so that you can make sure that your students are attempting good stress and intonation as well getting the correct answers. Nominate **A** and **B**.

Answers

A I went to the airport but I couldn't catch the plane.
B Oh dear! Had you forgotten your passport?

A I was homesick while I was living in New York.
B Poor you! Had you never lived abroad before?

A I met my boyfriend's/girlfriend's parents last Sunday.
B Oh! Hadn't you met them before?

A My grandfather had two sons from his first marriage.
B Really? I didn't know he'd been married before.

A I told everyone the good news.
B Hadn't they heard it already?

A As soon as I saw him I knew something was wrong.
B Oh dear! What had happened?

2 **T.21** Play the tape for students to listen and check their answers. Encourage them to pay particular attention to the stress and intonation.

3 Students now practise in pairs, and practise the stress and intonation from the tape. Ask them to choose one or two and make them into longer conversations.

SUGGESTION

You could record a few of the conversations and play them back to the class, or choose some pairs to act out their conversations at the front of the class.

LANGUAGE REVIEW (SB page 28)

Narrative tenses

If you haven't done this already, read this aloud to the class. They could be encouraged to translate some of the sentences into their own language.

Ask them to read the Grammar Reference section for homework, and again whilst they are doing some of the exercises in the Workbook.

ADDITIONAL MATERIAL

Workbook
Exercises 6–9 These give more practice of the Past Perfect.

● VOCABULARY (SB page 29)

Art, music and literature

This vocabulary section is a word-sort on art, music and literature. It is important to do it at this point because it both sets the scene and introduces some necessary vocabulary for the following reading texts.

SUGGESTION

Set homework *before* the vocabulary lesson, asking your students to write a few notes about their favourite book, poem, piece of music or painting, because this features in exercise 4 of the activity and is also a prelude to the reading texts.

1 Ask students to work in pairs or small groups. Make sure they realize that all the words are nouns. Ask them to draw the columns on a piece of paper and then write in the words. Check with the whole class.

Answers

ART	MUSIC	LITERATURE
painter	composer	poem
oil painting	instrument	author
palette	band	chapter
sketch	tune	biography
brush	orchestra	detective story
portrait	bugle	fiction
drawing	banjo	play
	pop group	novel
	pianist	

2 This is a collocation activity. Give students a few minutes to consider the verbs in pairs before you go through them together as a class. Make sure that they realize that all the words are verbs. You could write a couple of examples on the board to help, for example, *an author writes a novel   we read a novel*

Answers

read and write	a poem, a chapter, a biography, a detective story, fiction, a play, a novel
write	an author writes books, a composer writes music
compose	a tune, a poem
play	an instrument, a tune, a bugle, a banjo; a pianist plays a tune
play in	a band, an orchestra, a pop group
draw	a sketch, a portrait
paint	an oil painting, a portrait; a painter paints a picture with a brush
conduct	an orchestra, a band
hum	a tune
tune	an instrument, a banjo

3 This exercise puts some of the collocations into context. Encourage students to do it quite quickly in pairs, then get feedback.

Answers

a Agatha Christie **wrote** many famous **detective stories**.

b I couldn't put the book down until I'**d read** the last **chapter**.

c I don't know the words of the song but I can **hum** the **tune**.

d The only **instrument** I can **play** is the piano.

e Picasso often **painted/drew** unusual **portraits/sketches** of his girlfriends.

f The **biography** of Princess Diana **was written** by the journalist, Andrew Morton.

g Listen! The show is starting. Can you hear the **orchestra/band/pop group**? They'**re tuning** their instruments.

h My brother is a soldier. He **plays** the bugle in the army **band**.

i Before I painted the picture I **drew** a quick **sketch** in pencil.

4 This will work much better if you have set it as homework prior to the lesson, as suggested. Ask the class to talk about it in small groups first and then compare with the whole class. Encourage them to ask each other questions. You could also tell them about your favourites.

SUGGESTION

Remember that this discussion is designed to set the scene for the reading activity about the writer, the painter and the musician. Therefore if you are not doing this until a later lesson, it is a good idea to defer the discussion until then, and have it before the pre-reading task.

● READING AND SPEAKING (SB page 29)

The writer, the painter and the musician

Pre-reading task

SUGGESTION

T.22 Put on Scott Joplin's *The Entertainer* from the very start of the lesson – at first just as background music whilst you ask what students know about the other two famous people, Agatha Christie and Pablo Picasso. Turn it up when you focus on Scott Joplin himself. This is not just a pleasing and motivating start to the reading activity, but probably Scott Joplin is the least well-known to your students and the tune helps identify him because it is very well-known.

1 Write the names of the three famous people on the board and ask *Which is the writer? The painter? The musician?* Ask for any general information about why they were famous. Now ask students to open their books and look at the book titles and picture of *Guernica*. Play *The Entertainer*. Ask if they know any more of their works. They may well do for the first two but probably not Scott Joplin.

NB 'Guernica' was a small Basque town in northern Spain which was almost totally destroyed by a bombing attack in 1937 during the Spanish Civil War. Picasso's painting of the scene is now in the Prado Museum, in Madrid.

2 Ask them to discuss the questions in groups. You could at this point form the three groups you will need to do the actual reading activity. Tell them they will find out the answers to the questions when they read.

Reading

SUGGESTION

Before the reading lesson, divide the class into the three groups A, B, C, and set a vocabulary exercise for homework, one exercise per group. Use the exercise given in the photocopiable materials on page 120 in this Teacher's Book. Ask students to use their dictionaries to find the meanings of the underlined words in each sentence.

This is a jigsaw reading activity, which should generate a lot of free speaking. The writer is Agatha Christie, the painter Picasso, and the musician Scott Joplin. The class is divided into three groups, and each group reads about only *one* of the people and then they swap information about the other two with students from the other groups.

Put the students into three groups, **A**, **B**, **C**, if you have not already done so, and then allocate the texts. Check that someone in each group has a dictionary to look up words which they can't guess from the context.

Go round the groups as they work and help them. Get them to make very brief answer notes and give the groups about ten minutes to answer the questions.

Then ask students to swap information with members of the other groups.

Answers

1. A Agatha Christie was born in Devon (a very beautiful county in South West England).
   B Pablo Picasso was born in Malaga, Spain.
   C Scott Joplin was born in Texas, USA.

2. A She was born in 1890.
   B He was born in 1881.
   C He was born in 1868.

3. A She was beautiful but very shy. She didn't go to school but was educated at home by her mother. Her father died when she was only eleven and she was very upset.
   B He showed his talent early. He learned to draw before he could talk. His first word was *lápiz* (pencil). He was very spoilt because he was the only son. He hated school and would only go if he took one of his father's pigeons. He painted a beautiful pigeon at 13 and his father gave him his own palette.
   C He came from a very poor family. He played the violin and bugle and piano. He played at first by ear and didn't learn music until he was 11. His mother died when he was 14 and he went to St. Louis.

4. A Her divorce from Archibald Christie and her mother's death in the same year caused her a lot of pain but also seemed to lead to some of her best writing. Her second husband was an archaeologist who also needed detective skills.
   B His father, who was an amateur artist and drawing teacher, encouraged him by buying him his own palette.
   C His father worked extra hours to buy him a piano. His old German music teacher gave him free lessons. Music in St. Louis inspired him.

5. A Her father's death. Working in a hospital dispensary in World War I. Her mysterious disappearance after her mother's death and her divorce. The opening of *The Mousetrap*. Her second marriage.
   B Watching his father paint. Painting a pigeon. The bombing of Guernica.
   C Getting a second-hand piano. Learning to play classical music as well as blues and spirituals, with his old German teacher. Going to St. Louis. Working on the Mississippi waterfront.

6. A She wrote 79 novels and several plays. She has sold more books than Shakespeare. She wrote her first detective novel, *The Mysterious Affair at Styles*, in 1920. Her two main detectives were Hercule Poirot and Miss Marple. She wrote her masterpiece *The Murder of Roger Ackroyd* when she was very unhappy. Her play *The Mousetrap* is the longest running show in the world.
   B He was not a traditionalist painter. He is best known for his 'Cubist' pictures, using geometric shapes. *Guernica* is a masterpiece. He created over 6,000 paintings, drawings and sculptures. His paintings are worth millions of pounds.
   C His music is known as Ragtime – a mixture of classical European and African beat. It is played by both black and white musicians. He wrote about 50 piano rags. His most famous tune *The Entertainer* was the musical theme of the film *The Sting*.

7. A She died in 1976.
   B He died in 1973.
   C He died in 1917.

8. A She wrote 79 novels. Her father died when she was 11, and she was missing for 11 days. She has written 4,680,000 words. Her first book came out in 1920. She was divorced in 1926. *The Mousetrap* opened in 1952.
   B He created 6,000 paintings, drawings and sculptures. He got his first palette aged 13. He painted *Guernica* in 1937.
   C He didn't learn to read music until he was 11. He wrote 50 rags. His mother died in 1882 when he was 14.

Comprehension check

1. Ask students now to read *quickly* through the other texts. This should *not* take very long. They have already found out a lot of information about the other two famous people from the students from the other groups.

   The idea is that they also help each other with unknown underlined words from the texts.

2. There are two sentences about each person. Ask students first to recognize which one the each question refers to. Students work in pairs. Forming questions can be quite a challenging activity, so you will need to go round and help them, particularly with **b**, **c**, and **d**.

   Go through the whole exercise in open pairs in a class feedback.

Answers

a What was Agatha Christie like?

b Why was cigar smoke blown into Picasso's nose?

c How did Scott Joplin's father get (the) money/afford to buy him a grand piano?

d Why did Agatha Christie dislike/hate/have bitter feelings towards the media?

e When did Picasso paint *Guernica*?

f Where did Scott Joplin go when his mother died/ when he was 14/ to seek his fortune?

Language work

This focuses on the Past Simple passive. It is a good idea to do the language work exercises altogether, or with the class in small groups, so they can help each other and move the lesson forward more quickly. Alternatively, you could set this and the note-taking element of the following activity for homework.

1 Read aloud the example. Then ask students to give you other examples from the texts. To help them, you could give the exact number to find in each one.

Answers

Agatha Christie
was born, was educated, was found, was determined (past participle and adjective)

Pablo Picasso
was born, was blown, was spoilt (past participle and adjective), was allowed, were made (up of)

Scott Joplin
was born, was known, was played, were filled, were settled

Tell students to read the Grammar Reference section on page 144.

2 Do this as a class.

Answers

a Agatha Christie **was** educated at home. She **didn't** go to school.

b She **was** found in a hotel in Harrogate, after she **had** been missing for 11 days.

c She **didn't** stop writing while she **was** suffering from a nervous breakdown.

d Pablo Picasso **didn't** like going to school unless he **was** allowed to take one of his father's pigeons with him.

e His father **didn't** paint again after Pablo **had** completed the picture of the pigeons.

f Some paint **was** spilt on the French minister's trousers when he **was** visiting Picasso.

g Scott Joplin left home after his mother **had** died.

Note-taking and discussion

The research and note-taking is best set as homework, and followed up in class with discussion in pairs. Students can report interesting points made by their partners to the whole class. This could of course lead to their writing a short biography.

You could also tell them about a famous person of *your* choice and get them to ask you questions about him or her.

ADDITIONAL MATERIAL

Workbook Unit 3

Exercises 10 and 11 Further practice of the Past Simple passive. The exercises include some very short texts which pick up on the theme of biographies of the famous.

Video Report 2 is about the life of Agatha Christie.

● WRITING AND LISTENING (SB page 32)

Adverbs in a narrative

This combines listening, reading and writing skills. We suggest that the whole activity should be done in pairs.

1 Do this not only to set the scene, but because the notes will be needed for the subsequent writing activity.

> **SUGGESTION**
> You could ask students to think about their worst holiday for homework immediately before the lesson. This will give them time to collect a few thoughts and save valuable lesson time.

2 Tell students that now they are going to hear about someone else's worst holiday. This is a true story. Ask them to read the first part and then work in their pairs to insert the adverbs. This is quite challenging so go round and help as they do it. Go through it with the whole class.

NB *There is sometimes more than one possibility as to where the adverbs can go. However, this is probably the most natural sounding version.*

Answer

The holiday that wasn't

Just after Christmas two years ago, Jack and Liza *suddenly* decided to go away *somewhere* for New Year. They didn't want to stay in a hotel with crowds of people and *so* they were *really* delighted when they saw an advertisement in the Sunday Times for a holiday flat in a village near Oxford.

However, it was no ordinary flat. It was on the top floor of an old Tudor mansion. They booked it *immediately* and on New Year's Eve they set off in the car. *Although* it was raining *heavily* and freezing cold, they were happy and excited.

They had been driving for *nearly* three hours when they *finally* saw the house in the distance. It looked magnificent with *incredibly* tall chimneys and a long, wide drive. They drove up to the huge front door, went up the steps, and knocked *loudly*. Nothing happened. They knocked again *more loudly*. *Eventually* the door *slowly* opened and a small, wild-looking, old lady stood there.

3 **T.23** Before you play the tape, ask students to guess what happens next. You could put their suggestions on the board and tick any that prove to be true as you listen.

Answers
- The old lady was wearing old, dirty, torn clothes and bandages.
- She was carrying a cat and a large glass of whisky.
- The house was old, dark and dirty. There were cats everywhere.
- When she was leading them upstairs two huge dogs nearly knocked them over.
- When they saw the rooms they couldn't believe their eyes because the furniture was broken, there were no curtains and the only heating was a small electric fire. Also there was only one power point.

4 Ask students to read the end of the story and complete it as before.

Answer
When they got outside again the rain had turned to snow. They ran to the car, laughing *hysterically*. They felt that they had been released from a prison and now they *desperately* wanted to be with lots of people. They drove to the next village and *fortunately*, *just* as midnight was striking, they found a hotel with a room for the night. 'Happy New Year!' cried Jack, as he kissed the surprised receptionist *warmly* on both cheeks. 'You have no idea how beautiful your hotel is!'

5 Students could begin this in class and complete it for homework. If you have time, you could ask them to read and check each other's work later in class while you circulate and help with the correction. Ask some of them to read their stories aloud.

ADDITIONAL MATERIAL

Workbook Unit 3
Exercise 13 This is a further exercise on adverbs.

PostScript (SB page 34)

Giving opinions

This could be used at any stage in the unit after the reading texts. It provides practice in giving opinions about books, films, people, food, etc. Students could work in pairs for the whole activity.

1 You may need to do the first one with the class as an example.

Answers
a *It*   = a play
b *one* = a book/novel
c *It*   = a film
d *She* = an actress or film star
e *they* = the parents   *them* = their children
f *It*   = a holiday
g *They* = pizzas
h *It*   = a football match

As you go through the answers, ask your students which words in the sentences helped them reach a decision.

2 **T.24** Students match them, then listen to check their answers. Ask them particularly to listen for stress and intonation, and practise it in pairs afterwards.

Answers

Did you like the film?	c
What did you think of the play?	a
Did you enjoy your pizzas?	g
Do you like Ben Brown's novels?	b
What do you think of their children?	e
What was your holiday like?	f
What did you think of Hannah Smart?	d
What was the match like?	h

3 This is a freer personalized activity to practise. Do the example in open pairs to illustrate the idea. Then ask them to write down some things they did last week.

Go round and monitor as they do it, and note any interesting conversations. Round off the lesson by getting a few pairs to act out their conversations, or record some and play them back.

Don't forget!

Workbook Unit 3

Exercise 14 Prepositions of time *in*, *at*, *on*.

Exercise 15 Pronunciation – an exercise on homophones, words that sound the same but have different meanings.

Wordlist This is on page 157 of this Teacher's Book for you to photocopy and give your students.

Video Report 2: The life of Agatha Christie

Stop and check There is a Stop and check revision section for use after each quarter of the Student's Book.

Stop and check 1 is on pages 136–7 of this Teacher's Book. You need to photocopy it. The key is on page 151.

SUGGESTION

You can use the Stop and check any way you want, but here is one way.

- Give it to your students to do for homework, preferably when they have enough time, for example, a weekend.

- In class, ask them to go over the test again in groups of five or six people. They should try to agree on definitive answers. If they can't agree, they should ask you.

- You provide the answers and any necessary explanations.

Doing the right thing

Modal verbs (1)
Requests and offers

Profile

Student's Book

Language
- modal auxiliary verbs (past and present)
- obligation, permission
- requests, offers
- negative forms
- forming questions
- filling in a form

Pronunciation
- *have to*
- *must/mustn't*
- word formation and changes in stress

Vocabulary and everyday English
- adjectives describing character
- word formation
- requests and offers

Workbook
- extra grammar – *can/be able to, could/managed to*
- vocabulary – nationality words (*France – French – The French*)
- pronunciation – sentence stress
- multi-word verbs – separable or inseparable?

Video
- *Wide Open Spaces* Episode 2
- Report 5 about a famous English public school is also relevant (but see Unit 9).

Photocopiable materials for this unit (TB page 120)
- This is an extra reading and speaking activity on etiquette (see TB page 45).

Introduction to the unit

The topics for this unit are authority and obeying rules – school rules and social rules – and entertaining friends in different countries. These themes fit the target language of the unit, which is expressing obligation and permission.

There is a lot to get through in this unit. Not only are the two Presentations quite meaty, there are many extra skills activities. Students are invited to talk about the age at which they can do various things (for example, get married) in their countries, and school rules. There is an interview with a man in his late seventies, where he recalls his days 'at the Big Boys school'. Prior to the reading, there is a discussion about nationality stereotypes.

So don't get 'bogged down' in this unit. Keep things moving!

Language aims

Grammar
Modal auxiliary verbs

Your students probably had some familiarity with the grammar in Units 1–3. Without doubt they had come across the two Present tenses and the three Past tenses before. When we were trying this material out ourselves, our class had quite a shock when they reached Unit 4. Modal verbs are a much more difficult area to understand. There are subtle differences of meaning (*must* versus *have to*), problems of form (*mustn't* versus *don't have to*), as well as problems of confusing modal auxiliary verbs and full verbs. Suddenly, language learning didn't seem quite so easy for our students!

It is possible that they hadn't come across modal auxiliary verbs as a system before. They had no doubt encountered *can* and *should*, and probably *must* and *might*. *Have to* is often taught at lower levels as an all-purpose way of expressing obligation, thus avoiding the problems of sorting out *must* versus *have to*, which is not easy.

Modal auxiliary verbs present problems of all kinds, but now is the level to start sorting them out. Don't expect students to have mastered the area by the end of the unit. They will continue to have a lot of problems. Some areas of the language, like the Present Perfect, take a long time to assimilate. Practice, practice, more explanation, more exposure and more practice is what is necessary!

There is an introduction to modal auxiliary verbs on page 146 of the Grammar Reference section. At some stage of the unit, draw students' attention to this, as it should enable them to begin to perceive a pattern in the form and use of these verbs.

Vocabulary

There are two lots of vocabulary input. The first comes prior to the reading, and is an input of adjectives that describe character. This is to set up the discussion on nationality stereotypes. The second comes after the reading, and concerns word formation and dictionary entries.

PostScript

The functions of requests and offers are presented and practised. This is not only because they are high frequency functional areas, but because they offer the chance of furthering students' understanding of modal auxiliary verbs.

Workbook

- Extra grammar – *can* and *be able*, *could* and *managed to*
- Vocabulary – nationality words – *Italy, Italian, the Italians*
- Pronunciation – sentence stress
- Multi-word verbs – separable or inseparable?

Notes on the unit

Test your grammar (SB page 35)

This particular *Test your grammar* exercise is short. The idea is simply to raise students' awareness of a few of the problems presented by modal auxiliary verbs. Don't fall into the trap of using this opportunity to tell the class everything you know about these verbs.

1 Ask students to look at the sentences. Ask if they know what *can, must* and *should* are called.

2 Ask students to make the sentences negative, into questions, into the third person singular.

This exercise highlights the fact that modal verbs don't use *do/does* to form the negative and the question; that there is no *-s* in the third person singular; that *have to* also expresses obligation, but it's a full verb, not a modal verb.

> **Answers**
> You can't go.
> You mustn't go.
> You shouldn't go.
> You don't have to go.
>
> Can you go?
> Must you go?
> Should you go?
> Do you have to go?
>
> He can go.
> She must go.
> He should go.
> She doesn't have to go. *She has to go*
> *Have to* is the verb that operates differently.
> It is a full verb.

PRESENTATION (1) (SB page 35)

can, have to, and *allowed to*

These three items shouldn't present too much of a problem, but they are enough to challenge students! It is the act of bringing them together to compare and contrast them that makes them difficult.

Can will be very familiar to students. It is a more informal way of expressing *allowed to*, which in this unit is only used in the passive.

Have to in the positive is less of a problem than in the negative. Students seem quite happy with *have to* in the positive, until it is contrasted with *must*, when things start getting very tricky. This is dealt with in the Practice section of Presentation (2). The concept of absence of obligation as expressed by *don't have to* is quite difficult to convey, and many languages express this idea with a paraphrase such as *It isn't necessary to ...*

Notice the pronunciation of *have to* /hæf tu:/.

1 Discuss the problems of the teenage years for both parents and children. This might go on for quite a while! Don't let it dominate the lesson, however.

2 **T.25** Listen to Megan and Laura talking about being a teenager. Ask *What are some of the things they like, and some of the things they don't like?* You might want to point out that Megan and Laura use *you* to refer to all teenagers in general, not a specific *you*.

Answers
They like the fact that they don't have to go to work or pay bills. They are free to go out. They don't have to do the housework.
They don't like the fact that they don't have enough money. They have to wear a school uniform.

3 Students work in pairs to complete the gaps. Let them use their memories and their knowledge of grammar to puzzle out what should go in the gaps. Don't let them just copy from the tapescript.

Answers
a You **don't have to** go out to work.
b You **don't have to** pay bills.
c You **can** go out with your friends.
d I always **have to** tell my Mum and Dad where I'm going.
e We **don't have to** do the housework.
f You **aren't allowed to** buy what you want.
g Adults **have to** worry about bills.
h We **have to** wear a stupid school uniform.
i We **can't** wear make-up.
j We **aren't allowed to** chew gum!

SUGGESTION

Before you move on, you need to do some work on checking meaning, form and pronunciation. Ask questions such as:

Is it necessary for teenagers to go out to work?
Can they work if they want to?
Is it necessary for teenagers to do the housework?
Is it necessary for them to wear a school uniform?
What are some of the school rules?
Is it OK for them to wear make-up?
What about chewing gum?
Do 'can't' and 'not allowed to' mean the same?

The above questions are to establish meaning. You now need to drill the sentences to establish form and pronunciation. Ask for individual repetition of the sentences in this exercise and correct all mistakes. You could get question and answer drills going across the room in open pairs, for example

Do teenagers have to go out to work?
No, they don't.
Do they have to do the housework?
No, they don't.
Does Megan have to tell her parents where she's going?
Yes, she does.
Are children allowed to chew gum at school?
No, they aren't.

---

4 Read the introduction. The first part of this exercise is aimed to get some controlled practice of *have to*.

Answers
Barbara doesn't have to work on Thursdays and Fridays.
She has to do the shopping and the cooking.
She has to take Laura to dancing.
Malcolm has to work full-time.
He doesn't have to do anything in the house.

Answer the three questions at the bottom of the page. They are designed to get more practice of the target structures, but with the students talking about their own families. Decide how much you want to correct. Presumably if the topic takes off and the students are interested, you won't want to correct all the time. Equally, if there are some howling errors, you'll want to intervene.

● **Grammar questions**

Students work in pairs to answer the grammar questions. They will probably find the first one easy because the sentences relate directly to what they've just been talking about. However, the second set of sentences may prove trickier as they try to puzzle out if it is essential or merely desirable to go to England to learn English. Be prepared to intervene and nudge.

Answers
– Children **have to** go to school.
  Adults **don't have to** go to school, but they **have to** go to work.
  Old people **don't have to** go to work.
  Teenagers **have to** study for exams.

– The correct sentences are:
  a You mustn't drive on the right in Britain.
  b You don't have to go to England to learn English.

PRACTICE   (SB page 36)

1 Grammar and speaking

1 This is a manipulation exercise. Do it first as a class, then in pairs. It shouldn't take long. Correct carefully.

Answers
a I don't have to go.
   Do I have to go?
   I had to go.
b She doesn't have to work hard.
   Does she have to work hard?
   She didn't have to work hard.   *She had to*
c He can't do what he likes.
   Can he do what he likes?
   He couldn't do what he liked.
d We aren't allowed to wear what we want.
   Are we allowed to wear what we want?
   We weren't allowed to wear what we wanted.

2 Ask students to look at the chart. Set this up by telling the class some sentences about you and your life, then ask them to work in pairs to produce some sentences about themselves. Add *son* and *daughter* to the list of people if some of your students have children.

Monitor the pairs, then get some feedback as a class. Look at the questions at the bottom of the page, and try to get a mini-discussion going.

3 Students work in pairs to make questions.

> **Answers**
> a How often does she have to go abroad?
> b What time do you have to leave?
> c How long did you have to wait (for)?
> d Why do you have to take your car to the garage?
> e Why did Peter have to stay in bed for a week?

2 Signs

Students produce sentences using *can, can't, not allowed to, have to* and *don't have to* from the signs. Make sure they know the verb *to browse*, and that they will need to use *you* meaning 'people in general'.

Do this exercise first in pairs so that all students have to work to produce sentences, then as a class to check.

> **Answers**
> a You can't/aren't allowed to take photographs.
> b You can come into the shop and look, you don't have to buy anything.
> c Adults have to pay £5, but children don't have to pay anything.
> d You can't/aren't allowed to park here.
> e You have to wear a seat-belt. *must*
> f You can't/aren't allowed to skateboard.
> g You can't/aren't allowed to light fires.
> h You have to eat it before 16 June.

3 Listening and speaking

Remember not to do all the Practice activities one after the other. Intersperse them with some freer activities, and/or something completely different.

Look at the picture. Ask students to describe what they can see. They may decide to describe the age of the children, their clothes and haircuts, the furniture, the number of children, etc.

1 **T.26** You could set this activity up by asking students about their parents' schooling. *Where did your parents go to school? Was it strict? What were some of the rules? Did they like it?*

Read the introduction, and ask students to check the four words in their dictionaries.

Students listen and take notes under the headings. They don't have to write complete sentences, just notes.

> **Answers**
> **knitting** – All the children had to learn to knit.
> **paper and pencils** – They weren't allowed to use paper and pencils until they were seven.
> **chalk and a slate** – They had to use chalk and a slate for the first two years.
> **the 'Big Boys' school** – He went to the 'Big Boys' school when he was ten.
> **exams** – He didn't have to take any exams to go to the 'Big Boys' school.
> **walking to school** – They had to walk to school.
> **a bike** – He didn't get a bike until he was fourteen.
> **leaving school** – Everyone had to leave school at fourteen.
> **talking in class** – They weren't allowed to talk in class.
> **writing lines** – He had to write one hundred lines because he arrived late to school.
> **homework** – He never had to do any homework.

Play the tape again with students reading the tapescript on page 130 of their books.

2 In groups, students talk about their school rules. Again, be careful about correcting. Don't interrupt the flow of conversation, but do correct howlers.

ADDITIONAL MATERIAL

Workbook Unit 4
Exercises 1 and 2 *have to/don't have to*
Exercises 3 and 4 *can/allowed to*
Extra grammar *can/be able, could/managed to*

Video Report 5 is about Rugby, a famous English public school.

PRESENTATION (2) (SB page 37)
must and *should*

> **PROBLEMS**
> These two items aren't that problematic, and students may well have come across them already, but perhaps not as compared and contrasted items. Stress that *must* expresses strong obligation, and *should* expresses milder obligation, in other words, advice.

1 **T.27a** Students listen to Jim and his mother. Practise the four-line dialogue in open and possibly closed pairs. Be careful with the pronunciation of both the positive and the negative.

/ˌjuː məs ˈraɪt/   /ˌjuː mʌsn ˈluːz/

Check the meaning of *must* with questions.
Is it important that Jim writes? Is it very important?
Can Jim's mother tell him what to do?

Students work in pairs to make similar dialogues. Do one or two as a class first, so students know what they have to do.

T.27b Play the tape to check their answers.

2 **T.28a** Students listen to Jim and Anthony. Ask questions to check understanding of *should,* for example
Does Jim say, 'We must take travellers' cheques'?
What does he say?
What's the difference between 'must' and 'should'?
Which is stronger?
Which is more of a suggestion?

Read the instructions for the dialogues. Do the first one as an example.

I think we should take plenty of sun cream. It'll be really hot.

Students work in pairs to match an idea in **A** with a line in **B**.

T.28b Play the tape to check their answers.

● Grammar questions

Read the sentences as a class. Ask the questions, and monitor the students carefully to see if they understand or not.

> **Answers**
> – The first sentence expresses strong obligation.
> – The second sentence expresses a suggestion.
> – Jim's mother is more forceful because she has greater authority.

PRACTICE   (SB page 38)
1 Giving advice

Read the instructions and the example as a class. Students work in pairs to think of suggestions.

> **Sample answers**
> a I think you should phone the bank and cancel your cheques.
> b I don't think he should drive. I think he should take a taxi.
> c I think you should tell the waiter.
> d I don't think you should buy so many new clothes.
> e I think they should wait a few years.
> f I think you should try to find one you like.

2 *must* or *have to*?

We strongly suggest that the class reads the Language Review on page 39 before doing this exercise. The difference between *must* and *have to* is very subtle, and sometimes both are possible. It is very difficult to explain this, and learners don't generally like to be told 'It depends how you look at it and what you're thinking of'. They prefer the certainties of right and wrong.

You could do the first two as a class, quite slowly and carefully. Then ask students to do the rest in pairs.

> **Answers**
> 1 a I'm telling myself that this is important.
>   b This is why I can't come out with you. Sorry.
> 2 a It would be really nice!
>   b Another boring business trip. Yawn!
> 3 a I want to look good.
>   b It's the rule.
> 4 a It says on the notice board.
>   b One student is talking to another.
> 5 a I haven't done them for ages.
>   b It needs lots and lots of water.

3 Roleplay

This activity might make a good warmer.

Students work in pairs to think of a job and ask and answer questions. You could give them some suggestions, for example traffic warden, lion tamer, chocolate tester, tour guide.

You could ask some of the pairs to act out their dialogue. You could also turn this activity into a quiz in which Student **A** must guess Student **B**'s job.

4 Correcting mistakes

This activity is just another small check to see how students are getting on with the new input. Ask them to do it in pairs, then get some feedback.

> **Answers**
> a Can you help me a minute?
> b What time do you have to start work?
>   (In some regions, this question is acceptable.)
> c I must go now. Bye-bye.
> d We aren't allowed to wear jeans at school.
> e We can't do what we want.
> f I don't have to do the washing and ironing …
> g You can't smoke in here. It's against the rules.
> h My mother has to work …

ADDITIONAL MATERIAL

Workbook Unit 4
Exercises 6–8 *must/should/have to*

LANGUAGE REVIEW (SB page 39)

Modals to express obligation

Read this together in class, and/or ask students to read it at home. If you have a monolingual class, you could use L1 and ask students to translate some of the sentences. Encourage questions and queries at this point. Don't worry if you get the impression that students are still not happy about the areas presented in this unit. There is a lot to absorb, and it will take time.

Ask students to read the Grammar Reference section at home.

● READING AND SPEAKING (SB page 39)

This is a light-hearted magazine article on international business behaviour. It is prefaced by a discussion on nationality stereotypes. No matter how tolerant we think we are, prejudices lurk!

> **SUGGESTION**
> You might like to do the vocabulary exercise on nationality words in the Workbook (page 28) before you do this reading text. The vocabulary will be revised in the speaking and reading here.

Pre-reading task

1 Students work in pairs to identify the nationalities in the cartoons.

> **Answers**
> a German – leather trousers, beer and sausages
> b French – romantic, smart, poodle
> c Italian – pasta, vines and wine
> d English – *The Times*, bowler hats, suits

2 Discuss these questions as a class.

> **Answers**
> The stereotype English man wears a suit, possibly has a moustache, reads *The Times* and carries an umbrella. He talks about the weather, but never about his feelings. He has a stiff upper lip, which means he must never show his feelings.
> The stereotype English woman wears tweeds and looks like the Queen. She likes dogs and going for walks in the countryside. She bakes cakes and does good deeds to help people less well-off than herself.

3 Students use their dictionaries to check new words and decide which words go with which nationality. This is, of course, extremely subjective! There are no definitive answers, just a good basis for discussion.

> **Possible answers**
>
> | American | Japanese | German |
> | --- | --- | --- |
> | hard-working | hard-working | hard-working |
> | friendly | punctual | punctual |
> | hospitable | reserved | formal |
> | casual | formal | nationalistic |
> | enthusiastic | quiet | |
> | talkative | respectful | |
>
> | French | Italian | British |
> | --- | --- | --- |
> | emotional | easy-going | reserved |
> | outgoing | friendly | lazy |
> | sociable | emotional | formal |
> | enthusiastic | lazy | quiet |
> | sophisticated | outgoing | tolerant |
> | well-dressed | sociable | respectful |
> | nationalistic | fun-loving | serious |
> | romantic | enthusiastic | nationalistic |
> | | well-dressed | |

Discuss the questions at the bottom of the page as a class.

Reading

Read the introduction as a class. The feel of the sub-title and the illustrations suggest something more light-hearted than serious. You might want check some vocabulary before they read.

tip (= suggestion)	*to signal*	*manners*	*wink*
soles of your feet	*bang on time*	*to exceed*	*status*
roll up your sleeves	*taking it easy*	*etiquette*	

1 Students read the article and then write down one thing about each nationality.

> **Answers**
> **American**
> They arrive 15 minutes early.
> They put their feet on the desk.
> People like to find a geographical link with each other.
> They eat a hamburger with two hands very quickly.
>
> **Japanese**
> They don't like to eat and work at the same time. They don't drink at lunchtime.
> You mustn't put your feet on the desk.
> You mustn't blow your nose in public.
> A young man must never try to complete a deal with an older man.
> They exchange business cards when they first meet.
> They don't shake hands, they bow.
>
> **German**
> They arrive on time.
> They like to talk about business before they eat.
> You can't take off your jacket and roll up your sleeves.
>
> **French**
> They like to eat first and then talk about business.
> You have to shake hands with everyone you know in a café.

Italian
They may arrive up to an hour late.

British
They may arrive 15 minutes late.
They think everyone understands their customs.
They are happy to have a business lunch with a drink.
You can take off your jacket and roll up your sleeves.
They are cool and reserved. They talk about the weather.

2 Students share what they have written, either in small groups or as a class.

Before you do the Comprehension check, you might want to read the article aloud, or ask students to read a paragraph out loud. This gives you the opportunity of asking questions to check vocabulary.

Comprehension check

Students discuss their answers in pairs.

Answers
1 The Germans are the most punctual; the Italians are the least punctual.
2 Because a lot of people understand the English language.
3 The Japanese, the Germans and the French.
4 Animals such as horses.
5 Italian or British; German or American; Japanese; American; French; Thai; Russian
6 Don't put your feet on your desk. Don't blow your nose in public. Exchange business cards when you first meet someone. Do this with both hands. Don't shake hands, bow. Your first bow of the day should be lower than when you meet after that.
7 **(Sample answers)**
   a Hello. What terrible weather we're having. Isn't it awful for the time of year? So wet and miserable.
   b Hi! Where are you from? I'm from Denver, Colorado. Where d'you say you're from? Houston, Texas? I went there once. Nice place. I have an uncle who lives there. Didn't stay there long.
8 In France you have to shake hands with all your friends.
   In the Middle East you must never use your left hand for greeting, eating, drinking or smoking.
   In Thailand you should clasp your hands together when you greet someone.
9 Because he/she will give it to you.
   Because it is polite to drink as much as your hosts.
   Because you should spend at least five minutes saying hello.
   Because she/he will be too busy eating.

Discussion

Discuss all four questions as a class. Obviously this activity will work best with a multi-lingual group.

● VOCABULARY AND PRONUNCIATION
(SB page 42)

Word formation

It is very important for students to see how they can make a word change word class, usually via a suffix, as they can enlarge their vocabulary considerably. It will add to their powers of expression, and enable them to understand more when listening and reading. You can devise similar exercises yourself after you've done a text in class.

1 Ask students to look at the dictionary entry and see how the different parts of speech are given. Ask students if their dictionaries are the same.

Students practise saying the words in phonetic script.

2 Students use their dictionaries to find the different parts of speech.

Answers

Verb	Noun
be'have	be'haviour
ar'range	ar'rangement
meet	'meeting
ad'vise	ad'vice
di'scuss	di'scussion
feel	'feeling
deal	'dealing ?
ac'cept	ac'ceptance
tip	tip
ad'mire	admi'ration

Noun	Adjective
'foreigner	'foreign
shock	shocked
height	high
re'spect	re'spectful
'difficulty	'difficult
re'serve (bank)	re'served
'stranger	strange
of'fence	of'fensive

reservation

Ask one or two students to say the words back to you so that you can check pronunciation.

3 Students rewrite the sentences, using the word in italics in a different word class.

Answers
a She advised me about which clothes to wear.
b What's the height of that wall?
c Children should never speak to strangers.
d I had a feeling that there was someone watching me.
e It was very difficult for us to find the way here.
f My son behaved very badly at the party.
g There are a lot of foreigners in town at the moment.
h I was so shocked that my hair turned white.

● LISTENING AND SPEAKING (SB page 42)

Entertaining friends

If you have the facilities to have three groups working with a tape recorder each, this activity could easily and profitably be done as a jigsaw.

1 Discuss the questions as a group.

2 **T.29** Students listen and take notes. These are real people, not actors, so students will need to listen carefully. Sumie and Rosa speak very good English, but they have accents.

You might want to check some vocabulary, or ask students to look up some words in their dictionary.

to spray pudding to take pot luck to show off anchovy

	Sumie	Rosa	Leslie
the kind of invitation	Sounds quite formal	An informal meal	Sounds quite informal
the time of day	At the weekend, about 7.00 in the evening	Late evening, about 8.30 or 9.00	Usually the evening, but it can be lunchtime.
the preparations that the host or hostess makes	They tidy the front garden and the entrance hall and spray it with water.	She just cooks!	The host invites people to bring something to eat, maybe a starter, a main course, salad or vegetable, or dessert.
the presents that people take	We don't know what, but it is chosen very carefully.	Maybe a bottle of wine, or something for pudding (dessert)	The food! Some guests may bring a bottle of wine.
the food and drink served	If the guests are foreigners, they serve Japanese food like *sushi*, *tempura* or *sukiyaki*. If the guests are Japanese, they serve all kinds of international food.	Spanish omelette, with potatoes, onions, eggs. Spanish ham, olives, anchovies, mussels They drink wine or beer.	It's a surprise. It depends what people bring.

3 Students work in groups to compare information. Go round the groups, monitoring and helping.

4 Discuss the questions as a class.

SUGGESTION

To give more practice on etiquette in Britain, an extra exercise is provided in the photocopiable materials on page 120 of this Teachers' Book.

● WRITING (SB page 43)

Filling in a form

Form filling was chosen for this unit's writing input because of the connection with authority and obligation.

1 Read the introduction as a class. Ask students to use what they see in the picture to answer the questions.

2 Students work in pairs to match a line in **A** with a question in **B**.

Answers
1 e	4 i	7 d
2 h	5 c	8 b
3 g	6 a	9 f

Practise the questions orally, making sure that students' voices start high.

3 Do exercise 3 on the board, answering the questions about *you*, then ask students to do the same for themselves.

4 Students fill in the form, probably for homework. You might want to photocopy the form so that you can more easily collect it in and mark it.

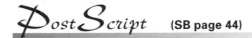

PostScript (SB page 44)

Requests and offers

Like all the PostScript activities, this one doesn't necessarily have to be done last. It is probably a good idea to break up the rest of the unit and do this during a lesson.

Students will be familiar with a few basic ways of making requests and offers. These activities are aimed at increasing their range, both receptively and productively. You could ask students to read the Grammar Reference section on page 148 on requests and offers as homework before you do this lesson.

1 Students work in pairs to match a line in **A** and a line in **B**, and then say who is talking and where the dialogues are taking place.

Answers

a Sure …
   (a driver to a garage attendant; at a petrol station.)

b Certainly, sir …
   (a customer to a waiter; in a restaurant)

c Yes, indeed …
   (a customer to a shop assistant; in a shop)

d Halves or pints?
   (a customer to a barman/barwoman; in a bar/pub)

e One moment …
   (a caller to a telephone operator; on the telephone)

f That's great …
   (friends or acquaintances; after a meeting/party)

g Not at all …
   (people in a room/office, or on a train)

h I'm afraid …
   (a caller to a telephonist)

2 **T.30** Play the tape to check answers. Ask students to practise the dialogues in pairs, paying attention to voice range and intonation.

Practise the dialogues in open pairs across the room. Ask students to close their books. Indicate which two students you want to talk, and say a one word prompt, for example, *pub*, *restaurant*, *phone*, *station*. The students must recall the dialogue.

Direct students to the Grammar Reference section. This is short enough to do in class. If you prefer, you could set it for homework prior to the lesson.

3 **T.31** Students listen to the six dialogues and answer the questions.

Answers

1 At home, husband and wife
   Do you think you could …?

2 In a shoe shop, customer and shop assistant
   Can you …?

3 At home, father and daughter
   Turn …, will you?

4 In an office, work colleagues
   Would you mind …?

5 In an office, businessman and secretary
   Could you …?

6 In the street, paper seller and pedestrian
   you wouldn't … would you?

Roleplay

Students work in pairs to prepare their dialogues. When they are ready, ask them to come to the front and act out their dialogues, preferably without a script. It can be nice sometimes to record students, with a camcorder if possible, and give feedback and correction as you view.

Don't forget!

Workbook Unit 4

Exercise 10 Pronunciation – sentence stress

Exercise 11 Multi-word verbs – separable or inseparable?

Wordlist This is on page 158 of this Teacher's Book for you to photocopy and give to your students.

Video *Wide Open Spaces* Episode 2: Nick and Maddy visit Maddy's parents to ask for financial help. Things do not go quite as expected.

Report 5 about Rugby, one of the most famous English public schools.

On the move

Future forms
Travelling around

Profile

Student's Book

Language
- future forms – *will*, *going to*, Present Continuous
- *I think I'll … / I don't think I'll …*
- forming questions
- sending faxes

Pronunciation
- the South West, the South East, etc.

Vocabulary and everyday English
- geography of Britain
- the weather – noun, adjective, verb
- travelling by (public) transport
- dialogues in hotels

Workbook
- extra grammar – *someone*, *anyone*, etc.
- vocabulary – *make* or *do*?
- prepositions of place
- pronunciation – spelling and phonetic script

Video
- Report 3 *The Sea*

Photocopiable materials for this unit
- **TB page 121** Role cards for the roleplay on SB page 48.
- **TB page 122** Map of the British Isles for the listening exercise on SB page 50.

Introduction to the unit

The theme of this unit is travelling. The reading text is about a group of American tourists on a lightning tour of Europe; there is a vocabulary and listening exercise on the geography of Britain and the weather; the writing section focuses on sending a fax to a hotel; finally, the PostScript is about transport, and dialogues in a hotel.

This is another challenging unit for students. Sorting out the various future forms that exist in English is invariably difficult for both teacher and learner. As with other complex areas of the language, students need a lot of exposure and a lot of practice.

Language aims

Grammar
Future forms

PROBLEMS

It is often said that English does not have a future tense. Instead, it has four or five main *forms* that refer to the future. What dictates the speaker's choice of form depends on aspect, that is, how the speaker views the event, and not certainty or proximity to the present, which is what students mistakenly often believe. It is the abstract nature of aspect that makes the area difficult, and the fact that often more than one form is possible – it depends how you see it!

Another factor which influences the choice of future form is when the decision is made – before the moment of speaking, or actually at the moment of speaking. In many languages, the spontaneous intention or offer is expressed by a present tense, but this is not possible in English.

I'll give you a lift to the station.
*I ~~give~~ you…

This use was practised in the PostScript section of Unit 4.

This unit looks at three ways of referring to the future, *will*, *going to* and the Present Continuous. Your students will probably have come across all three at some time, but it is unlikely that they are using them correctly. Students often grossly over-use the Present Simple to refer to the future, and they use *will* where English would more naturally use *going to* or the Present Continuous.

COMMON MISTAKES

A ***What ~~do you do~~ tonight?
B ***I ~~watch~~ TV.

A *The phone's ringing.*
B ***OK. I ~~answer~~ it.

A *Have you decided yet?*
B ***Yes. ~~We'll go~~ to Spain.

A ***When ~~you go~~ home?
B ***~~I'm go~~ home soon.

Try to stress the following:
- Use *will* for future facts, and intentions or offers made at the moment of speaking.
- Use *going to* for intentions made before speaking.
- Use the Present Continuous for arrangements between people.

Be vigilant in the correction of mistakes. Try asking the class before a weekend or a holiday what they are planning to do, and monitor their use of future forms.

Vocabulary

The vocabulary input is the lexical set of the weather, looking at nouns (*the sun*), adjectives (*It's sunny*) and verbs (*The sun's shining*).

PostScript

The PostScript section deals with language used when travelling on different kinds of transport. It also practises dialogues in a hotel.

Workbook

- Extra grammar – compounds such as *someone, anyone, everyone, no one*
- Vocabulary – *make* or *do*?
- Pronunciation – spelling and the phonetic script
- Prepositions – *in, at, on* for place

Notes on the unit

Test your grammar   (SB page 45)

This particular *Test your grammar* section is in the form of a joke. It is recorded, so you have the choice of having students listen and read at the same time, or you can read it aloud, or they could read it silently to themselves. Hopefully they will get the joke! Students underline the verbs that refer to the future. In our experience, students can easily identify the forms, but are unable to say what the

difference between them is. If students look worried, reassure them that this is the aim of Unit 5. Keep any explanations of use very short at this stage.

Answers
<u>shall</u> – used to express a suggestion
we'<u>ll ask</u> – a decision made at the time of speaking
we'<u>ll go</u> – same
we'<u>re taking</u> it – Present Continuous for an arrangement
we'<u>re going to have</u> – *going to* for a planned intention

You could ask students to read the joke aloud in pairs.

PRESENTATION (1)   (SB page 45)

going to and *will*

1   Read the introduction. Students read the example. Drill this around the class, correcting any mistakes.

Look at the second item on the list as a class, and ask for suggestions. Elicit *He's going to pay the electricity bill*, maybe say it a few times yourself to act as a model, then drill this around the class, too. This is to establish the form and pronunciation of *going to*.

Ask students in pairs to make other sentences.

Answers
He's going to fill up the car with petrol.
He's going to pay the electricity bill.
He's going to get/pick up the plane tickets from the travel agent.
He's going to take some books back to the library/get some books out of the library.
He's going to have a hair-cut.
He's going to take the dog out for a walk.
He's going to buy some sugar.
He's going to buy some tea.
He's going to buy some cheese.
He's going to buy some yoghurt.
He's going to buy two avocados.
He's going to buy some apples.
He's going to buy a melon.

Get feedback as a class. Correct carefully.

SUGGESTION
You could get a little question and answer drill across the class in open pairs, such as:

A *What's he going to get from the travel agent?*
B *He's going to get the plane tickets.*

A *What's he going to do at the library?*
B *He's going to get out/borrow some books.*

A *Where's he going to take the dog for a walk?*
B *He's going to take her to the park.*

A *What's he going to buy at the shops?*
B *He's going to buy some sugar and some cheese.*

2 **T.33** Students read and listen to the dialogue. Ask a couple of students to read it aloud.

● Grammar questions

Students work in pairs. Then get feedback as a class.

> **Answers**
>
> – John uses *going to* to express what he has already decided to do.
>
> He uses *will* to express what he decides to do at the moment he's speaking.
>
> (You could mime looking at the list to illustrate *going to*, and touching your forehead and clicking your fingers to illustrate a sudden idea.)
>
> – I'm going to the shops ...
> Jo and Andy are coming round ...

PRACTICE   (SB page 46)

1 Dialogues

Read the instructions as a class. Get two or three pairs of students to say the little dialogue between Anna and John to establish a model, and correct all mistakes, including pronunciation and intonation. Then ask students to work in pairs to produce similar dialogues using the prompts.

You might want to check/teach the names of the various shops that John is going to visit. Students might not know the following:

off-licence   hardware shop   video shop   stationer's

> **Answers**
>
> A Could you get a newspaper?
> J OK. I'll go the newsagent's and buy one.
>
> A Could you get a bottle of wine?
> J OK. I'll go to the off-licence and buy a bottle.
>
> A Could you get a joint of beef?
> J OK. I'll go the butcher's and buy it.
>
> A Could you get a film for my camera?
> J OK. I'll go to the photo shop/chemist's and buy one.
>
> A Could you get some shampoo?
> J OK. I'll go to the chemist's and buy some.
>
> A Could you get a tin of white paint?
> J OK. I'll go to the hardware shop and buy it.
>
> A Could you get a video?
> J OK. I'll go to the video shop and get one out.
>
> A Could you get some felt-tip pens?
> J OK. I'll go to the stationer's and get some.

Get some feedback as a class. Ask *Why does John use 'will' and not 'going to'?* Stress that John is deciding as he is speaking. Don't let this go on too long. Students are probably fed up with John's lists by now.

2 Listening

The aim of exercise 1 was controlled practice of *will* for spontaneous intentions. The aim of this exercise is controlled practice of *going to* for planned intentions. Note that there are one or two examples where we avoid saying *going to go* or *going to come*.

Ask students to look at the picture and say what they can see.

Read the example dialogue as a class – you could ask two students to do this. Drill the three *going to* sentences, correcting carefully.

Remind students that we don't usually say *going to go* or *going to come*. Play the tape. Pause after each dialogue so that students have time to write. Ask students to compare their answers in pairs.

Get feedback as a class. Encourage other students to comment on what each other says, for content and linguistic correctness.

> **Answers**
>
> 1 They're going to get married.
> They're going to get married in a church.
> They're going to have the reception in a hotel.
> They're going to Bali for their honeymoon.
>
> 2 They're going to have a party.
> About twenty or thirty people are coming.
> They're going to eat caviar and drink champagne.
> They're going to dance.
>
> 3 They're going to move house.
> The removal men are coming at 7.00 in the morning.
> They're going to move to the country.
> They're going to have a baby.

3 *I think I'll...*

1 The aim of this exercise is to practise *will* for a future fact or prediction. In fact, for many of the sentences in this exercise, it could be argued that *going to* is also possible, but we don't suggest you say this. Stress that *will* in this exercise is to express future facts, that is, predictions, and not intentions or offers.

Read the instructions and the example. Do question **b** in column **A** as a class. Ask for a sentence with *it/be a nice day tomorrow*. Elicit *I think it'll be a nice day tomorrow*, say it yourself, then drill it. Ask the class to match it with a sentence from column **B**, and drill the two sentences.

Ask students to continue in pairs. Get feedback, and insist on good pronunciation. Point out that *get a move on* means 'hurry up'.

Answers

b I think it'll be a nice day tomorrow. The forecast is warm and dry.

c I think I'll pass my exams. I've been revising for weeks.

d I think you'll like the film. It's a lovely story, and the acting is superb.

e I think we'll get to the airport in time. But we'd better get a move on.

f I think you'll get the job. You've got all the right qualifications.

2 Read the instructions. Point out that we don't say *I think I won't…* . Instead, we say *I don't think I will…* (This is called 'transferred negation', but there's no need to say that to your students.)

Read the example, and drill it around the room. Again, ask for a sentence with *it/be a nice day tomorrow*. Elicit *I don't think it'll be a nice day tomorrow*, say it yourself, then drill it. Ask students to do the others in pairs. Point out that *not your cup of tea* means 'not something you would like'.

Get feedback, correcting as necessary.

Answers

I don't think it'll be a nice day tomorrow. The forecast said rain and wind.

I don't think I'll pass my exams. I haven't done any revision at all.

I don't think you'll like the film. It's not really your cup of tea.

I don't think we'll get to the airport in time. There's too much traffic.

I don't think you'll get the job. You're too young and you've got no experience.

3 Read the instructions. Ask students to make true sentences about themselves.

This activity can very easily be personalized and made topical. Think of some prompts that you could put on the board regarding things and events that may happen soon in your personal situation. It could be *Real Madrid/win the cup*, or *Watson/become President* or *Maria/pass her driving test*. Ask students to make predictions about these things.

4 Grammar

Remember as always that the controlled practice activities should not be done as a block, one after the other. They should be interspersed with freer activities.

Students work in small groups to underline the correct verb form. If students manage to do this without too many mistakes, you're beginning to get somewhere with this tricky area of future forms!

Answers

a I'll get

b I'll send

c I'm going to take

d We're going to get married

e I'm going to watch   I'll come

f I'll do

ADDITIONAL MATERIAL

Workbook Unit 5

Exercises 1–4 All these exercises practise the input of this unit.

PRESENTATION (2) (SB page 47)
Present Continuous

NB Of course, the form of the Present Continuous will be familiar to your students, and they may know in theory that it can be used to refer to the future, but it is unlikely that they use it accurately and appropriately on the occasions when a native speaker would. The Present Continuous for future is used a lot, but with a limited range of verbs, and it is worth pointing this out. The verbs are all to do with moving, meeting, activities and entertainment, for example,

'seeing friends'   'going swimming'
'catching a train' 'having lunch'   'playing tennis'

1 Read the introduction to Nina Kendle and her secretary. Look at her diary. Make sure students realize that it is 9.30 in the morning.

Ask students to answer the three questions. Do this very carefully. They should be able to answer the first two easily, but they might well make mistakes with the third as it requires students to use the Present Continuous for the future. It is unlikely that they will do this.

Answers

– She's in a factory.

– She's visiting a factory.

– She's having lunch with a designer, seeing a customer, and then spending the rest of the afternoon in her office.

2 **T.35** Students listen to the dialogue between the secretary and the businessman.

3 Students look at the conversation and fill the gaps. Let them try to puzzle this out. Don't let them copy from the tapescripts.

For the same reason, get some feedback and encourage students to comment on each other's offerings before you give the answers. You could play the tape again, or students could look at the tapescripts.

Ask one pair of students to say the dialogue so you can check they've got the right answers, then ask the class to practise the dialogue in pairs. This will provide some repetition practice of the Present Continuous for the future.

● Grammar questions

Do these questions as a class.

Answers
– Present Continuous.
– **a** refers to the present. **d** and **e** refer to the future.
– They are with *will* because they are both decisions made at the moment of speaking.

PRACTICE (SB page 48)
1 Roleplay

You will need to photocopy the Student **A** and Student **B** information on page 121 of the Teacher's Book. There are three pairs of role cards.

Read the instructions carefully, and review some expressions used on the phone.

Give out the role cards. Ask if there are any questions. Give students a few minutes to plan what they're going to say. Remind students that their dialogues will be very similar to the one between Alan Middleton and Nina Kendle's secretary.

Monitor the roleplays, but be careful with correction. If you overcorrect, the students might stop talking. You could note down common mistakes and deal with them when students have finished.

Get three pairs of students, one for each situation, to do their roleplays again in front of the class. Encourage the others to comment and correct.

This activity will test students on their use of the future tense quite intensively, so let's hope students do well!

2 Discussing grammar

Students could do this activity in pairs or small groups. Get feedback. Encourage students to tell you why that answer is correct.

Answers
a Are you doing
b I'll answer
c are you going   We're going
d I'll see
e it'll rain
f We're having   are you going to invite
   I'm going away

3 Arranging to meet

Don't do this activity on the same day that you do the two previous practice activities. Students need to do some freer work, as well the controlled type.

1 Read the instructions as a class. Working on their own, students fill in their diary for the weekend. Stress that they need to leave *some* free time!

2 Students work in pairs to decide why they want to meet, then do the roleplay and find a time and a place to meet. This will be done quite quickly by some pairs, whilst others will take longer.

You could finish the activity off by asking *So where and when are you going to meet?* The answers should use either *going to* or the Present Continuous.

ADDITIONAL MATERIAL

Workbook Unit 5
Exercises 5 and 6 Practise all three future forms.

LANGUAGE REVIEW (SB page 49)
Future forms

Read the Language Review together in class, and/or ask students to read it at home. If you have a monolingual class, you could use L1 and ask students to translate some of the sentences. Encourage questions and queries at this point. Don't worry if you get the impression that students are still not happy about the areas presented in this unit. There is a lot to absorb, and it will take time.

Ask students to read the Grammar Reference section at home.

● LISTENING AND VOCABULARY

(SB page 50)

A weather forecast

The topics of the geography of Britain and a weather forecast might not seem very interesting but students often want to learn about the country behind the language. Many learners know of London only, and nothing of other towns or locations.

It is not just the English who like to talk about the weather! The weather is something that affects us all. Allow enough time for this activity. The listening tasks are quite dense.

NB Britain, or Great Britain, consists of England, Scotland and Wales. The British Isles consists of Great Britain and Ireland. The United Kingdom consists of England, Wales, Scotland and Northern Ireland. (The other part of Ireland is called the Republic of Ireland, or Eire.)

1 **T.36a** Students look at the map of the British Isles. Encourage comments and questions.

Ask students just to tell you the main areas of the British Isles so they can practise the pronunciation – the South West, the South East, etc. You could ask students questions such as *Where's Birmingham?* to get the answer *Birmingham's in the Midlands*. If you have a good class, you could teach geographical terms such as *Dublin is on the east coast of Ireland*; *Swansea is on the south coast of Wales*.

Ask students to draw a line between the Bristol Channel and The Wash. This line marks a major division in the geography of Britain, as the speaker on the tape explains.

Listen to the tape. Students answer the three questions. We suggest you play only the first half of the tape, stopping at …*growing crops and cereals*.

PROBLEM

There is a lot of vocabulary on the tape that students might not know. They will no doubt be able to answer the three questions adequately, so you can decide if you want to explore the unknown words or not. You could pre-teach items such as *climate, agriculture, hill, backbone, crops, cereal, coastline, wild ponies, heavily populated, wheat, valley, mining, moor, mist*. Or, you could play the tape again with students reading the tapescript, stopping at these words and checking/teaching them.

Answers
– To the north we can find higher lands and mountains, more rain, and sheep and cows.

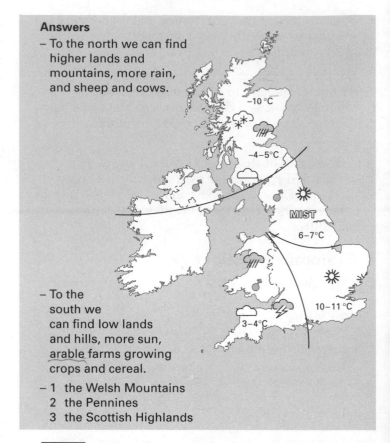

– To the south we can find low lands and hills, more sun, arable farms growing crops and cereal.

– 1 the Welsh Mountains
  2 the Pennines
  3 the Scottish Highlands

2 **T.36b** Students listen to the second half of the description and take some notes about the areas and places. This requires only one or two words for each.

Answers
- The South West has beautiful countryside and coastline. Dartmoor is very beautiful, it has wild ponies.
- The South East is gentle, there is fruit-growing, it is where a lot of people live. *vast*
- East Anglia is flat, and has big fields of wheat and potatoes.
- The Midlands used to have a lot of heavy industry.
- Wales has mountains in the north and valleys in the south.
- In the North West there is the Lake District and the *cities* towns of Liverpool and Manchester.
- In the North East there used to be a lot of ship building and mining. *lakes*
- Scotland has lochs, moors, mountains and not many people. *–empty, rich, green*
- Ireland is famous for its rain, grass, romance and mists.

3 Students work in pairs to put the adjectives in order.

Answers
boiling   hot   warm   chilly   cold   freezing

Ask three or four students to repeat the words, so you can check pronunciation. Ask *What's the weather like today?*

4 Students work in pairs or small groups to complete the chart.

PROBLEM

Students will probably know one word to go with each symbol, but not all the parts (verb, adjective and noun). As soon as there is potential for confusion, it happens! So you can expect students to get the different parts of speech confused. They make mistakes, such as *It's sunshine today. *It was rain yesterday. *The weather was sun.

Answers

Verb	Adjective	Noun
The sun's shining.	It's sunny.	sunshine
It's raining.	It's rainy.	rain
It's snowing.	It's snowy.	snow
The wind is blowing.	It's windy.	wind
	It's showery.	shower
	It's cloudy.	cloud
	It's stormy.	storm
	It's foggy.	fog
	It's misty.	mist

You now need to practise these items. You could do a little sketch of the symbols on the board, and point to them one by one. Students have to give you all three items for each symbol. Correct all mistakes carefully.

5 Before you play the tape, ask students to look at the map and notice the lines which divide the British Isles into four weather regions. (Photocopy the map on page 122 for your students to write their answers.)

T.37 Students listen to the weather forecast, and make marks on the map. Ask students to compare answers in small groups before you give the answers.

It's probably easier to correct the answers verbally rather than looking at everyone's map. Ask questions such as *What's the weather going to be like in the North West and the North East?*

Answers

(See the map of the British Isles on page 52.)

---

6 Students work in pairs to write a weather forecast. This could take a while to make it good, so allow enough time, and go round monitoring and helping.

SUGGESTION

You could take this opportunity to tell your students about a trip you made to Britain or the United States. If you have some pictures, students would no doubt be interested.

If you come from Britain or another English speaking country, tell your class about your area.

● LISTENING AND READING   (SB page 51)

This text is the main reading exercise for Unit 5. We decided to have it on tape too because it consists of an interview in direct speech, and your class might be interested to hear some American accents. The article appeared originally in a British national newspaper.

Pre-listening task

1 Discuss the questions as a class. Students might have a lot to say, and they might not.

2 Read the instructions as a class. Direct students' attention to the title of the article *If it's Tuesday … we must be in Munich*. This is an old joke about a kind of holiday where you see so many places in such a short time that you don't know where you are.

Listening

1 Look at the pictures. Which can students recognize?

Answers

1 Eiffel Tower (Paris)	6 Prado Art Gallery (Madrid)
2 Glockenspiel (Munich)	7 Gondola (Venice)
3 Leaning Tower of Pisa	8 Belgian lace (Brussels)
4 Big Ben (London)	9 Cuckoo clock (Switzerland)
5 Statue of David (Florence)	

Note The following answers apply to the first two impressions of the Student's Book.

Answers

1 Eiffel Tower (Paris)
2 Mannequin Pis or 'Pissing boy' (Brussels)
3 Leaning Tower of Pisa
4 Big Ben (London)
5 Statue of David (Florence)
6 Cuckoo clock (Switzerland)
7 Gondola (Venice)
8 Prado Art Gallery (Madrid)
9 Glockenspiel (Munich)

---

2 **T.38** Students read the introduction in the box on page 51, then listen to the interview on tape *before* they read it. They put a tick in the box if the place or thing in the pictures is mentioned.

Answers

They mention the following:

The Munich Glockenspiel	A gondola
A cuckoo clock	The Leaning Tower of Pisa
Belgian lace from Brussels	The Statue of David

SUGGESTION

You could ask students to put the pictures in order, 1–9, of the Schumachers' itinerary. Give them the first place, London, and last place, Madrid.

---

3 Students answer the questions first in pairs, then as a class.

> **Answers**
> It's called the Express Tour because they see so many countries so quickly.
> They have already been to England, Belgium, France, Switzerland.
> They're going to Austria (but not stopping), Italy and Spain.
> Now they're in Germany.

Reading

Students read the article and answer the four questions. Allow students enough time to do this, don't rush them.

> **Answers**
> – Ruthie Schumacher and her husband, Bob, their son, Gary, and his wife, Gayle.
> – Ruthie and Gayle, but Gary seems quite enthusiastic, too. Ruthie loves the castles, the sense of history, and shopping. Gayle thinks this is the best holiday ever. She's looking forward to seeing the Leaning Tower of Pisa.
> – Bob doesn't seem to be enjoying it. He doesn't say very much, and when he does, he moans.
> – *real interesting* (British English 'really interesting')
> *goose bumps* (BE 'goose pimples')
> *sidewalk* (BE 'pavement')
> *vacation* (BE 'holiday')
> *bathroom* (BE 'toilet')

Comprehension check

Students work in small groups to answer the questions.

> **Answers**
> 1 a False. This is the first time.
>   b True.
>   c False. They saw it this morning.
>   d True.
>   e False. She thinks that it might have been frustrating to only see Paris from the bus without being able to walk around. But Gary misunderstands the question and thinks that the frustration might have come from not being able to go to the toilet.
>   f False. They couldn't get one because the shop was closed for lunch.
>   g False. Gary says that they think their lunch break is more important than money.
>   h True.
>   i False. They are driving through Austria, but they aren't stopping.

>   j False. They're going to have a few days in Italy.
>   k True.
>   l False. They are flying home from Madrid.
> 2 Gary corrects Ruthie about the boat trip. The interviewer corrects Ruthie about the statue of David. Gayle corrects Gary about the order of the countries they have visited, but Gary thinks he's right.

Language work

Students work in pairs to form the questions. Note that quite a few test students in the formation of future forms.

> **Answers**
> a **Have they** ever **been abroad** before?
> b **Where does/did the** interview take place?
> c When **did they see the Munich Glockenspiel**?
> d **What did Ruthie buy in London**?
> e **What is she going to buy** in Venice?
> f Why **does she like shopping**?
> g **They're driving through Austria on their way to Venice.**
> h How long **are they going to stay** in Italy?
> i **What are they going to see in Florence**?
> j Where **are they flying** home from?
> k How **will** Bob **feel** when he gets back to the States?

Class survey

Students probably need a change of focus by now, having worked hard on the reading and listening.

Get students to stand up. Many of them are probably tired, and would far rather sit down!

If they can be encouraged to get on their feet, this activity will be more fun and generate more noise.

● WRITING (SB page 54)

Sending a fax

This exercise will introduce students to the organization of a fax message in English. They are probably quite similar in other languages.

1 Read the introduction as a class. Students fill in the first part of the fax on their own, then check with a partner.

Answers

FAX TRANSMISSION

From	Janet Cooper
To	Hotel Plaza, Alicante
For the attention of	Receptionist
Page 1 of	1
Date	(Today's date)
To fax no	00 34 6 527 15 02
From fax no	01923 285446

2 Students put Janet's words in the right order. Let students do this in pairs. It doesn't take long.

3 **T.39** Students listen and check.

4 Students write the reply for homework. It might look as though we have given students too much help with this, but such letters and faxes consist mainly of formulaic expressions, so we thought it best just to give them. Students would be most unlikely to get them right on their own.

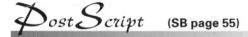

PostScript (SB page 55)

Travelling around

> **SUGGESTION**
>
> You could launch this activity with a short chat about public transport in your country, such as
>
> *How do you travel around?*
> *How do you get to school?*
> *What's the cheapest form of transport?*
> *Are the buses/trains reliable?*
> *What's the traffic situation like?*

1 Read the introduction as a class. Students match a dialogue with a means of transport.

Answers

Do you think it'll be a rough crossing? – **ferry**

Excuse me, I think you'll find those seats facing the front are ours. – **train**

Two to the British Museum, please. And could you possibly tell us when it's our stop? – **bus**

Can you take us to Euston Station, please? – **taxi**

I'll get a couple of coffees from the buffet car. – **train**

That's all right, you can keep the change. – **taxi**

No, no! He said turn left at the pub, not right! – **car**

Excuse me, are we landing on time? – **plane**

Which line is it for Oxford Circus? – **underground**

2 Students match a line in exercise 1 with a reply.

T.40 Students listen and check their answers, then practise some of the dialogues with a partner. Insist on good pronunciation.

Roleplay

Read the introduction and example as a class. Students prepare their roleplays. Notice that the roleplay should revise the functional areas of requests and offers, which were practised in the PostScript of Unit 4.

Ask some of the pairs to act out their roleplays to the rest of the class. Encourage comments from the others.

Don't forget!

Workbook Unit 5
Exercise 7 Compound words like *someone, anyone*
Exercise 8 Vocabulary *make* and *do*
Exercise 9 Prepositions *in, at, on* for place
Exercise 10 Pronunciation – spelling and phonetic script

Wordlist This is on page 159 of this Teacher's Book for you to photocopy and give to your students.

Video Report 3: A report on the way the sea has affected life and jobs in Britain.

Likes and dislikes

Like
Verb + *-ing* or infinitive?
Signs and soundbites

Profile

Student's Book

Language
- *Do ... like / would ... like*
- *like* as a preposition
- *What ... like?*
- verb + *-ing* or infinitive
- descriptions
- comparatives practice
- relative clauses

Pronunciation
- intonation in *Wh-* questions
- practising intonation in dialogues

Vocabulary and everyday English
- international food
- collocations (adjectives + people, places, food)
- instructions, warnings, advice, written signs, messages

Workbook
- extra grammar – *as ... / like ...*
- vocabulary – synonyms and antonyms
- pronunciation – sentence stress
- multi-word verbs + objects

Video
- *Wide Open Spaces* Episode 3

After Units 4 and 5, where the language aims were quite challenging, students should find Unit 6 a bit easier.

This unit is mainly about descriptions – asking for descriptions and giving descriptions. In Presentation 1 various questions with *like* as a verb and a preposition are introduced, and in Presentation 2 various verb patterns are examined.

The reading activity is about English food, and in the discussion that follows students are asked to talk about food in their country and where they like to eat. The listening is a jigsaw activity, comparing living in New York and living in London. In the tapescripts there are many examples of comparative adjectives. If you think your class would benefit from it, you could do some further remedial work on comparatives and superlatives; or you might decide they have a reasonable grasp already.

In the writing activity, students read a description of a kitchen, and are invited to write about their favourite room.

Language aims

Grammar

Like

Students will of course be familiar with *like* as a verb, although they might well confuse *like* and *would like*.

> **COMMON MISTAKES**
> A **Do you like a Coke?*
> B *Yes, please.*
> A *Would you like a Coke?*
> B **Sometimes.*
> A *Do you like swimming?*
> B **Yes, that's a good idea. Let's go.*
>
> Another common mistake is with the short answer.
> A *Do you like Coke?*
> B **Yes, I like.*

There are more problems with *like* as a preposition, and more specifically with the question *What ... like?* This is a very common question. Students will have come across it many times already, but it is unlikely that they are using it.

> **PROBLEMS**
>
> • On a surface level, the question *What is X like?* asks for a comparison: *Compare X to something that I am familiar with.* The answer could be a comparison, but it is more likely to be a general description. So on a deeper level, the question means *Tell me some relevant features about X because I don't know anything about it.*
>
> • Students confuse *What ... like?* with *How ...?* and *like* as a verb.
>
> A *How's your mother?*
> B *~~She's very kind. She's taller than me.~~*
>
> A *What's your mother like?*
> B *~~She's like cooking and reading and relaxing.~~*
>
> • Students usually appreciate that *What does he look like?* asks for a physical description, but they probably won't realize that *What's he like?* may be asking for a description of either his appearance or his character, or both.

Verbs + *-ing* or infinitive?

Students will undoubtedly know that there are a lot of verbs followed by another verb. These simply have to be learned. There is a list of verb patterns at the back of the Student's Book.

Vocabulary

The important area of collocation is practised, with adjectives that commonly go with people, places and food. This is partly in preparation for the reading text that follows on English food.

PostScript

This activity focuses on examples of language, some spoken and some written, that students will encounter in an English-speaking environment, for example *Keep out of reach of children* on a medicine packet, and *Dry clean only* on a shirt.

Workbook

• Extra grammar – relative clauses and *as* versus *like*
• Vocabulary – antonyms and synonyms
• Pronunciation – sentence stress
• Multi-word verbs – verbs + objects

Notes on the unit

Test your grammar   (SB page 56)

1 It is important that students see the difference between *like* used as a verb and *like* used as a preposition.

Do the first two as a class, then ask students to do the others in pairs. It shouldn't be terribly difficult.

> **Answers**
> In sentences **a**, **d** and **g**, *like* is a verb.
> In sentences **b**, **c**, **e** and **f**, *like* is a preposition.

2 This second question tests students on the verb pattern of one verb – *stop*. Most verbs can be followed by one pattern only; a few can be followed by both the infinitive and *-ing* with no change in meaning; and a few can be followed by both with a change in meaning. *Stop* is one of these.

The aim is simply to start students thinking about one verb followed by another verb.

Students will either know the answer or they won't. You could prompt by saying 'In picture 1, what did they stop doing?' The answer is they stopped walking down the street. 'In picture 2, what did they stop doing?' 'They stopped talking.'

> **Answers**
> *They stopped to talk to each other* is picture **a**.
> *They stopped talking to each other* is picture **b**.

PRESENTATION (1)   (SB page 56)
Questions with *like*

1 Read the introduction as a class, and ask the question.

2 In pairs, students read the conversation, putting one of the questions into each gap. We suggest that you don't give an explanation of each question before students read the conversation. Let students do it to see how much they know. There are plenty of exercises that explain and practise the questions in the next section.

T.41 Students listen and check their answers. In pairs, they practise the conversation.

● Grammar question

Students do this question first in pairs, then as a class.

> **Answers**
> a What does she look like? (preposition)
> b What does she like doing? (verb)
> c What's she like? (preposition)
> d How is she?
> e What would she like to do? (verb)

PRACTICE (SB page 57)

Students might feel that they know all these questions already, although they continue to make mistakes with them. It is unlikely that intermediate students are using the *What ... like?* question correctly and appropriately.

On the other hand, they might be confused at seeing the five questions together. Either way, there are plenty of exercises.

1 Questions and answers

Students match a question and an answer. This should be quite easy.

> **Answers**
> a He likes swimming and skiing, and he's a keen football fan.
> b He's really nice. Very friendly and open, and good fun to be with.
> c He's quite tall, average build, with straight brown hair.
> d He isn't very well, actually. He's got the 'flu.

> **SUGGESTION**
> Practise the same four questions about someone your class all knows, perhaps an actor, a musician, a sportsman or woman, a member of the class. Students must give the answers to the four questions.

2 Listening

T.42 Students listen to the short descriptions, and in pairs write a question for each.

Get feedback and ask for suggestions before you give the right answer. Make sure students' voices start high on the questions.

> **Answers**
> 1 What's he like?
> 2 How is she?
> 3 What does she like doing?
> 4 What's the weather like where you are?
> 5 What does she look like?
> 6 How is he?
> 7 What's she like?
> 8 What was your holiday like?
> 9 What sort of books do you like?

3 Descriptions

Be careful with this exercise. The questions may look very easy, but they are full of potential areas of confusion.

Encourage your students to ask *you* the questions **a–e** first, and you can answer them about *you*. Then ask one or two students the questions with the class listening, and finally ask students to do it in pairs.

ADDITIONAL MATERIAL

Workbook Unit 6
Exercises 1–2 These practise the language in this Presentation.
Exercise 3 This is extra input on *as* versus *like*, and a practice activity.

PRESENTATION (2) (SB page 58)

Verb + *-ing* or infinitive?

1 Students read the letter and underline the correct verb form. Do this in pairs, then get some feedback.

2 **T.43** Students listen and check their answers. Ask a student to read the letter aloud, and correct any pronunciation mistakes.

> **SUGGESTION**
> To reinforce the point, go through the exercise again, asking students to say what pattern follows each verb. Say the verbs in the infinitive, for example *want*, *enjoy*, *manage*, and students must reply *Plus infinitive*, or *Plus -ing*.
>
> This should highlight some problems, for example, *stop* has both patterns with a difference in meaning.

● Grammar question

Do this question as a class.

> **Answer**
> *stopped* + *-ing* means 'I stopped doing the activity'.
> *stopped* + infinitive means 'I stopped the activity in order to answer the telephone'.

PRACTICE (SB page 58)

1 Grammar and listening

1 Students put the verbs from the Presentation text in the right box. Ask them to draw the boxes on a separate piece of paper as they will add to the list in the next exercise.

Ask them to do this in pairs then get feedback as a class.

> **Answers**
>
> | 1 | 2 |
> |---|---|
> | love doing | want to do |
> | enjoy doing | manage to do |
> | try doing | stop to do |
> | stop doing | hope to do |
>
> | 3 | 4 |
> |---|---|
> | want someone to do | make someone do |
> | invite someone to do | let someone do |

2 Read the instructions carefully, as this exercise is quite tricky. Do the first two or three questions as a class.

T.44 Students listen to the sentences and put the verbs in the correct box.

Answers	
1	**2**
finish doing	promise to do
can't stand doing	continue to do
like doing	forget to do
hate doing	refuse to do
	choose to do
	need to do
	agree to do
	manage to do
3	**4**
tell someone to do	
ask someone to do	

3 Students look at the list of verb patterns on page 158 and check their answers.

2 Discussing grammar

Students work in pairs.

1 Students underline the verb that isn't possible.

Answers	
a didn't mind	d enjoy
b made	e wanted
c refuse	f decided

2 Students change the sentences using the above verbs. Do this first in pairs, then as a class. It should be quite easy.

Answers	
a didn't mind mending	d enjoy going
b made her son turn down	e wanted me to do
c refuse to go	f decided to work

ADDITIONAL MATERIAL

Workbook Unit 6
Exercises 4–6 These all practise verb patterns.

LANGUAGE REVIEW (SB page 59)
Asking for descriptions
Verb patterns

Read these sections together in class, and/or ask students to read it at home. If you have a monolingual class, you could use L1 and ask students to translate some of the sentences. Encourage questions and queries at this point.

Ask students to read the Grammar Reference section at home.

● VOCABULARY AND PRONUNCIATION
(SB page 59)
Words that go together

This should be a satisfying lesson as collocation is an interesting and useful area. This activity also sets up the reading to follow on English food.

> **SUGGESTION**
> You could begin by saying that many words go together. Ask for words that go with *turn off*, for example, *a light*, *an oven*, *a stereo*; words that go with *egg*, for example, *fry*, *boil*, *break*; words that go with *happy*, for example, *Christmas*, *birthday*, *ending*.

1 Students work in pairs or small groups to decide which four words cannot go with the noun in the centre. They will need their dictionaries.

Allow plenty of time for this. There is a lot to explore, and many related questions can arise.

Answers
People – *expensive, antique, high, crowded* don't go. We talk about *antique furniture*.
Towns – *young, antique, excited, capital* don't go. We talk about *a new town* and *a capital city*.
Food – *disgusted, wealthy, tasteful, starving* don't go. *Tasteful* means 'showing ability to choose the best kind', for example, *tasteful decoration*.

2 Students put a suitable adjective in the gaps. Ask them to work in pairs.

NB *In this activity and the jigsaw listening on page 62 there is a lot of in-built practice of comparatives and superlatives. We chose not to have a Presentation section on these because students should be pretty familiar with them by now. If you see that students are having problems, however, you might decide to have a remedial lesson on it.*

3 **T.45** Students listen and check their answers.

Ask students to practise the sentences in pairs across the room. Correct pronunciation mistakes.

● READING AND SPEAKING (SB page 60)

The topic of food is usually one that is guaranteed to generate interest and discussion, so allow enough time.

Pre-reading task

1 Students work in pairs to think of typical meals from the countries. If they can't think of one from a particular country, tell them to move on.

Sample answers
France – everything! Boeuf bourgignon, coq au vin, bouillabaisse, onion soup, cheese, salads
India – curry, rice
Switzerland – fondue, chocolate, rosti
England – roast beef and Yorkshire pudding, roast lamb, sausages, fish and chips, custard
Turkey – kebabs, figs
Spain – omelette, paella, tapas
America – burgers and French fries, steak, turkey
Italy – pasta, osso bucco, spaghetti bolognese
Mexico – taco shells, chilli con carne, peppers
Greece – lamb, salad, yoghurt, calamare

Discuss the question about what influences a country's food. You might have to prompt with ideas such as climate, agriculture, farming, culture, tradition.

2 Students read the quotes about English food. They all have the same opinion of English food – it's no good!

Reading

Students read the article quickly, and match a paragraph with a summary.

Answers
Para. 1 – There's everything except an English restaurant
Para. 2 – The British love-affair with international cooking
Para. 3 – Historical and climatic influences on British cooking
Para. 4 – The legacy of World War II
Para. 5 – Where there is hope for the future

NB *A poppadom is eaten with Indian curries. It is a kind of large crisp that is made of flour.*
Lasagne is an Italian dish, consisting of pasta, mincemeat and cheese.
Shepherd's pie is an English dish, made of mincemeat in a sauce topped with mashed potato.
Lancashire hotpot is made with lamb chops, kidney and sliced potatoes.
Bread and butter pudding is made with bread, raisins, egg, milk and sugar.

Comprehension check

Students read the article more carefully, and in pairs answer the multiple choice questions. Get feedback and invite discussion before you provide the right answer. Ask *Why?* so that they have to justify their answers. Remember that multiple choice questions almost invite doubt, but in so doing they require very precise thinking.

Answers		
1 b	3 a	5 b
2 c	4 c	6 c

Discussion

Answer the two questions as a class. This could go on for quite a while, depending on the interests of your students.

Language work

Students work in pairs to answer the questions.

Answers
1 *like* as a verb – Why do they now like cooking in wine and olive oil? (para. 2)
   like as a preposition – English kitchens, like the English language (para. 3), cooking British food is like speaking a dead language (para. 4)
2 difficult to find (para. 1), easier to find (para. 1) able to produce (para. 3)
3 prefer cooking (para. 2), like cooking (para. 2)
4 choose to eat (para. 2),
   had to forget (para. 4)
   learn to do (para. 4),
   managed to recover (para. 4)
   began to believe (para. 4),
   try to serve (para. 5)

ADDITIONAL MATERIAL

Workbook Unit 6
Exercise 9 This is a vocabulary exercise on synonyms and antonyms.

● LISTENING AND SPEAKING (SB Page 62)

New York and London

This is a jigsaw activity, so the skills of both speaking and listening are practised. You will need two tape recorders, and ideally two rooms, so that one group can take themselves off to listen to their tape. The speaking practice comes when the groups tie up with a partner and compare information.

Pre-listening task

Students look at the pictures of New York and London and answer the questions. Hopefully some of your students will have been to one of the cities, and/or other students will know something about them.

Listening

T.46a **T.46b** Students work in two groups, **A** and **B**, and read the introduction relevant to them. They usually want to listen more than once, maybe three times, to make sure they have all the information. They take notes for the next exercise.

Comprehension check

Answers	Bob and Sheila	Terry
1 People	New York is cosmopolitan, but not as mixed as London. Nationalities stay in their own areas. People are ruder, pushing on the streets, fights getting on a bus. The taxi drivers are the rudest in the world. Bob also says that Americans are friendly. They made a lot of friends. They say that Americans are more open.	The average Englishman is cold and not very open. In the States people start conversations in the street. Americans are more spontaneous and enthusiastic. But the English improve as you get to know them. Once you've made a friend, it's a friend for life. English people think Americans are inferior because they get excited by everything. American people stand closer when they're talking.
2 Shops	Open till 10.00 at night, so Bob could work and lead a normal life. Gimbles department store open till 9.00. Some super-markets open 24 hours a day. Most shops don't open till 10.00 or 11.00 in the morning. Everything is open on Sunday.	It's easier to spend money in the States. Shops are open all the time. The shops are open later now than when she first arrived.
3 Work and holidays	People work later. The public holidays are shorter, only the banks are shut. Bob worked on the sixty-third floor.	Americans work a lot harder. For Americans their work is the most important thing in their lives. Holidays are longer in England. The whole country closes down for two weeks at Christmas and New Year. Americans live to work, like the Japanese.
4 Transport	The taxi drivers are the rudest in the world. The subways are unusable. They are dirty and uncomfortable.	The taxi drivers are wonderful.
5 General opinions	They liked it a lot. They had a wonderful time. Life is easier. You could do what you liked when you liked. New York is a dangerous place, but they never had any problems. They made a lot of friends.	Life is easier in the States. It's easier to make money and it's easier to spend it. But she loves living in England. It's safer, more relaxed, more enjoyable. England doesn't have the dramatic beauty of the States, but it's very pretty and charming in a way she finds comforting.

Speaking

Students find a partner from the other group and compare information. There is usually no need for you to check understanding, but you might want to ask a few questions just to make sure.

● WRITING AND SPEAKING
(SB page 63)

Describing a room

Ask students to read the Grammar Reference section on relative clauses for homework prior to this lesson.

> **SUGGESTION**
> Do a word sort before doing this activity.
> Put these words on the board. Students must decide which rooms they go with.
>
> | | | |
> |---|---|---|
> | *cooker* | *settee* | *bath mat* |
> | *shower* | *wardrobe* | *washing machine* |
> | *mug* | *sink* | *fireplace* |
> | *rug* | *desk* | *bedside table* |
> | *kettle* | *lamp* | *chest of drawers* |
> | *saucepan* | *towels* | *bookshelves* |

1 Students think of their favourite room and draw a plan of it. They write down a few words to describe it, and talk to a partner.

2 **T.47** Students read and listen to the description of the kitchen. They check new words in their dictionaries, or use the illustration to work out the meaning.

3 Students find the four mistakes.

> **Answer**
> The table is rectangular, not round. (oval) The trees are apple trees, not pear trees, and you can see two of them through the window. The menu on the notice-board is for a Chinese restaurant, not an Indian restaurant.

4 Students find the relative pronouns *which* and *where*.

> **Answer**
> *where we cook* refers to the kitchen
> *which lead to* refers to troubled times
> *which is the focal point of the room* refers to the table
> *which looks out* refers to the window
> *which is old-fashioned* refers to the pulley
> *which tells* refers to the notice-board
> *which means they come* refers to the fact that all our friends use the back door

Students read the Grammar Reference section on page 149.

5 Students work in pairs to link the sentences.

> **Answers**
> a The blonde lady who's wearing a black dress is my wife.
> b There's the hospital where my sister works.
> c The postcard that arrived this morning is from Auntie Nancy.
> d I passed all my exams, which made my father very proud.
> e Did you meet the girl whose mother teaches French?

6 Students describe their favourite room for homework.

ADDITIONAL MATERIAL

Workbook Unit 6
Exercises 7 and 8 These give further practice of relative clauses.

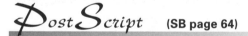

PostScript   (SB page 64)

Signs and soundbites

There is no productive task to this exercise, and no extension. It is simply for recognition of signs and snippets of conversation that students will come across if they are living in an English-speaking environment.

Ask students to work out where they might see or hear the words. Then have a class discussion.

> **Answers**
> Government health warning *Tobacco seriously damages your health* – **on a cigarette packet**
> *Vacant* – **on a toilet door**. It means it is empty. If there is someone in there, the sign reads *Engaged*.
> *Coming next on Capital* – traffic news and the weather – **a radio station**
> *Is service included?* – **in a restaurant**
> *Keep out of reach of children* – **on a bottle or a packet of medicine**

> *Services 20 miles* – **on a motorway**
> *Yours faithfully, Veronica Vazey* – **at the bottom of a formal letter**
> *Dry clean only* – **on an item of clothing**
> *A table for four, please* – **in a restaurant**
> *Pay and display* – **in a public car park**. You buy a ticket from a machine, and show (= display) the ticket in your windscreen
> *The management accepts no responsibility. Coats and other articles left at owner's risk* – **in a public place such as a pub or restaurant**
> *Visitors are requested to keep to the paths* – **in a park**
> *No, I'm just looking, thank you* – **said in reply to a shop assistant asking 'Can I help you?'**
> *For external use only* – **on a medicine bottle or a pot of skin cream**
> *Don't forget to give my love to everyone at home* – **at the bottom of an informal letter or postcard**

Don't forget!

Workbook Unit 6
Exercise 10 Multi-word verbs + objects
Exercise 11 Pronunciation – sentence stress

Wordlist This is on page 160 of this Teacher's Book for you to photocopy and give to your students.

Video *Wide Open Spaces* Episode 3: Maddy's boss asks her out to lunch and gives her some good news.

Stop and check There is a Stop and check revision section for use after each quarter of the Student's Book.

Stop and check 2 for Units 4–6 is on pages 138–9 of this Teacher's Book. You need to photocopy it. The key is on page 151.

> **SUGGESTION**
> You can use the Stop and check any way you want, but here is one way.
> • Give it to your students to do for homework. They'll need plenty of time for it.
> • In class, ask them to go over the test again in groups of five or six. They should try to agree on definitive answers. If they can't agree, they should ask you.
> • Provide the answers and any necessary explanations.

Progress tests There are Progress tests at the end of Unit 6 and Unit 12.

Progress test 1 for Units 1–6 is on pages 144–6 of this Teacher's Book. You need to photocopy it. The key is on page 153.

These Progress tests serve the same function as the Stop and check tests, but teachers sometimes like to have their own checks of progress.

The world of work

Present Perfect active and passive
On the telephone

Profile

Student's Book

Language
- Present Perfect
- comparing Present Perfect and Present/Past Simple
- time expressions – *for, since, in, ago*
- writing formal letters

Pronunciation
- intonation and questions

Vocabulary and everyday English
- multi-word verbs – practice of basic aspects
- making phone calls
- messages on an answer machine

Workbook

- extra grammar – *been* or *gone*
- revision of tenses
- pronunciation – phonetic script and word stress
- nouns and prepositions
- vocabulary – words with more than one meaning

Video

- Report 4 *Taxi!*

Photocopiable materials for this unit (TB page 123)
- An extra exercise on the Present Perfect.
- Role cards for the PostScript activity on SB page 75.

This unit marks the beginning of the second half of *New Headway Intermediate*. The first half included revision and extension of many of the basic tenses of English, but did not dwell on the one tense which is undoubtedly the most difficult for students to gain overall mastery of – the Present Perfect. It is therefore appropriate that the second half begins with a comprehensive study of all the main uses of this tense. The themes of work and news are useful vehicles for this.

The skills work includes reading texts about young people who have chosen jobs that do not meet with the full approval of their parents. There is a listening and discussion about retirement, and a focus on writing formal letters and making telephone calls, including leaving messages on an answering machine.

The vocabulary does some work on multi-word verbs.

Grammar

Perfect tenses

It is useful to understand the nature of Perfect tenses, as they can cause students such problems. The Present Perfect is particularly difficult.

Perfect tenses in English bring together different times. They express an aspect which is not dictated solely by the time when something happened, but show how one time relates to another time. The word *Perfect* means 'before', so the Past Perfect means 'before a time in the past', and relates one past time to another past time.

When I arrived at the station, the train had left.

Present Perfect means 'before now' and relates past to present.

I've lived in London for six years.
(I lived there six years ago, and I still live there now.)

You've cut your hair.
(I see now evidence of something you did in the past.)

The Present Perfect

Students at intermediate level will undoubtedly be familiar with the form of the Present Perfect. They will have met it quite frequently, but they will not as yet have assimilated its uses, all of which relate past time to present time. This unit aims to bring together *all* of its uses, giving students a comprehensive view to refer back to. The unit is therefore constructed as follows.

Presentation (1) deals with two of its uses, unfinished past and life experience. Presentation (2) covers the third use, giving news/present evidence of past events. It also covers the Present Perfect passive. Throughout the presentations, the Present Perfect is compared and contrasted with the Past Simple and there are many discriminatory exercises.

Time expressions which are used with the different tenses are also revised and contrasted: *for*, *since*, *in*, *ago*, etc.

PROBLEMS

- The same verb form (auxiliary *have* + past participle) exists in many other European languages where it is often interchangeable with other past tenses. However, its uses in English are very specific (see above) and it is *not* interchangeable with the Past Simple.
- The Present Perfect joins past and present in a way other languages do not feel the need to. They express the same ideas by using a past tense or a present tense. Students' mistakes are invariably as a result of this.
- *for* and *since* are often misused.

COMMON MISTAKES	CORRECTED
* I ~~have seen~~ him yesterday.	I saw him yesterday.
* He ~~has been~~ there last year.	He went there last year.
* ~~Did you ever~~ go there?	Have you ever been there?
* She is a teacher since six years.	She's been a teacher for six years.
* I ~~live~~ here since 1995.	I've lived here since 1995.
* How long ~~do you know~~ Mary?	How long have you known Mary?

NB *This unit deals with the Present Perfect Simple only. The Present Perfect Continuous is dealt with in Unit 10.*

Vocabulary

This focuses on multi-word verbs, sometimes called phrasal or prepositional verbs. Students will be familiar with many of these. Indeed if they have been following the *New Headway Intermediate* Workbook, they will have already had considerable systematic coverage of the area. This vocabulary section selects certain basic aspects of both their form and use and practises these.

PostScript

Different types of telephone conversations are practised and useful telephone phrases are introduced. Students also learn how to leave a message on an answer phone in English.

Workbook

- Exercise 4 The difference between *been* and *gone*.
- Exercise 8 Tense review – This is a general review of tenses based on someone's curriculum vitae. This can be a useful guide to students as to how to set out their own curriculum vitae.
- Exercise 11 Vocabulary – This focuses on homonyms – words with more than one meaning.
- Exercise 12 Pronunciation – This focuses on word stress and practice at recognizing phonetic script.
- Exercise 13 Nouns + Prepositions.

Notes on the unit

Test your grammar   (SB page 65)

The *Test your grammar* has a dual purpose.

It revises the Present Simple and the Past Simple and contrasts their uses with the Present Perfect tense.

It is also a personalized activity, where students report back on their partners. It is a nice idea to do this half way through the course, and particularly useful if the class is newly formed or has new members.

As always with the *Test your grammar* sections, do *not* be tempted to go into any detail over the tense usage. The students are asked simply to form them and name them.

1   Go round the class as they work in pairs and gently correct any grammar mistakes, but generally show more interest in the personalized side of the activity than the grammar.

Sample answers
a I'm a student.
b For two years. Since 1995./I don't have a job, I'm a student.
c I worked in a bank./I was at school.
d I live in a flat. I don't live in either, I live on a boat.
e For six months.
f Six months ago.
g For two years./Since the beginning of the term.
h Two years ago./Five weeks ago.
i Yes, I have./No, I haven't.
j I went in 1990./Ten years ago.

---

2 Ask a few students to report back. They are now
   practising the third person, e.g. *Peter's a businessman.*

3 Ask the class to name the tenses.

> **Answers**
> a, d are Present Simple.
> c, f, h, j are Past Simple.
> b, e, g, i are Present Perfect Simple.

PRESENTATION (1) (SB page 65)

Present Perfect Simple

This presentation illustrates two uses of the Present
Perfect, the unfinished past and experience. They are
compared with the Present Simple and Past Simple.

1 Ask quickly about your students' jobs. Then ask them
   to look at the advertisement for the business journalist
   and encourage their comments. Would they like this
   job? Why? Could they apply for it? Do they have any
   of the necessary qualifications?

NB *Check that your students know the meaning of
'qualifications'. You might also want to pre-teach
'apply for', 'applicant' and 'application'.*

2 **T.48** Ask your students to look at the photograph
   and read about Nancy Mann. Play the tape of the
   complete interview and ask if they think she will get
   the job and why. Does she have many of the right
   qualifications?

3 Ask students to turn the page and read the first part
   of the interview, and work with a partner to complete
   it with the correct auxiliary verb. This section
   compares the unfinished past use of the Present
   Perfect with the Present Simple and Past Simple.

> **Answers**
> I Who **do** you work for at the moment, Ms Mann?
> N I work for the BBC World Service.
> I And how long **have** you worked for the BBC?
> N I**'ve** been with the BBC for five years. Yes, exactly
>   five years.
> I And how long **have** you been their German
>   correspondent?
> N For two years.
> I And what **did** you do before the BBC?
> N I worked as an interpreter for the EU.

Play the first part again and ask them to listen and check
their answers. Do the grammar questions immediately.

● Grammar questions

Ask students to consider the questions in pairs. Then go
through them with the whole class.

> **Answers**
> – Yes she does.
> – No, she doesn't.
> – Nancy says:
>   *I* **work** *for the BBC World Service.*
>   because she works for them now. (Present Simple)
>   *I've* **worked** *for them for five years.*
>   because she is talking about past time and present
>   time. She began working for them five years ago and
>   she still works for them now. (Present Perfect)
>   *I* **worked** *as an interpreter for the EU.*
>   because she doesn't work for them any more. It is
>   finished past time. (Past Simple)

4 Ask students to read and complete the second part of
   Nancy's interview. This section compares the life experience use of the Present Perfect with the Past Simple.

> **Answers**
> I As you know, this job is based in Geneva. **Have** you
>   ever lived abroad before?
> N Oh yes, yes I **have**.
> I And when **did** you live abroad?
> N Well, in fact I **was** born in Argentina and I lived there
>   until I was eleven. Also, I lived and worked in
>   Brussels for two years when I **was** working for the EU.
> I That's interesting. **Have** you travelled much?
> N Oh yes, yes indeed. I**'ve** travelled all over western
>   and eastern Europe, and I**'ve** also been to many
>   parts of South America.
> I And why **did** you go to these places?
> N Well, mostly for pleasure, on holiday, but three
>   years ago I went back to Argentina to cover various
>   political stories in Buenos Aires for the BBC.

Play the second part again and ask your students to
check their answers. Do the Grammar questions
immediately.

● Grammar questions

Ask students to do this in pairs, then go through the
questions with the whole class.

> **Answers**
> *Have you ever* **lived** *abroad?*
> The Present Perfect is used because the interviewer is
> asking about a general experience in Nancy's life.
> *When* **did** *you* **live** *abroad?*
> The Past Simple is used because the interviewer is
> asking about a specific time in the past.
> *I've* **been** *to many parts of South America.*
> The Present Perfect is used because Nancy is talking
> about a general experience in her life.
> *... three years ago I* **went** *back to Argentina ...*
> The Past Simple is used because Nancy is talking
> about a specific time in the past.

PRACTICE   (SB page 66)

1 Biographies

Ask the class to look at the pictures of some of the scenes from Nancy's life. Ask them some general questions about them.

1 Do two examples with the whole class, they are <u>underlined</u> below. Then ask them to work in pairs to complete the exercise. Point out that they will learn more information about her – this activity does not simply go over what she said in the interview.

Answers
a <u>She was born in Argentina in 1959.</u>
b She went to boarding school in England from 1970 to 1977.
c She studied French and German when she was at Oxford University.
d She hasn't spoken Spanish since she was in Buenos Aires three years ago.
e <u>She's worked in both eastern and western Europe at various times in her life.</u>
f She worked in Brussels for two years, from 1989 to 1991.
g She's worked for the BBC for the last five years.
h She hasn't worked abroad since her son was born four years ago.
i She married for the first time when she was twenty-one.
j She's been married three times.
k She married for the third time last year.

2 **T.49**   Play the tape for students to listen and check their answers. Ask them to read her biography aloud around the class. You could ask them a few questions about the different tenses used.

3 Ask students to work in pairs and write similar tables of their lives for their partners to match. In doing this they will get practice of the first and second persons. Round off the activity by asking one or two to tell the class about their partners.

> **SUGGESTION**
>
> It is a very nice idea to launch this activity by writing similar information about *your* life on the board, and asking students to match the events with the time expressions. This can be great fun!

2 Time expressions

This is a short revision activity and should be done very quickly. You could simply do it with students reading aloud sentences round the class. Alternatively, you could make it like a race, putting students into pairs and seeing which pair finishes first.

Answers
a I was born **in** 1961.
b I went to university **for** three years.
c I passed my driving test fifteen years **ago**.
d I've had a car **since** 1983.
e Now I've got a BMW. I've had it **for** two years.
f I met my wife **in** 1985.
g We've been married **for** nine years.
h Our first daughter was born six years **ago**.
i We've lived in the same house **since** 1990.

ADDITIONAL MATERIAL

Workbook Unit 7
Exercise 5 This includes a useful table about which time expressions can be used with the different tenses.

3 *Have you ever ...?*

1 The verbs in this exercise are not only needed for the next exercise but also for Presentation (2). Do it quite quickly with the whole class or with the class in small groups. Remind them that there is a list of irregular verbs on page 157 of the Student's Book. You could use this when checking their answers.

2 Practise the example dialogue in open pairs across the class. Encourage good pronunciation. Then put them into closed pairs. Make it clear that they need not do the whole list, but choose the questions which interest them. Go round and check as they do it, perhaps nudging forward the dialogues yourself with further questions.

3 Ask various members of the class to report back on their partners, thereby practising the third person.

> **Sample answer**
> Sandra has never had an operation and she's never been on TV, but she has slept in the open air lots of times. She went camping in the mountains when she was a Guide, and last summer she fell asleep on the beach after a barbecue.

ADDITIONAL MATERIAL

Workbook Unit 7
Exercises 1 & 2 These give further discriminatory practice between the Present Perfect Simple (for life experience and unfinished past) and the Past Simple.

PRESENTATION (2) (SB page 67)

Present Perfect active and passive

This presentation section has a dual purpose. It illustrates the third use of the Present Perfect, the importance now or evidence now of a past event, often used when giving news. It also introduces the Present Perfect passive.

1 Ask students to read the newspaper headlines. Help them with new words. The following might be new to them: *floods* /flʌdz/, *chaos* /ˈkeɪɒs/, *kidnapped* /ˈkɪdnæpt/ and *redundant* /rɪˈdʌndənt/.

2 **T.50a** You may have to play the tape twice for your students to fill in the gaps. Ask them to check with a partner before you ask for feedback.

> **Answers**
> a The murderer Bruce Braden **has escaped** from Parkhurst Prison on the Isle of Wight.
> b After the heavy rain of the last few days, floods **have brought** chaos to drivers in the West Country.
>
>   *NB The West Country is an area in the far south west of Britain. It is made up of two very beautiful counties, Devon and Cornwall.*
>
> c Amy Carter, the kidnapped baby from Leeds, **has been found** safe and well in a car park in Manchester.
> d Two thousand car workers from a US car factory **have been made** redundant.

● Grammar questions

Ask students to do these in pairs, then go through the questions with the whole class.

> **Answers**
> – Students should be able to answer the first two questions but not the second two.
>   Bruce Braden has escaped from prison.
>   Floods have brought chaos to the West Country.
>   We don't know who found Amy Carter.
>   We don't know who made the workers redundant from the car factory. (We can guess it was the manager or the owner, but we don't know for sure.)
> – The verb forms in the first two sentences are Present Perfect active. In the second two they are Present Perfect passive.

3 **T.50b** Now comes the comparison with the Past Simple, active and passive. Having introduced the news in the Present Perfect with no specific time reference, the announcer now gives further and more specific information about the news stories, using the Past Simple and with past time references. Ask students to read and listen. You may have to play the tape twice before they are able to fill in the gaps.

> **Answers**
> a Last night the murderer Bruce Bradfield *en* **escaped** from Parkhurst Prison. Prison officers **found** his cell empty at six o'clock this morning.
> b Early this morning floods **brought** chaos to many roads in Devon. Drivers left their cars and **walked** to work through the flood water.
> c Late last night the kidnapped baby, Amy Carter, **was found** safe and well in a car park in the centre of Manchester. The car park attendant **heard** a noise coming from a rubbish bin and he **found** Amy wrapped in a warm blanket.
> d Two thousand car workers from the General Motors factory in Detroit **were made** redundant yesterday. The management **gave** them no warning. The men were shocked and furious when they **heard** the news yesterday evening.

● Grammar questions

Ask students to answer these with a partner. Then go through them with the whole class. You can accept any explanation which shows they are on the right track. In a monolingual class they could use L1.

> **Answers**
> – In exercise 3 above, the Past Simple is used because specific past times are given.
> – In exercise 2 on page 67, the Present Perfect is used because only the main facts of the news are given without any time details. It is important just to learn what happened – not when, how, etc.

You could read through the Language Review on page 69 at this stage. It might help consolidate the uses before the practice.

PRACTICE (SB page 68)

1 Here is the news!

NB Newspaper headlines are often written in shortened form and in the Present Simple. This is the dramatic use of the tense, it adds immediacy and colour to a story. If a passive is needed, only the past participle is used in the headline. In radio news headlines the Present Perfect active and passive replaces these.

1 Ask students to look at all the newspaper headlines, point out that the first is in the Present Simple, and the second contains just a past participle. Illustrate how newspaper headlines translate into radio headlines by going through the two examples.
   Now ask the students in pairs to work on the other newspaper headlines and rewrite them as radio headlines using Present Perfect active and passive.

   Ask students to read aloud their answers in feedback.

Sample answers

a Gloria Gumm, the famous Hollywood film star, <u>has left</u> $3,000,000 to her pet dog.

b The Mona Lisa <u>has been stolen</u> from the Louvre in Paris.

c Seven people <u>have been killed</u> in a train crash in northern Sweden.

d Princess Lucia <u>has run away</u> with a palace gardener.

e President Larotti of Estovia <u>has been forced</u> to resign.

f The Olympic athlete, Ben Fleet, <u>has failed</u> a drug test at the Ottawa Games in Canada.

2 Ask them to choose two and continue them as full news stories. Remind them that they will probably need to use the Past Simple.

Sample answer

Gloria Gumm, the famous Hollywood film star, has left $3,000,000 to her pet dog. Gloria, who died two months ago, aged 87, left the money to Fifi, her French poodle. She didn't leave anything to her seven ex-husbands. Her present husband, the twenty-year-old pop singer, Rocky Stone, was left her house in Malibu.

Ask them to read aloud some of their stories to the rest of the class.

> **SUGGESTION**
>
> If you have the time and the facilities, it can be very worthwhile and great fun for students to create a complete news programme, with announcers and reporters. This can either be recorded or videoed. You could do this instead of exercise 3.

3 The idea here is to have some topical discussion to round off the lesson. It can be brief.

2 Giving personal news

> **SUGGESTION**
>
> You can make this exercise even more personal for your students if you substitute or add to the list with actual examples that relate to their lives.

This is a personalized activity continuing the theme of giving news. Students ask and answer the questions in pairs. Go round and monitor as they do it. You could reinforce the comparison with the Past Simple by asking some further questions when you tune in to their conversations, such as: *What did you see at the cinema? Did you enjoy it? Did you do well in your exam? What did you get for your birthday?* etc.

Ask a few students to report back on some of their partner's activities, and encourage the rest of the class to question further in the Past Simple.

Answers

Today …
Have you travelled by bus?
Have you done any work?
Have you had a coffee break?
Have you had lunch yet?
Have you done any exercise?

This week …
Have you been to the cinema?
(Careful *been* not *gone*!)
Have you done any exercise?
Have you played a sport?
Have you watched TV?
Have you washed your hair?

This year …
Have you had a holiday yet?
Have you moved house?
Have you had your birthday yet?
Have you taken any exams?
Have you applied for a new job?

3 Discussing grammar

NB *These two exercises benefit from being discussed in class because meanings need clarifying.*

1 Tell your students that there are several possibilities with different meanings. Also, the grammar might be possible but the meaning is highly unnatural, a point you can make with *never* and the first sentence. Discuss in a final full class feedback.

Answers

a I've **just/already** washed my hair. (*never* is not really probable!)

b Have you **ever** played basketball?

c He hasn't **ever** learned to drive. He hasn't learned to drive **yet**.

d They've **just/already** finished the exercise.

e She's **never/already** learned a foreign language. (*just* is not really possible.)

f We've **just/already/never** met your teacher.

g Have they finished doing the washing-up **yet**? (This is the most natural here.)

h Has it stopped raining **yet**? Has it **just** stopped raining?

2 Ask students to work in pairs to decide which is the correct verb form. Discuss the answers in a final feedback session.

Answers

a The Prime Minister of Italy <u>has resigned</u> and a new Prime Minister <u>has been elected</u>.

b The Italian people <u>were told</u> of his resignation on television yesterday evening.

c I <u>have lost</u> my glasses. <u>Have you seen</u> them anywhere?

d 'Where <u>has</u> Liz <u>gone</u> on holiday?' 'She's in Paris.'

e 'Where <u>did</u> Liz <u>go</u> on holiday?' 'She went to Paris.'

f '<u>Has</u> John ever <u>been</u> to Paris?' 'Oh, yes. Five times.'

g A huge earthquake <u>has hit</u> central Japan. Nearly 1,000 people <u>have been killed</u>. It <u>happened</u> mid-afternoon yesterday.

LANGUAGE REVIEW   (SB page 69)

The Present Perfect
The Present Perfect passive

If you haven't done this already, read these aloud to the class. They could be encouraged to translate some of the sentences into their own language.

Ask them to read the Grammar Reference section for homework, and use it whilst they are doing some of the exercises in the Workbook.

ADDITIONAL MATERIAL

Workbook Unit 7

Exercises 3–7 These give further practice of all uses of the Present Perfect Simple.

Exercise 8 This is a general tense review.

Exercises 9 & 10 These practise the Present Perfect passive.

● READING AND SPEAKING   (SB page 69)

The three articles come from a popular daily newspaper. They are making the point that times have changed a great deal in respect of people having servants. People who come from families that in the past had servants, have become servants themselves. An example is always made of Princess Diana, who used to look after small children, before she married Prince Charles and became the Princess of Wales.

NB In Britain, as in many other countries, the word 'servant' these days is in fact rather old-fashioned and conjures up images of past times. People may have help in their homes, but they talk about having 'home-help': someone to help with the children, clean the house, do the garden, etc. Nobody, except perhaps royalty and the exceptionally rich, has servants. Gone are the days of butlers, cooks and maids.

Pre-reading task

1 Students seem to like doing this. Make it fun! Ask them first to look at the picture to stimulate ideas. Be sure students really do close their eyes and give them a few minutes to visualize life as very rich person 100 years ago. As they sit with closed eyes, read the questions aloud to encourage their imaginations.

You could prompt with further more concrete questions, such as *Have you ever spoken to your parents about life when their grandparents were young? What do you know about your family 100 years ago?*

2 Ask students to work in small groups and share ideas. Go round and listen so that you can call on students with interesting ideas in the feedback.

3 Conduct this with the whole class. Give them some examples from your own life if you have any, for example, *I once worked as an au pair in Germany*.

Reading

The modern servant

This is a jigsaw reading activity.

1 Divide the class into three groups, **A**, **B**, **C** and allocate the texts. Check that someone in each group has a dictionary to look up unknown words. Go round the groups as they work and help them with new words. Get them to make very brief answer notes, otherwise the activity will go on too long. Give the groups about 10 minutes to answer the questions **a–e**.

SUGGESTION

Ask students to swap information with other groups about **a–e** and get feedback before asking them to do exercise 2.

Answers

Amanda – the Nanny

a Two nannies she had when she was a child, especially the traditional one.

b To study law at university.

c They laughed and thought it was just a childish phase. They rowed.

d Yes. They weren't angry for long, they encouraged her. They're proud that she's done so well and is an independent thinker.

e Being a nanny is now socially acceptable, after all Princess Diana was one!

Giles – the Cook

a He's always been interested in food. His grandparents' cook. Doing cookery at school and a cookery course.

b To be a farmer.

c Silence and questions but they didn't get angry. They were understanding.

d Yes, a little. They're very proud now because he's opened a restaurant. His grandfather still thinks he's mad. His father thinks it's good to do what you enjoy, because not many people do these days.

e The father was brought up with a butler and cook, but now anyone with a job they enjoy is lucky.

Hugo – the Gardener
a His family's gardener when he was a child. Working in a garden centre one summer holiday.
b To study archaeology at Oxford University.
c They were furious. They didn't speak to him for months.
d Yes. They've learnt to accept it, not only because he's happy, but because his university friends have found it difficult to find good jobs.
e All kinds of people do all kinds of work and the world is better as a result.

2 Ask students to read their text again and find which of phrasal/multi-word verbs it contains. Ask them to underline them.

Answers

bring up (1)	The Nanny (line 53)
	The Cook (line 48)
bring up (2)	The Cook (lines 33–34)
carry on	The Gardener (line 29)
drop out	The Gardener (line 5)
fall out	The Gardener (line 48)
get on with	The Nanny (line 27)
get over	The Cook (line 52)
give up	The Cook (line 45)
	The Gardener (lines 24–25, 45)
go through	The Nanny (line 34)
grow up	The Nanny (line 31)
look after	The Nanny (line 11)
	The Cook (lines 48–49)
make up (1)	The Cook (line 26)
make it up (2)	The Nanny (line 45)
	The Gardener (lines 52–53)
pick up	The Cook (line 19)
	The Gardener (line 17)
put off	The Cook (line 32)
be taken aback	The Cook (line 50)
	The Gardener (line 38)
take after	The Nanny (line 50)
turn out	The Nanny (line 55)
take over	The Cook (line 24)

Later, students will compare with the other groups the multi-word verbs in their article.

NB *This is a foretaste of further work to come on multi-word verbs in the vocabulary section of this unit. It would be useful to ask your students to read the Grammar Reference section on multi-word verbs (SB page 151–2) for homework before you proceed to the vocabulary section.*

Comprehension check

Ask students to find a partner from each of the other two groups.

1 Get them to through questions **a–e** together (if they have not done this already) and compare and swap information about the people.

2 Ask everyone to read the other two articles quickly, (they should be able to because they have already learnt a lot about the other people from their partners) and decide if the following statements are true (✓) or false (✗). They should compare the correct answers to the false ones.

Answers
a Only Giles and Hugo were influenced by the servants in their families when they were children. (✗)
(Amanda was also influenced by the two nannies.)
b Amanda wanted to be a nanny because she liked the uniform. (✗)
(No, because she got on well with children.)
c Giles wanted to be a cook because the meals were so bad at boarding school. (✗)
(No, because he learnt cookery instead of sport.)
d Hugo did well in his holiday job because he had learnt a lot about plants from the gardener. (✓)
e All of the parents were very angry when they were told about the choice of career. (✗)
(No, Giles' parents didn't get angry but his grandfather did.)
f Hugo's parents were the least angry. (✗)
(No, they were furious. They refused to allow him in the house. Giles' parents were the least angry.)
g All of the parents have become friends with their children again. (✓)
h Giles' grandfather has not forgiven him for becoming a cook. (✓)
i Some of the children have regretted their decision not to go to university. (✗)
(None of them did, especially as some of their friends have had difficulty finding good jobs.)
j Hugo has already become a millionaire. (✗)
(No, he hasn't become one yet, but his sister thinks he will before he's 40.)

3 Students show each other which multi-word verbs appear in their articles, and discuss their meaning and which ones appear in more than one article.

Answers
See answers to Reading, exercise 2 above.

Roleplay

Divide the class into groups of three and allocate roles, **A**, **B** and **C**. Give them time to think and collect their ideas before you start the roleplay.

SUGGESTION

You could do this by putting *all* the **A**s and **B**s together to discuss ideas and *all* the **C**s together to do the same before they do the roleplay.

Go round and monitor the actual roleplays. Ask some groups to do it in front of the others. You could record and/or video them if you have the facilities.

ADDITIONAL MATERIAL

Video Report 4: London taxi drivers

SUGGESTION

You could exploit the use of the Present Perfect in the reading texts on pages 70–1 of the Student's Book by doing the photocopiable exercise on page 123 of this Teachers' Book.

● VOCABULARY (SB page 72)

Multi-word verbs

SUGGESTIONS

• You could ask your students to read through the Grammar Reference section on multi-word verbs (SB page 151–2) for homework before this lesson. This is useful following their work on multi-word verbs in the reading texts.

• It might be useful for you to read the Grammar Reference section yourself before doing this lesson, to remind yourself of the different types.

NB Multi-word or phrasal verbs are covered systematically in the Workbook. The different types are practised in a variety of exercises in every second unit.

Students have already done some work on multi-word verbs as part of their work on the reading texts. The sentences quoted here are examples of three different types. Read them aloud to your class. Point out that …

• in the first example you can't say *look ~~us~~ after*. It is inseparable, it must be *look after us*.
(This is Type 3 in the Grammar Reference section.)

• in the second example *give up* is separable. You can say *give up smoking* **or** *give smoking up*, but a pronoun always separates, *give her up*, *give it up*.
(This is Type 2 in the Grammar Reference section.)

• the third example has no direct object.
(This is Type 1 in the Grammar Reference section.)

1 **Meaning**
This exercise focuses on meaning and the fact that one multi-word verb can have many meanings. These can be both literal and non-literal (idiomatic). Make sure

that your students understand this before they do the exercise. It may be a good idea to do the first one with them as an example.

Ask students to work in pairs. Go round and monitor them as they work, helping their discussion where necessary. Conduct a feedback with the whole class.

Answers
1 **b** is literal.   **a** and **c** are idiomatic.
  a means 'a plane has left the ground'.
  c means 'started to be successful'.
2 **a** is literal.   **b** and **c** are idiomatic.
  b means 'mentioned a point in the conversation'.
  c means 'raised and looked after children'.
3 **b** is literal.   **a** and **c** are idiomatic.
  a means 'improved'.
  c means learned informally, not in lessons.

SUGGESTION

Ask your students to look at and explain the cartoon which illustrates sentence **c**. Its humour is because of the confusion of literal and idiomatic meaning.

4 **c** is literal.   **a** and **b** are idiomatic.
  a means 'recover from'.
  b means 'make someone understand'.
5 **c** is literal.   **a** and **b** are idiomatic.
  a means 'looked for and found'.
  b means 'improved'.

2 **Verbs with two particles**
These are Type 4 in the Grammar Reference section.

This can be done quite quickly. Give students a few minutes to go through it, then check with a partner and finally with you.

Answers
a get on with   b run out of   c look forward to
d go out with   e put up with
c, e same **a, b, d** different

3 **Separable or inseparable ?**
Ask students to work in pairs and consult a dictionary to do this. Check it in a class feedback session.

Answers
  S = separable   **I** = inseparable
a **S** I've just looked *it* up in my dictionary.
b **I** He's looking after *them* while I'm away.
c **S** She has brought *them* up really well.
d **S** We picked *it* up very quickly.
e **I** I don't think they'll ever get over *it*.
f **S** He's taken *it* up because he has a lot of free time since he retired.

● LISTENING AND SPEAKING (SB page 73)

Thomas Wilson
- a retired man -

Pre-listening task

Put the first question to the whole class and get feedback from one or two students. Then put them into small groups to go through the other questions. Ask them to report back from their groups. This has proved to be quite a generative speaking activity, many students seem to like talking about the older members of their families.

Listening

T.51   Ask students to comment on the photographs of Thomas and Philippa, his granddaughter, who is sixteen. Ask some questions about them, for example: *Did Thomas have an important job? Do you think he misses it? Do you think Philippa is happy? How do you think her life is different from her grandfather's?*

Ask them to listen and say who sounds the happier and why.

> **Answer**
> Thomas seems very active and happy. He doesn't complain, even though he misses his wife and his dog. Philippa seems less happy with her life. She complains about not going to interesting places and only having exams and work to look forward to.

Comprehension check

Before your students do this, you may have to play the tape again. Only you can be the judge of your students' listening ability. Do the grammar part of question one together, i.e. the choice of which tense is correct. This is to revise the difference in meaning between the Present Perfect and the Past Simple.

> **Answers**
> 1 a How long has he been retired? **Four years**. (He is still retired, is not dead.)
>
>   b How long did he work for the textile company? **Forty years**. (He doesn't still work there.)
>
>   c How long was he married? **Thirty-five years**. (His wife has died. He's a widower.)
>
>   d Who did he go to Wales with? **With his friends, Ted and Marjorie**. (He is not in Wales now.)
>
> 2 Because it's an excuse for a walk and he has made some good friends at the golf club.
>
> 3 He has visited/been to Australia, the Caribbean, Spain, Morocco, Turkey and Wales. Two years ago he went to Australia to see his son Keith and family.
>
> 4 Because he has just come back from a cruise round the Caribbean.

> 5 Rover – his dog, who died.
>   Keith – his son in Australia.
>   Miriam – an American lady he met on the cruise.
>   Kylie – his Australian granddaughter.
>   Helen – his daughter, Philippa's mother.
>
> 6 The deaths of his wife and his dog.
>
> 7 She complains about not going to interesting places and only having exams and work to look forward to.
>
> 8 He's talking about life. You only get one life, so don't wish it away, make the most of it.

Discussion

Ask students to consider the questions in groups before you have a full class discussion. Again, this often proves to be a subject many students have a lot to say about – especially the subject of the kind of retirement they would like for themselves!

● WRITING (SB page 74)

Formal letters

The unit comes full circle and ends with Nancy Mann's formal letter of application for the job.

1 The gaps should be easy to fill – they are all revision of grammar or vocabulary in this unit. Ask students to do it and compare their answers with a partner.

> **Answers**
>
> 17 Hillside Rd
> Chesswood
> Herts. WD3 5LB
> Tel 01923 284171
> Fax 01923 286622
> Thursday 17 January
>
> David Benton
> Worldwatch UK Ltd
> 357 Ferry Rd
> Basingstoke RG2 5HP
>
> Dear Mr Benton
>
> I saw your advertisement for a Business Journalist in today's Guardian newspaper. I am very interested in the job and I think that I have many of the necessary qualifications.
>
> I studied politics and modern languages at Oxford University. I am fluent in French, German and Spanish. I have travelled widely in Europe and South America, and I have worked as a business journalist for the BBC for the last five years.
>
> I enclose a copy of my curriculum vitae. I look forward to hearing from you soon. Please let me know if you need more information.
>
> Yours sincerely
>
> *Nancy Mann*
>
> Nancy Mann

2 Students remain in their pairs to do this. Go round and help them as they will probably need it. Give them about ten minutes to do it and then go through the answers with the whole class.

> **Answers**
> **– Formal beginnings and endings**
> Dear Sir or Madam, Dear Madam, Dear Sir(s) … Yours faithfully (When you don't know the name.)
> Dear Mr/Ms/Miss/Mrs Smith … Yours sincerely (When you know the name.)
> Dear Simon/Sally Smith …Yours sincerely (This is becoming more frequent when writing to strangers but **not** Dear *Mr Simon Smith*.)
>
> **– Informal beginnings and endings**
> Dear Mary …
>   love/regards/kind regards *John/Elizabeth*
>
> Dear John …
>   love *Mary*
>   yours/with best wishes *Peter/Elizabeth*
>   all the best *Michael*
>
> – In the top right hand corner.
> – On the left, above the name.
> – 17 January 1996 or 17/1/96
> – She signs her name directly below the ending. She prints it below her signature.
>
> Para. 1 – says where she saw the advertisement and introduces herself.
> Para. 2 – gives details about why she is suitable for the job.
> Para. 3 – is the conclusion, with details about anything enclosed in the letter and the hope for further contact.

3 This could be begun in class and finished for homework. Remind students to use Nancy Mann's letter as the model.

PostScript (SB page 75)

On the telephone

This is to give practice of both formal and informal telephone conversations. It includes suggestions about how to leave a message on an answer machine, which can be difficult even in L1 for many people!

1 Students could work in pairs to do this.

> **Answers**
> a Hi, Annie … (This is an answer machine.)
> b Yes please. This is …
> c Yes, please. I'm sure …
> d Good morning …
> e Thank you …
> f No, I'm sorry …

2 **T.52** Play the tape for students to listen and check.

> **Answer**
> b, c, d, e are business calls
> e is a mixture: wife to secretary, then wife to husband.

3 These are some useful expressions for the telephone, which students can draw on later for the roleplay activity. There are four very short dialogues. Ask students to read them aloud in open pairs across the class. Make it more fun by encouraging them to use good stress and intonation.

Leaving a message on an answer phone

1 Read through the introduction with the class.

Now ask everyone to think of someone or somewhere they really want to ring. They ring and get the answer machine.

Ask them to follow the instructions and rehearse a suitable message in their heads.

Now *you* pretend to be the answer machine. Address individual students with: *Please leave your message after the tone.*

Invite the student to respond with their message. Now ask students to do the same in pairs.

2 The role cards are on page 123 for you to photocopy. Put students into pairs, **A** and **B**, and give out the cards. Give each student time to read the card and work out what they will say before starting the roleplay. Ask some of the students to act out their roleplays. You could record some of them and play tem back, encouraging students to comment and correct.

Don't forget!

Workbook Unit 7

Exercise 11 Vocabulary. An exercise on homonymes – words with more than one meaning.

Exercise 12 Pronunciation – Word stress.

Exercise 13 Nouns + Prepositions.

Wordlist This is on page 161 of this Teacher's Book for you to photocopy and give to your students.

Video Report 4 A documentary about London taxi drivers.

Imagine!

Conditionals
Time clauses
would
Making suggestions

Profile

Student's Book

Language
- first, second, zero conditionals
- various conditional forms
- time clauses – *when, as soon as, before, until*
- *I'd rather …/I wouldn't mind …*

Pronunciation
- intonation and *Wh-* questions
- *it'd*

Vocabulary and everyday English
- base and strong adjectives
- modifying adverbs (*very, absolutely*)
- making suggestions
- linking devices – *although, however,* etc.

Workbook
- extra grammar – *wish, if only*
- vocabulary – money
- multi-word verbs with more than one meaning
- pronunciation – *oo* and *ou*

Video
- *Wide Open Spaces* Episode 4

Photocopiable materials for this unit (TB page 124–132)
- Maze cards for the Speaking activity on SB page 82.

Introduction to the unit

The theme of this unit is imaginary situations, possible ones in the case of the first conditional and unreal ones in the case of the second conditional.

There has been much talk and controversy in Britain since the introduction of the National Lottery in 1994. Winning large amounts of money seems to have terrible effects on most people. The reading text in this unit is a magazine article which takes an amusing look at the lives of such people. On a more serious note, the listening texts are three charity appeals, and students are invited to say how much they would give to each. The speaking activity is a maze, and students have to talk their way out of the problem of being millionaires! The PostScript section presents various ways of making, accepting and rejecting suggestions.

Language aims

Grammar
Conditionals

English language teachers often talk about the first, second, third and zero conditionals. Various commentators have taken issue with this, saying that this is a gross over-simplification – there aren't just four, there are many, many more. What they mean is that there are numerous permutations – imperatives, alternative modal verbs and tenses in the result clause, and *unless, should, provided,* and alternative tenses in the condition clause.

Nevertheless, for the intermediate student it is worth pointing out that beneath all the various permutations there is a basis on which all the others are formed.

PROBLEMS

Conditional sentences present students with all sorts of problems, both form and meaning. They rarely begin a sentence with *if* and get all the ensuing bits right. This is perhaps because there are two clauses (result and condition) with different tense rules for each, the form probably differs from their own language, and because the choice of first versus second conditional can depend on how the speaker views the likelihood of the event. Both first and second conditionals can refer to present and future time.

COMMON MISTAKES

- **If it will rain, I'll stay at home.*
  Many languages use a future tense in the conditional clause to refer to a future condition, which is quite logical. However, English doesn't.

- **If I see Peter, I tell him the news.*
  This is an example of learners resorting to a ubiquitous Present Simple/verb stem tense to refer to any time.

- **What you do if you win a lot of money?*
  *If he asks me, I not say anything.
  This is an assortment of form and meaning mistakes.

- **When Germany wins the world championship, I'll be very happy.*
  German has only one word to express both *when* and *if*, so speakers of German can confuse the hypothetical nature of *if* and the certainty of *when*.

- *If I lose my job, I'll …*
  If I lost my job, I'd …
  The choice of conditionals is sometimes dictated by how possible or impossible the speaker sees the condition.

- In the zero conditional, *if* does not express hypothesis. It means *when* or *whenever*.
  If I can't get to sleep, I read a book.

As with so many areas at the intermediate level, students will have been introduced to first and second conditionals before, but they still make mistakes, and will continue to do so. This is not a reason to stop trying to help them! One step back and two steps forward.

Time clauses

The problems here are similar to those in the first conditional. English does not use a future verb form in the time clause.

| I'll do it | when
as soon as
before
until | she arrives. | (Not *she will arrive) |

would

As well as seeing *would* in the second conditional, students are also introduced to *I'd rather …* and *I wouldn't mind … .*

Vocabulary

Two related areas of lexis are examined, firstly base and extreme adjectives such as *big* and *huge*. The second area is the intensifying adverbs that go with the different base and extreme adjectives, for example *very big* and *absolutely huge.*

PostScript

Making suggestions is a very broad functional area, and it is examined in this PostScript section. Ways of making, accepting and rejecting suggestions are practised. Some suggestions include the speaker (*Why don't we …?, Let's …, Shall we…?*), others don't (*I think you should…, Why don't you…?, If I were you, I'd…*). Some suggestions are relatively mild (*I think you should…*), and others imply that the speaker really does know best (*You'd better…*).

Workbook

- Extra grammar – *wish* and *if only*, present and past
- Vocabulary – money: *salary, bankrupt, broke*
- Pronunciation – ways of pronouncing *oo* and *ou*
- Multi-word verbs – verbs with more than one meaning

Notes on the unit

Test your grammar (SB page 76)

Ask students to look at the pictures.

1 Students put the words in the right order. This is harder than it looks, so be prepared to help. Don't forget that these *Test your grammar* sections are aimed to orientate students and focus their attention on the grammar to come – they are not designed to be a way of actually teaching the grammar.

Answers
a if I get up late, my Dad gives me a lift.
b if I pass the test, I'll buy a new car.
c if I won a million pounds, I'd travel round the world.

Unit 8 Imagine! **75**

2 Ask students to think about the three questions in pairs before you answer them as a class. Don't worry if they don't all get the right answers – you're about to present the area thoroughly!

Answers
a is always true.
b expresses a future possibility.
c is possible but improbable.

PRESENTATION (1) (SB page 76)
First conditional and time clauses

For the second time we meet Jim and his mother, who we first met in Unit 4. He still hasn't set off on his trip round the world, but it's getting closer!

Students look at the picture. Ask your class
Do you remember this boy? What's his name?
Where's he going? Who with? (Anthony)
What's his mother like? (She worries a lot.)

1 **T.53a** Read the introduction as a class. You could play the dialogue and then ask students to fill the gaps; or, you could decide to ask students to fill the gaps first, then play the tape to check. This second approach is more challenging.

Students practise the dialogue in pairs.

SUGGESTION

At this point you need to do some controlled practice of the first conditional, to reinforce the form and the pronunciation, and to make sure that students can make the structure before the slightly freer practice in exercise 2. Students will do exercise 2 in pairs so you need to be reasonably sure that they can do it.

Drill the question *What will you do if you run out of money?* around the room, then the answer *We'll get a job, of course.* Practise this in open pairs.

Do the same with the following: *What will you do if you get lost? If we get lost, we'll ask someone the way.*

Correct mistakes of form and pronunciation very carefully.

2 Students make similar dialogues between Jim and his mother, using the prompts. Do the first positive sentence and the first negative sentence as a class, so that students know what they have to do.

Get some feedback. There should be some funny suggestions for Jim's replies to his mother's concerns. Correct mistakes carefully.

3 **T.53b** Students listen to the second part of the conversation. Again, you might choose to ask students to put the verb in the correct tense *before* they listen.

Students practise the dialogue in either open or closed pairs. Make sure their intonation is good.

Grammar questions

Answer the questions as a class. The first question is aimed primarily at speakers who confuse *when* and *if.*

Answers
– *If* expresses a future possibility.
  When expresses a future certainty.

– *If we get lost, ...*   ✔
  If we'll get lost, ...   ✗
  When we go, ...   ✔
  When we'll go ...   ✗
  As soon as we arrive ...   ✔
  As soon as we'll arrive ... ✗

PRACTICE (SB page 77)
1 Completing a conversation

1 Read the introduction as a class. Students work in pairs or small groups to complete the conversation. This is quite a difficult exercise, so monitor carefully and help where necessary.

Answers
J Goodbye, darling! Good luck with the interview!
S Thanks. I'll need it. I hope the trains are running on time. **If** the trains **are** delayed, **I'll get** a taxi. **If I'm** late for the interview, **I'll be** furious with myself!
J Just keep calm! Phone me when you can.
S I will. **As soon as** I **come** out of the interview, **I'll give** you a ring.
J When **will** you **know if** you've got the job?
S They**'ll send** me a letter in the next few days. **If** they **offer** me the job, **I'll accept** it, and if I accept it, we**'ll have to** move house. You know that, don't you?
J Sure. But we'll worry about that later.
S OK. What are you doing today?
J I can't remember. **When** I **get** to the office, **I'll look** in my diary. I don't think I'm doing much today.
S Don't forget to pick up the children **when** you **get back** from work.
J I won't. You'd better go now. **If** you **don't hurry,** you**'ll miss** the train.
S OK. I**'ll see** you this evening. Bye!
J Bye, my love. Take care, and good luck!

T.54 Students listen and check their answers.

2 In pairs, students ask and answer questions. Again, this is a challenging exercise, especially in forming the question and changing the sentences from first and second person to the third person. Monitor carefully and correct as necessary. Get feedback as a class.

> **Answers**
> a How will she feel if she's late for the interview?
>   She'll be furious with herself. (*feel furious* sounds odd)
> b When will she phone Joe?
>   She'll phone Joe as soon as she comes out of the interview.
> c When will she know if she's got the job?
>   In the next few days.
> d What will she do if they offer her the job?
>   She'll accept it.
> e What will they have to do if she accepts the job?
>   They'll have to move house.
> f What will Joe do when he gets to the office?
>   He'll look in his diary.
> g What will happen if Sue doesn't hurry?
>   She'll miss the train.

ADDITIONAL MATERIAL

Workbook
Exercises 1–4 These all practise the input of this unit so far.

PRESENTATION (2) (SB page 78)

Second conditional and *would*

1 Answer the two questions as a class. Don't worry if not very much discussion ensues.

T.55 Students listen to the people and discuss their ideas about who says what.

> **Answer**
> a 3   b 8   c 6   d 1   e 2   f 5   g 7   h 4

Then play the first few lines again. Write some notes on the board to give students an idea of what to do, for example, *boat trip round the world   relax   fly*

Now play the rest of the tape. The last little boy speaks very quickly, but he's very funny.

> **SUGGESTION**
> Practise some of the sentences, drilling them around the class, correcting mistakes very carefully.
> You could use these sentences.
> *I'd go on a boat trip around the world.*
> *I'd like to relax.*

> *I'd buy all the toys in the world.*
> *I'd take the children to Disneyland.*
> *I'd buy a football team.*
> *I wouldn't give up my job.*
> *I'd go to the moon.*

For the last few, you could get a two-line dialogue practised in open pairs.
What would you do if you won two million pounds?
I'd take the children to Disneyland.

2 Play the first two extracts again. Students complete the sentences. The aim here is to focus on the contractions *I'd* and *it'd*, the short answer *I wouldn't*, and two other expressions with *would – I'd rather …* and *I wouldn't mind …*

Check the answers, then ask them to practise saying the sentences. Correct mistakes carefully.

You might want to play the rest of the interviews again, with students reading the tapescript at the same time.

Grammar questions

Read the sentence aloud.

• Answer the question as a class. This is a tricky question, one that students probably hadn't been asking themselves, so they will have to stop and think carefully.

> **Answer**
> The past tense forms *had* and *would* don't show past time, they show unreality.

• Read the final two points as a class. *I'd rather* may seem strange to the class because *rather* isn't a verb and doesn't look like a verb. We suggest that you don't go into this – teach it as an idiom.
• *I wouldn't mind* may seem strange because it is a negative way of expressing a positive idea.

NB *There is an exercise on 'I'd rather' in the Workbook. You might want to do it in class to try to get this structure in use. However, we haven't provided any practice of 'I wouldn't mind …' because we feel it would be an unexpected structure for students of this level to use, so they might be misunderstood. It's up to you if you want to give more practice of this and draw students' attention to it.*

PRACTICE (SB page 78)

1 Discussion

This is potentially quite a long activity, so you need to decide how long you want it to last. Of course, students might have nothing to say at all, in which case you'll just have to move on!

The prompts are to make questions. You could establish these first by drilling them. This activity is perhaps best done as a class so everyone can hear what the other would do with the money. You will have to decide how much you want to correct. You don't want to stop the flow, and the fun, but equally you don't want to hear horrendous mistakes go uncorrected.

2 Various conditional forms

1 The aim here is to show students some of the many variations that can occur in both the condition clause and the result clause.

Students work in pairs to match a line in **A** with a line in **B** and a line in **C**.

Get some feedback before you play the tape.

T.56a Students listen and check their answers, then practise the sentences in pairs.

Ask students to identify some of the different verb forms.

> **Answers**
> In the condition clause ...
> Present Perfect *If you've finished ...*
> could *(... if I could afford it)*
>
> In the result clause ...
> imperative *(don't wait ..., tell him ...)*
> might *(I might do ...)*
> have to *(you have to have a visa)*
> Notice the different pronunciations of *have* here (1st *have* /hæf/, 2nd *have* /hæv/).
> must *(you must give me a ring)*
> can *(you can have a break)*
> should *(you should go to bed)*

2 **T.56b** Students hear some questions and decide which conditional they are. Read the Caution Box about the zero conditional first.

> **SUGGESTION**
> Stop the tape after each question and ask the class to decide which conditional it is. Do this partly as a class, and partly in pairs. This exercise is quite challenging, so be prepared to help and nudge.
>
> Ask students to look at the tapescript to practise asking and answering the questions. They can then answer the questions at their own pace.

3 Dialogues with *will* and *would*

Read the instructions as a class. This is quite a difficult exercise, too, because students have to decide how probable the future situations are for themselves.

Students work in pairs to ask and answer the questions. Do the first one as a class, otherwise students might spend so long deciding whether they will be able to do the exercise or not that they won't do it!

Get some feedback and encourage the others to comment and correct.

LANGUAGE REVIEW (SB page 79)
First conditional
Second conditional
Zero conditional
Time clauses

Read the Language Review together in class, and/or ask students to read it at home. If you have a monolingual class, use L1 and ask students to translate some of the sentences. Encourage questions and queries.

Ask students to read the Grammar Reference section at home.

ADDITIONAL MATERIAL

Workbook Unit 8
Exercises 5–8 These all practise the target language of Presentation (2).
Exercises 9 & 10 These practise *wish* and *if only*.

● READING AND A SONG (SB page 80)

This is a lengthy activity, so allow enough time.

Pre-reading task

1 Read the introduction as a class.

T.57 We included the song to launch the reading text and for fun. Don't get bogged down with the listening – take no more than a minute or two. Ask students to read the tapescript as they're listening as some of the vocabulary is strange.

2 Students work in pairs to decide which they think are good or bad suggestions.

NB *In the instructions for this exercise, we use the first conditional ('If you win a lot of money ...') and not the second. This is because the article is about people who have actually won huge amounts of money, so the condition is not improbable – it is possible. We include this note for your information, in case a smart student asks you.*

3 Students match a word in **A** with a definition in **B**.

Answers

A	B
envy	a feeling of discontent because someone has something that you want
to fantasize	to imagine, to dream
a jigsaw	a picture cut into pieces that you have to put together again
a windfall	a sum of money you receive unexpectedly
a purpose	an aim, a reason for doing something
to fritter away money	to spend money foolishly on small, useless things

Reading

Students read the article, and put the eight sentences in the right place. Ask students to talk about this in pairs when you think they have all read the article. If students want to use dictionaries, let them, but don't encourage them to look up every word they don't know.

When you get the feedback on where the sentences should go, ask *Why do you think that?* and encourage other students to comment.

Answers

a 6, b 2, c 3, d 5, e 1, f 7, g 4, h 8

> **SUGGESTION**
>
> You might want to read the article aloud yourself, or ask students to take it in turns to read aloud a paragraph. This gives you the opportunity of checking items of vocabulary as you go through it – but don't forget the vocabulary exercise on page 82 which tests some of the words in this text.

Comprehension check

1 As a class, ask students to say if they have changed their minds about any suggestions to give to people who have won a lot of money.

2 Students work in pairs or small groups to answer the questions.

Answers

a Much more about the negative side.

b **our work**
  People who win a lot of money might give up work, but then there is no reason to get up in the morning.
  our home and friends
  They might buy a bigger house, but then they leave their friends behind.

c Money can be spent employing all sorts of people who are trying to protect them.

d psychotherapist   charity   relative
  security guard   lawyer

e **Val Johnson**
  She won £850,000 in 1989.
  She went on a spending spree for four years.
  She married five times.
  She is penniless and unhappy.
  Alice Hopper
  She won £950,000 four years ago.
  It made her miserable.
  She left her job and her husband.
  She bought a villa and two bars in Spain.
  Her son was killed on a motorbike.
  She is now poor again.
  Malcolm Price
  He won £2.5 million.
  He said it wouldn't change him, and it didn't.
  He went to his local pub and didn't even buy his friends a drink.
  He is a lonely man.

f The husband says 'It won't change us'. The wife says she wants it to change them.

g They want computer games, CD players and motorbikes. The neighbour wants to borrow some money.

h The husband doesn't buy anything. The son buys a huge music system. The daughter buys a holiday in Barbados with her boyfriend. The wife buys a Rolls-Royce and a racehorse for her husband.

What do you think?

These questions are probably best done as a class, as it won't take so long. Students might be getting a bit tired of this article by now.

Answers

1 Because the different parts of our life, for example, our work, friends and house, all go together.

2 If something happens to one part of our lives, the other parts are affected, too.

3 Work gives our life structure, and something to do every day.

4 All the husband wants to do is fix the toilet seat, but nobody else is interested. They want to spend their money on much more exotic things.

5 He wants their life to be unchanged, presumably because they are happy. His wife is looking forward to spending lots of money.

6 Students answer this for themselves.

Vocabulary

> **SUGGESTION**
>
> You might chose to do this on another day so that students have a break from the article.

Students work in pairs to find the words in the text.

Answers

a rarely	f protect
b huge	g spending spree
c smash	h penniless
d neighbourhood	i groceries
e begging	j leak

SPEAKING (SB page 82)

A maze

Read the introduction as a class. You will need to photocopy the maze cards on page 124–32 of this Teacher's Book. You might want to stick them onto some card so that they last longer.

Read card number 1 in the Student's Book. Make sure that students know what they have to do.

Students should work in groups of four or five. You know your students best – so you decide how to organize them. Basically, this activity should be a lot of fun, so move your students around if all the lively ones usually sit together.

NB *The maze should generate a lot of speaking as students try to argue about what is best to do. With some groups, however, they will agree to go in one direction without talking about it. Hopefully, they will soon get the idea that the maze isn't at all serious.*

You will need to make a decision about correcting. You probably won't want to interrupt the flow of conversation as mistakes occur, so you could make a note of them and correct them later. There will no doubt be lots of mistakes with conditionals as students speculate about what will or would happen if they make a certain decision.

Different groups will finish at different times. If students seemed interested in the activity, they could go back and start again wherever they like – at the beginning, or at a point where they had to made an interesting decision. There are about sixteen different endings, so students could go down a completely different route and make completely different decisions.

When they have all come to the end, ask the groups to report to everyone where their decisions took them, and how their maze ended.

VOCABULARY (SB page 82)

Base and strong adjectives

NB *This is a very interesting area of the language. In their speaking, students rarely use intensifying adverbs, they tend to use just a single adjective. But a native speaker's language is full of such items. One feature of spoken language is that people exaggerate. We don't*

just say 'I'm hungry', we say 'I'm absolutely starving', 'I could eat a horse'. We don't say 'She was angry', we say 'She went completely off her nut', 'She went bananas', 'She hit the roof'. We are not suggesting that such idiomatic language should be taught to foreign learners, but it would be interesting if they could begin to use intensifying adverbs.

PROBLEMS

There are three main problems.

1 Students need to perceive the difference between base and strong adjectives. This isn't terribly difficult once students have had them explained.

2 There are big problems with collocation. Very few intensifying adverbs go with all adjectives. *Very* and *really* seem to go with all base adjectives, and *absolutely* and *really* go with all strong adjectives. But there are many other adverbs which seem to go with certain adjectives only, for example

deeply disappointed   totally blind
completely insane   utterly useless

It is best if students can begin to recognize and produce *very* and *really* with base adjectives, and *absolutely* and *really* with strong adjectives.

3 *Quite* means different things, depending on stress and the adjective.

It was quite 'good. (Stress on *good*)
This is positive. I liked it.

It was 'quite good. (Stress on *quite*)
This is negative. I didn't like it.

It was 'quite 'perfect. (Equal stress with a strong adjective) *Quite* means the same as *absolutely*. I liked it a lot.

---

1 Read the introduction as a class. If you have a monolingual class, you might point out a few examples in their language. This is a feature of many languages, not just English.

2 Students put a base adjective next to a strong adjective. Notice that, not surprisingly, there are many words to express *good* and *bad*.

Answers

big	enormous, huge
hot	boiling
tired	exhausted
cold	freezing
tasty	delicious
interesting	fascinating
bad	horrid, horrible ...
good	perfect, marvellous ...
dirty	filthy
surprised	astonished, amazed
angry	furious
funny	hilarious

frightened	terrified
pretty/attractive	beautiful
clever	brilliant

Note that *brilliant* means both *very clever* and *very good*.

When you are getting the feedback to this exercise, make sure that students' voices sound extreme and enthusiastic, especially with the strong adjectives.

Read the Caution Box as a class. We don't suggest you go into too much detail with *quite*, but the information is here to help you. Encourage students to try using *very*, *quite* and *really* with base adjectives, and *absolutely* and *really* with strong adjectives.

3 **T.58** Students listen to the dialogues, and complete them in pairs. The situations all suggest the use of one of the strong adjectives. Good pairs of students might be able to produce a dialogue with several examples.

LISTENING (SB page 83)

After the quite lengthy reading exercise, this listening should be relatively easy and straightforward.

Pre-listening task

1 Discuss this as a class.

2 Students do this first in small groups, and then as a class.

Listening

T.59 Students copy the chart on a separate piece of paper. They listen to three charity appeals and fill in their charts. Ask them to compare information in pairs before you give the answers.

What do you think?

Read the instructions as a class. Students think first on their own, and then discuss with a partner. You could end with some class feedback.

You will need to decide what your attitude to correction will be. In all this speaking activity, there should be quite a few second conditional sentences. If and when there are mistakes, how are you going to correct them? You don't want to stop the flow. Maybe you could make a note of them, and deal with them after the discussion.

WRITING (SB page 84)

Words that join ideas

Students find this area of the language quite difficult, so be prepared to help where necessary. You might prefer to do it in class rather than for homework.

1 Read the explanation carefully. Use L1 if you can.

2 Again, read this as a class, and use L1 if you can.

3 Students choose the words that fit best. Do the first two or three as a class, so that they get the idea of what they have to do.

Answers

a even	g although	m pretty enough!
b Unfortunately	h because	n because of
c at least	i as well	o Actually
d also	j of course	p Anyway
e so	k but	
f only	l either	

Answers

	Who or what the charity tries to help	How the charity helps	Some of their successes and/or problems
Amnesty International	It tries to release prisoners of conscience, men and women who are in prison because of their beliefs, colour, language or religion.	It tries to get fair trials by publicizing the cases and putting pressure on governments to practise human rights.	In their twenty years they have helped prisoners in over sixty countries, and have won peace prizes.
RSPCA	It tries to stop cruelty to animals in England and Wales. It also works for the welfare of animals in the wild, for example whales and badgers.	They find new homes for about 80,000 animals, treat over 200,000 sick animals, and investigate over 100,000 complaints of cruelty.	They are the world experts at cleaning birds that have been caught in oil spills. They receive no aid from the government.
Drought and Famine in Africa	It helps people in Africa who are suffering from drought and famine.	They supply towns and camps with food and medical supplies.	In some parts of Africa, it hasn't rained for three years. Refugees are going from the countryside into the towns looking for food. One thousand people a day are dying.

They need more food and medical supplies, doctors, nurses, blankets, tents and clothes. |

Making suggestions

> **SUGGESTION**
> You could ask your students to read the Grammar Reference section for homework before doing this activity.

Students will of course be using some of this language already to make, accept and reject suggestions. This activity aims to widen their performance in such a high-frequency functional area.

1   Students read about Maggie and Paul. You might need to explain that *broke* is colloquial for *having no money*.

    Students work in pairs to decide which of the suggestions are for Maggie and which for Paul. Do the first one or two as a class so that students get the idea of which ones include the speaker.

> **Answers**
> **For Maggie**
> Let's go to the cinema! (+ speaker)
> Why don't we go for a walk? (+ speaker)
> Shall we have a game of cards? (+ speaker)
>
> **For Paul**
> If I were you, I'd get a better-paid job.
> I don't think you should go out so much.
> Why don't you ask your parents?
> You ought to save some money every month!
> You'd better get a loan from the bank!

2   **T.60**   Students listen to Maggie and Paul. Ask students to recall some of the suggestions.

> **Answers**
> *Why don't we ...?*
> *Let's ...*
> *Shall we ...?*
> *If I were you, I'd ...*
> *you'd better ...*
> *Why don't you ...?*
> *you ought to ...*

NB *'Telly' is slang for 'television'; 'Neighbours' is an Australian soap opera popular with children; 'mate' is slang for 'friend'.*

3   Students listen and read the tapescript. Ask them to identify ways of accepting and rejecting suggestions.

> **Answers**
> **Accepting suggestions**
> That's a good idea!
> Why didn't I think of that?
>
> **Rejecting suggestions**
> I don't feel like ...
> Oh no! I couldn't bear it! I'd rather do anything but that!
> I couldn't do that.
> I'd rather not.
> It's a good idea, but I've already tried it.

4   This is an old-fashioned transformation drill as in Robert O'Neill's *English in Situations*, but presumably there are now generations of language teachers who don't know what such an exercise is for, or how it works!

    The aim of a transformation drill is to provide speaking practice of several structural forms. Students have to manipulate the first sentence to incorporate the prompt.

    Read the instructions as a class. Say the first sentence *Let's go to the cinema* yourself, then say *Why don't we ...?* and point to a student. He or she must say *Why don't we go to the cinema?* Make sure the pronunciation is good, then drill the same sentence around the classroom.

    Now say *I think we should ...*, and point to another student. She or he must say *I think we should go to the cinema*. Drill the sentence three or four times, then say *invite Pete to dinner tomorrow* and point to another student. The process is repeated till the end, then you can do the same with the second base sentence *Why don't you phone Pat?*

5   Students work in pairs to make dialogues for one or two of the situations. When they are ready, get feedback as a class.

Don't forget!

Workbook Unit 8

Exercise 11 Vocabulary – money

Exercise 12 & 13 Pronunciation – *oo* and *ou*

Exercise 14 Multi-word verbs – verbs with more than one meaning

Wordlist This is on page 162 of this Teacher's Book for you to photocopy and give to your students.

Video *Wide Open Spaces* Episode 4: Maddy and Nick, now in their country cottage, go to the pub to meet the locals. They are in for a surprise.

9 Relationships

Modal verbs (2) probability
So do I! Neither do I!

Profile

Student's Book

Language
- Modal verbs of probability (*must, might, could, can't, may*)
- present and past (*must/must've*)
- sentence combination

Pronunciation
- stress and intonation

Vocabulary and everyday English
- character adjectives
- negative prefixes
- agreeing and disagreeing

Workbook
- extra grammar – the continuous infinitive
- vocabulary – verbs and nouns that go together
- pronunciation – connected speech
- prepositions – adjective and preposition

Video
- Report 5 *Public School*

Photocopiable materials for this unit (TB page 133)
- Lucy and Pam's original letters to Susie (SB page 87).

Introduction to the unit

This is the second unit on modal verbs. Unit 4 dealt with modals of obligation and permission, and also their use in requests and offers.

NB Remind your students of the introduction to modal verbs in the Grammar Reference section of Unit 4, SB page 146–8, and ask them to reread this prior to starting Unit 9.

In this unit we focus on modals of probability, in both the present and the past. This is a main use of modal verbs, because *all* modals can be used to express different degrees of certainty or probability. However, at this intermediate level we limit the range of modals covered so as not to overwhelm the students.

The theme of the unit is relationships, not only between people but also between people and nature. The skills work includes a listening in which two people from two very different families talk about their childhood, and a reading, which is extracts from a book called *The Man who Planted Trees*. This is a beautifully simple story with a profound message. It illustrates how one man's relationship with nature can change the world.

NB You will need a couple of magazines for Presentation (1), and there is a practice activity (suggested in this book on page 86), which necessitates students bringing to class some photographs of various members of their families, past and present. Ask your students to look for these now, before you start the unit.

Language aims

Grammar

Modal verbs of probability

Presentation (1) covers modal verbs of probability in the present with *must, could, might, can't* + the infinitive. *May* is included in the Language Review and the Grammar Reference section but not given as much prominence as the others in the body of the unit.

Presentation (2) covers the same modal verbs, but in the past *must have, could have, might have, can't have* using the perfect infinitive.

PROBLEMS

The use of *must* and *can't* to express strong possibility/ probability do not usually cause problems of concept as similar forms exist in many languages. However, it is more difficult to get students to use *might* and *could* to express weaker probability as there are no comparable forms. They often use the words *perhaps* or *maybe* in direct translation from L1, but this can sound very *un*-English!

COMMON MISTAKES	CORRECTED
Maybe they'll come.	*They might come.*
Maybe she failed her exam.	*She might/could have failed her exam.*
Perhaps he has a break.	*He could/ might be having a break.*
Perhaps I left my bag on the train.	*I might have left my bag on the train.*

Vocabulary

The vocabulary takes the form of a personality quiz. This not only enlarges the students' repertoire of adjectives to do with character such as *moody* and *ambitious*, but also does some work on the negative prefixes *in-* and *un-*.

PostScript

The Postscript fits the theme of relationships in its focus on ways of agreeing and disagreeing.

Workbook

• Extra grammar – the continuous infinitive
• Vocabulary – verbs and nouns that go together
• Pronunciation – connected speech
• Prepositions – adjective + preposition

Notes on the unit

Test your grammar   (SB page 86)

This is a recognition only exercise assuming that students will have some awareness of this use of modals.

1   Do the example as a class. You could write the examples on the board. Ask questions such as: *Which sentence is definite/absolutely 100% sure? Which is quite sure but not 100%?* Mark them with a ✔ and a ? so that students understand exactly what to do.

Answers
a   She's having a shower. (✔)
    She could be having a shower. (?)
b   That pen's mine. (✔)
    That pen might be mine. (?)
c   He doesn't own a Rolls Royce. (✔)
    He can't own a Rolls Royce. (?)
d   You must have met my brother. (?)
    You've met my brother. (✔)
e   They haven't met the Queen. (✔)
    They can't have met the Queen. (?)
f   Shakespeare might have lived there. (?)
    Shakespeare lived there. (✔)

---

2   Ask the students to read them through again and answer quickly. *Don't* be tempted to go over this in depth with them now. They will practise it later.

Answer
a, b, and **c** are about the present.
d, e, and **f** are about the past.

PRESENTATION (1)   (SB page 86)

Modal verbs of probability in the present

1   Bring into class a couple of magazines with problem pages. Ask how many students read these pages, or *admit* to reading them. Give your own opinion to prompt students' opinions. Ask them to work in pairs or small groups to think of typical problems they have seen on such pages. Get feedback on their ideas.

2   The idea is that these replies will generate the need to use the language of probability and possibility because we can deduce the contents of the original letters from these answers. Ask students to work in pairs and read and discuss the probable problems. Give them about five minutes and then ask for some brief general feedback.

SUGGESTION
Use this feedback to highlight the grammar.

Sample answers

How old do you think Lucy is?	*She must be a teenager.*
Why do you think that?	*Because she listens to music ...*
How old do you think Pam is?	*She can't be a teenager, she must be older. She might be in her late twenties or thirties.*
Why do you think that?	*Because she's married ... etc.*

3 & 4

Now ask students to discuss with their partner who they think the sentences refer to and give reasons. Students are being asked to recognize the target language here, before they produce it in practice.

Go round and help. Get feedback as a class, being sure to ask for reasons for their decisions.

Answers and sample reasons

a **Pam** must be exhausted ... because she works hard, she does everything in the house and she can't sleep.

b **Lucy** must be in love with a pop star ... because she daydreams, cries when she listens to his music and writes him letters (he lives in California).

c **Pam** could be a doctor or a nurse ... because she cares for sick people and has a tiring and stressful job.

d **Lucy** can't have many friends ... because Susie tells her to go out more and find some friends.

e **Pam's husband** might be an alcoholic ... because she finds empty whisky bottles under the bed.

f **Pam's husband** must be unemployed ... because Susie says that perhaps he will feel better when he finds work.

g **Lucy's parents** can't have a very good relationship with their daughter ... they don't listen to her problems because they're so busy.

h **Pam and her husband** might not have any children ... because Susie doesn't mention any children in her reply.

i **Pam's mother-in-law** can't get on well with her daughter-in-law... because she doesn't do anything to help Pam. She wants her son to be with her.

j **Lucy** must be studying for exams next June ... because Susie wishes her luck and tells her to study hard.

k **Pam and her husband** might live near a busy road ... because Susie tells her to buy some earplugs so she can sleep.

l **Pam's husband** must snore ... because Susie tells her to buy some earplugs so she can sleep.

● Grammar questions

Read the statements to the class. Ask the question and get the students' ideas.

Answers
must be is most sure
could be and *might be* are less sure

Read the second question aloud.

Answer
I don't think it's possible that
she is in love = She **can't be** in love. or
She **might not** be in love.

Now ask them to look back to exercise 3 and find examples of the different modals.

SUGGESTION
Your students might like to read the original letters Lucy and Pam wrote to Susie. They are provided on page 133 for you to photocopy and give out.

PRACTICE   (SB page 87)

1 Controlled speaking

NB *This is purposely a very controlled speaking practice, which in fact gives each student the opportunity to produce quite a long piece of English, concentrating on correct form and pronunciation. There is so much emphasis on free speaking in many language classrooms that some less forthcoming students often end up producing only odd words for discussion, albeit fluent ones! All students can experience quite a lot of satisfaction from an opportunity to speak correctly and at length.*

You will need to do the first line as an example, then ask students to address each other in pairs. Go round and check their efforts; they will need your help. Round off the activity by asking two individuals, a Student **A** and a Student **B**, to read aloud their piece to the whole class.

Answers
Student A
Lucy **lives** in Scotland so she must **be** Scottish. She **writes** a lot of letters to a pop star in California, so she must **spend** a lot of money on stamps. She **stays** in her room and **listens** to his music all of the time so she can't **have** many friends or hobbies. She should **go** out more and **find/make** some friends and then she might **forget** the pop star. She could **try** to talk to her parents again, but they might not **listen** because they **are** very busy.

Student B
Pam must **be** very tired at the end of the day because she **has** a stressful job. She must **feel/be** sorry for her husband because he **is** unemployed but she must also **be/feel** very angry with him because he never **does** any housework. She could **ask** her mother-in-law to help but she can't **have** a very good relationship with her because her husband **spends** too much time at her house. Things might **be/get** better if he could **find/get** a job and if they could **talk** to each other.

2 Grammar and pronunciation

T.61   Students now have the opportunity to produce the target language in a more challenging exercise. Ask them to do the exercise in pairs. One student reads out the first sentence and the second student responds using the prompts.

Play the tape for them to check what they have been doing.

Finally, have a session across the class – you or a student say the sentences and students respond as naturally as possible with good stress and intonation.

Answers
a Mr and Mrs Brown never go on holiday.
   They **can't have** much money.
b The phone's ringing! It **might be** Jane.
c Paul's taking his umbrella. It **must be** raining.
d There are three fire engines!
   There **must be** a fire somewhere.
e I don't know where Hannah is.
   She **could be** in her bedroom.
f My aunt isn't in the kitchen.
   She **can't be cooking** dinner.
g Whose coat is this? It **might be** John's.
h We've won the lottery! You **must be joking**!

3 What are they talking about?

1 **T.62** Students work in small groups. Go through the example with the class. Play the tape pausing after each conversation so the groups can discuss the answers. Get feedback after each and encourage them to give reasons for their decisions. Be prepared to have to push students into using modals in their replies and not just *perhaps* or *maybe* all of the time.

Sample answers
a They must be in a pub. They could be in a hotel bar.
   They can't be at home or a restaurant because …
b He must be a taxi driver because … he can't be an actor or sales manager because … . He might be a company driver but I don't think so.
c She must be talking about meeting her boyfriend's parents because … . They can't be her own parents because … . It definitely isn't her first day in a new job and she isn't talking about her wedding day.
d She can't be a baby or an au pair because … . She must be an animal, probably a dog, because … . She might be a horse.
e They must be fishing because … . But they might be rowing or swimming in rough water. They can't be water-skiing because … .

2 Students stay in their groups to do this.

SUGGESTION
It would be interesting for students to bring in photos of their families, and have a mingle activity visiting other groups and commenting on who they think the people are. *You* could bring in photos of your relatives. Elicit *That must be …*, *He could be …*, etc.

ADDITIONAL MATERIAL

Workbook Unit 9
Exercises 1, 2, 3 Modal verbs of probability in the present.

PRESENTATION (2) (SB Page 88)
Modal verbs of probability in the past

NB *Because students hear only one side of the telephone conversation, they have to deduce what is being talked about. This gives practice of the modal verbs of deduction/probability in the past, because Andy and Carl are talking about a past event (a recent holiday). Students will hear both sides of the conversation at the end of the activity.*

1 **T.63a** Set the scene by asking students to look at the pictures of Andy and Carl. Ask them a few questions about them. Play the tape and ask students to read and listen at the same time. Then discuss with a partner what they think they are talking about.

Answer
They're talking about a holiday with friends.

2 This is a recognition exercise. Students can study the text in more detail as they do it. Go through the example carefully with them. Make it very clear that each time *two* statements about the conversations are possible and *one* is not. Circulate and help them do it. Give them about ten minutes to do it. Then check through with the whole class, asking for reasons for all their deductions.

Answers
a Where have they been ?
   – They must have been on holiday. (✔)
   – They can't have been somewhere sunny. (✗)
   – They might have been to Switzerland. (✔)
b What happened to Carl?
   – He must have broken his leg. (✔)
   – He could have broken his arm. (✗)
   – He must have come home early. (✔)
c How many people went on holiday?
   – There must have been at least five. (✔)
   – There might have been more than five. (✔)
   – There must have been three. (✗)
d Where did they stay?
   – They could have stayed on a campsite. (✗)
   – They must have stayed in a hotel. (✔)
   – They might have stayed with friends. (✔)
e What did they do on holiday?
   – They must have taken a lot of photos. (✔)
   – They could have been sunbathing. (✔)
   – They can't have been skiing. (✗)

f What did Bob write?
   – He might have written a letter to his wife. (✗)
   – He could have written a letter of complaint to the hotel. (✔)
   – He could have written a letter of complaint to the tour operator. (✔)
g How did they travel?
   – They must have flown. (✔)
   – They must have gone by train. (✗)
   – They might have hired a car. (✔)
h What arrived on the next flight?
   – It could have been Marcia's skis. (✗)
   – It must have been Marcia's suitcase. (✔)
   – It might have been Marcia's coat. (✔)

3 Students could do this in pairs but it is best to do it as a class, inviting members of the class to continue the story, beginning with the example. This way, you and students can correct the grammar and the story until a final version is decided upon. Don't expect students to produce as full a version as the following, but stretch them as much as you can.

Sample answer

Andy and Carl must be friends and they must have been on holiday together. They might have gone to Switzerland and it must have been sunny because they're brown.

Carl must have had an accident and broken his leg and come home early. There can't have been just three friends because they talk about five people, so there must have been at least five. They must have stayed in a hotel because they talk about Bob and Marcia's balcony, but they might have stayed with friends. They must have been skiing and taken a lot of photos. Bob can't have written to his wife because she was with him; he must have written to the hotel or the tour operator to complain about something. They can't have gone by train; they must have flown and they might have hired a car while they were there. The airline must have lost Marcia's suitcase, or it might have been her coat.

4 **T.63b** Now play the tape of both sides of the telephone conversation. Students should be interested to find out if all their deductions were correct. Ask how much they learn. Are there any surprises?

● **Grammar questions**

NB *These grammar questions not only ask about modal verbs of probability, they also remind students of the uses and past forms of other modal verbs which they studied in Unit 4.*

Read the questions aloud to the whole class and ask how the different pasts are formed. In a monolingual class you could translate some of the sentences.

Answers

	must	
He	can't	**have been** on holiday.
	could	
	might	

I **had to** buy some sunglasses.
I **had to** go home early.
I **could** see the sea from my room.

PRACTICE (SB page 90)

1 Pronunciation and speaking

1 This controlled oral practice is to give students more confidence in producing the correct form with good stress and intonation. Illustrate with the example, then go round and assist as students work in pairs.

Answers
a He must have been ill.
b You can't have bought it yourself.
c She might have overslept.
d You must have forgotten it.
e She can't have finished already.
f He must have cheated.
g You could have left it on the train.

2 **T.64** Play the tape. Focus the students' attention particularly on the stress and intonation. Practise some of the sentences in open pairs across the class.

2 Discussing grammar

These two exercises revise the modals of obligation and ability (Unit 4) and compare them with those of probability studied in this unit. Ask students to discuss their answers in pairs and follow this with a full class feedback after *each* exercise.

ALTERNATIVE SUGGESTION

If you lack time, you could set these exercises for homework together with the reading of the Language Review. The discussion could then follow in the next lesson and take less time. It is particularly important to allow discussion time for exercise 2 because of the number of possibilities.

Answers
1 a You **must have been** very cold when you were out skiing.
  b When I was at school we **had to do** homework every night.
  c He **couldn't have been** a member of his school football team. He was hopeless at all sports.
  d She **could swim/was able to swim** really well when she was just eighteen months old.

2 You need to emphasize the word *naturally* because certain possibilities would now be judged as very old-fashioned use of English.

NB Take great care not to get too bogged down when going through this exercise with your class! Take care particularly with e, f and h. At this level it is probably best not to go into any detail about old-fashioned alternatives.

Answers

a He **can't/could/must/might** have been born during World War II.

b **Can/Could** you help me with the washing up, please. (~~Might~~ you … sounds ridiculously 'posh' in a request nowadays.)

c You **can/can't/must/should** see the doctor immediately. (*Could* is only possible if part of a conditional sentence such as *You could see the doctor immediately, if you left now.*)

d It **can't/could/must/might** be raining.

e **Can/Can't/Could/Must/Shall/Should** we go out for a meal tonight? (~~Might~~ we … sounds ridiculous and old-fashioned nowadays.)

f I **can/can't/must/might/should** stop smoking. (*Could* is only possible if part of a conditional sentence such as *I could stop smoking, if I wanted to.* I ~~shall~~… said emphatically, sounds very pompous!)

g It **can't/could/must/might** have been Bill that you met at the party.

h I **can/can't/must/might/should** learn how to speak English. (*Could* is only possible if part of a conditional sentence such as *I could speak English, if I really wanted to.* I ~~shall~~… said emphatically, sounds very pompous!)

LANGUAGE REVIEW   (SB page 90)

must, could, might, can't

Read this through with the class. They could be encouraged to translate some of the sentences into their own language, especially in a monolingual class.

Ask them to read the Grammar Reference section for homework and also whilst they are doing some of the exercises in the Workbook.

ADDITIONAL MATERIAL

Workbook Unit 9
Exercise 3 This introduces and practises *must* and *can't* + *be* + *-ing* as in *He must be working late.*
Exercises 4 & 5 These practise modals of probability in the past.
Exercise 6 This is a poem which leads to practice of the modals.

● VOCABULARY AND SPEAKING
(SB page 91)

Character adjectives

1 The quiz is a means of introducing adjectives that describe people's characters. Ask students to work with a partner, after doing it on their own about themselves. Tell them to use their dictionaries.

2 Now each student does the quiz again, but this time about their partner. This can be great fun. Hopefully nobody will be too insulting!! End with feedback from the whole class about the results of the quiz.

3 Students do this together. Get feedback before they go on to the next exercise.

Answers

a – 9	e – 13	i – 11	m – 16
b – 7	f – 3	j – 14	n – 8
c – 2	g – 10	k – 5	o – 1
d – 15	h – 4	l – 12	p – 6

NB There will inevitably be some debate about which are positive and negative qualities.

b, c, j, l, n, o, p are possibly positive qualities.
a, g, i, k, are possibly negative.
d, e, f, h, m, could be both.

4 If you are short of time, you could do this with the whole class and go through it quite quickly.

Answers

a tidy	i hard-working
b pessimistic	j mean
c unsociable	k easy-going
d quiet/reserved	l lazy
e outgoing/sociable	m moody/temperamental
f outgoing/sociable	n unreliable
g patient	o depressed/miserable/sad
h unambitious	p insensitive

5 This rounds off the activity. You could begin it by describing someone yourself. Make it fun!

ADDITIONAL MATERIAL

Workbook Unit 9
Exercise 7 Vocabulary – verbs and nouns that collocate.

● LISTENING AND SPEAKING   (SB page 91)

Brothers and sisters

Pre-listening task

This is a mingling activity to set the scene for the topic of the listening, not really a serious class survey.

You could launch it by telling your students about *your* family. Then ask them to circulate (if space allows), asking as many people as possible about their brothers and sisters. Let this go on for about five minutes before asking them to sit down and getting feedback. You will want to draw particular attention to the more interesting families that emerge.

Listening and note-taking

T.65 Before listening to the first person, Jillie, you will need to explain *hand-me-down clothes*, means 'passed on from sister to sister, brother to brother, etc. in a family'; an *Eton suit*, simply means 'a very old-fashioned and formal men's suit'.

NB Eton is a very famous and expensive private boys' school (Prince William goes there.) School boys still wear these suits today. They have tails and white starched collars.

Ask students to listen and take notes. Stress that these must be short. You may have to play each tape twice for them to take notes successfully. Pause to give students the opportunity to compare notes with a partner and then ask for feedback.

Play the second tape. Students listen to Philippa, and take notes. Students compare Philippa's family with Jillie's, first with a partner and finally as a class.

> **Answers**
> **Jillie**
> – She is the youngest of nine. She has four sisters and four brothers.
> – She was happy for many reasons: she got on well with her brothers and sisters and her parents. They had old bikes and freedom. The only things she didn't like were the hand-me-down clothes and not going abroad because of so many children.
> – Yes, she's happy now. They are still a close and happy family. They have an annual family party. She gets on very well with her sister Joy. But only six out of the nine are still alive.
> – Before the older ones looked after the younger ones. Now the two youngest look after the oldest. When her husband died, her sister, Joy, and she became very close.
> – Her big sister, Joy, who took her on walks as a child, became a nun and then went to Australia for 23 years. Now they're very close again. She had rich cousins who envied their freedom because they had to dress in smart suits. About 35 of the family meet every year and there are baby twins now.

> **Philippa**
> • She has none. She's an only child.
> • She was quite happy when very young because she had lots of cousins to play with. Also, she had a best friend who lived next door. But then the friend moved. Being a teenager was very difficult because she had no one to talk to about her parents and she had too much attention and not enough freedom.
> • It is still difficult being an only child because when her father died there was nobody to help her look after her mother.
> • It was OK being an only child when very young, but it becomes more and more difficult. The family changed when her father died. Now, she's married with two children. She wanted two because she feels sorry for only children.
> • She had lots of cousins who lived in the same town. She had a best friend who moved. Her father died 10 years ago. She has two young children.

Discussion

You could put the class into small groups to collect their ideas. Then conduct a full class discussion. This can be really interesting when you get diverse opinions.

● READING AND SPEAKING   (SB Page 92)

THE MAN WHO PLANTED TREES

Pre–reading task

NB If there are any environmental or green issues in the news at the moment, have a brief discussion about them with your class to set the scene for this reading.

Read the quotation aloud and then put the students into small groups to consider the questions. Give them a few minutes, then ask for their conclusions and reasons. Withhold the correct answer until there has been a bit of debate on the subject.

They will probably not guess it correctly.

> **Answer**
> An American Cree Indian in the 19th century.

Reading

Read the introduction aloud to your students. It is unlikely that they will have heard of Jean Giono. In our experience, not even many French students have heard of him, although he is in fact quite well-known. Ask your students for the dates of the two world wars (1914–1918 and 1939–1945). Establishing these will help them follow the story.

Ask students to look at the illustrations and pre-teach vocabulary such as *acorn*, *oak tree*, *barren*, *stick*.

T.66a Play Extract 1. Ask your students to read and listen to it. Go through the first questions with the class.

NB We heard this story being read aloud on BBC Radio 4, and the atmosphere invoked was so magical that we are hoping to recreate something similar here.

Often the questions following the extracts are designed to elicit the target language of this unit, 'must be', 'can't be', etc. but the main aim is to enjoy and understand the texts.

Answers
Extract 1
1 1913. (The first line says 40 years ago and he wrote the story in 1953. World War I began in1914.)
2 It **must/might be** the Alps. (It *is* the Alps). He talks about the mountains and the dry, colourless, barren countryside so it **must be** the south of France.
3 He **must be** interested to find out why someone lives in such a wild, barren place. Perhaps he likes/He **might like** the feeling of peace.

T.66b–d Continue with the other extracts, varying whether you or a student reads aloud the introduction, and whether students work in pairs or as a class.

Extract 2
4 He **must have been** quite young, in his teens or twenties. He **can't have been** middle-aged or older because he's writing about something that happened 40 years ago. He sounds young and idealistic.
5 He'll be 85. He is 55 now in the story, so in thirty years time he'll be 85. It's 1913 now in the story, so in thirty years time it'll be 1943. (Ask your students what was happening in the world in 1943.)
6 His ambition is to live long enough to plant lots more trees. His vision **must be** of forests where now there is wilderness.

Extract 3
7 Because when he met Elzéard he (the writer) was only 20, and at that age someone over 50 seems old and likely to die soon.
8 The war hadn't affected Elzéard at all. He had just continued to plant his trees.
9 Because there was now a large forest. He was amazed at the size of the forest and the trees.
10 He thinks that it is amazing that just one man could do all this. Man could create like God and not be destructive.
    Ask your students what destruction the writer is referring to in question 10. It is World War I.

Extract 4
11 There have been two world wars. He's not pessimistic because when he sees the results of Elzéard Bouffier's work, not just forests but villages, he is convinced that despite such things as wars, humanity is still good – although there is evil in the world, there is also good.
12 Because of the trees, the land is not barren any more and people have returned to the villages. They can farm the land again and bring up their families in beautiful surroundings.
13 We learnt earlier that in 1943 he was 85. He dies in 1947. Therefore he is 89 when he dies. It is important that he had a long life because he was able to plant so many trees.

What do you think?   (SB page 94)

Put the students into small groups to discuss these questions. Then conduct a full class feedback. Withhold the answers until there has been some discussion.

Answers
1 It is *not* a true story, but it is based on a true story. In the complete story, Elzéard *was* married and had a son, but his wife and child were killed in an accident and this is when he started planting trees.
2 Possible adjectives: *calm, wise, contented, optimistic, reserved, easy-going,* etc.
3 Giono is saying that despite the terrible things man can do to man, we should remember that there are good men and women, too, and the actions of one person can have a good influence on many people.

● WRITING   (SB page 94)
Sentence combination

1 Ask students to read the sentences and then ask one of them to read aloud the paragraph below. Ask them for ways in which the sentences have been combined.

Answer
(The ways they have been combined are in **bold**.)
Elzéard Bouffier was a **poor, solitary shepherd, who** lived in the **barren mountains of southern France. His** love of nature **gave** him an incredible idea. During his life he planted thousands of acorns. **These** grew into a forest, **which** made the countryside rich and fertile again. Elzéard died when he was 89.

2 Students can benefit from doing these writing activities in class and comparing versions, but of course they could also be set for homework and compared later in class. Make it clear to your students that many different versions are possible.

Sample answers

a Alan Higgins, the famous millionaire writer from the north of England, who has written 25 novels, has gone to live in the USA. His novels have been translated into five languages and now Hollywood is going to make a film of his latest one. This will star Sunny Shaw, whose last film, *Hot Night in the Snow*, was a big box office hit.

b The city of Oxford, which is in the south of England on the River Thames, has a population of about 100,000. The city is famous because it has one of the oldest universities in the world. It also has lots of other old buildings, such as the Bodleian Library, and the Ashmolean Museum, which was built in 1683. Not many people know that Oxford was once the capital of England. Charles I made it the capital from 1642–1645.

3 Students can do this for homework. Give enough time to go over it in class, and ask students to read each other's work. Remember good pieces can be put on a classroom notice-board to be read by all.

PostScript (SB page 95)

So do I! Neither do I!

1 Introduce the lesson with your own opinions and invite students to agree or disagree, for example *I hate football. I love Indian food. I don't want to work this evening.*

It's fine if they just say something like *Me too!*

Now ask them to read the statements and complete the **You** column, not with words but just a (✔) or a (✘).

2 **T.67** Play the tape of Polly at the party and ask students to listen and complete the column for her with a (✔) or a (✘). Then, check through with students, asking *Is it the same or different for Polly?*

3 Play the tape again and ask them to listen carefully, this time to hear Polly's exact words and write them in the **Polly's words** column. Go through the answers with the class, pointing out the differences.

Answers

	Polly	Polly's words
I want to travel the world.	(✔)	So do I.
I don't want to have lots of children.	(✔)	Neither do I.
I can speak four languages.	(✘)	I can't.
I can't drive.	(✔)	Neither can I.
I'm not going to marry until I'm 35.	(✔)	Neither am I.
I went to America last year.	(✔)	So did I.
I have never been to Australia.	(✘)	I have.
I don't like politicians.	(✔)	Neither do I.
I am bored with the British Royal family.	(✔)	So am I.
I love going to parties.	(✘)	I don't.

Refer the students to the Grammar Reference section on page 153.

4 Ask them to work in pairs, and read out the statements from exercise 1, giving the correct response for them from the list in exercise 3. Go round and help. End with some open pair work across the class.

5 Ask everyone to write down a few statements about themselves and call upon individuals to read out examples, to which other members of the class must express their opinion.

NB *'Me too! Me neither!' are acceptable here as responses – especially as by this stage everyone will be tired! This is a complicated area and at best the lesson will have raised students' awareness and ability to recognize, even if they will not easily produce them in the normal flow of conversation.*

Don't forget!

Workbook Unit 9

Exercise 8 practises the way words run together in English pronunciation, and recognizing phonetic script, for example *He must've eaten all Ann's oranges.* /ˌhi məst əv ˈiːtən ɔːl ˈænz ˈɒrɪndʒɪz/

Exercise 10 Prepositions – adjectives and prepositions that go together, such as *interested in*.

Wordlist This is on page 163 of this Teachers' Book for you to photocopy and give to your students.

Video Report 5: A short factual report about Rugby, one of the most famous English public schools.

Stop and check There is a Stop and check revision section for use after each quarter of the Student's Book.

Stop and check 3 for Units 7–9 is on pages 140–1 of this Teacher's Book. You need to photocopy it. The key is on page 152.

SUGGESTION

You can use the Stop and check any way you want, but here is one way.

• Give it to your students to do for homework, preferably when they have enough time, for example, over a weekend.

• In class, ask them to go over the test again in groups of five or six people. They should try to agree on definitive answers. If they can't agree, they should ask you.

• You provide the answers and any necessary explanations.

Obsessions

Present Perfect Continuous
Time expressions
Complaining

Profile

Student's Book

Language
- Continuous tenses
- Present Perfect Continuous
- Present Perfect Simple and Continuous
- Present Perfect and Past Simple
- time expressions
- *How long are you here for?*
- *How long have you been here?*

Pronunciation
- stress in compound nouns
- intonation in *Wh-* questions

Vocabulary and everyday English
- compound nouns
- beginnings and endings of letters
- expressions of quantity
- complaining – *too ..., not enough*

Workbook
- extra grammar – continuous aspect
- suffixes and prefixes
- prepositions of time
- pronunciation – diphthongs

Video
- *Wide Open Spaces* Episode 5

Photocopiable materials for this unit
- **TB page 133** An extra exercise on prepositions of time.
- **TB page 135** An extra cued dialogue on time expressions.

Introduction to the unit

The theme of this unit is people who have obsessions – about learning to drive, about smoking, and about collecting things. This theme provides practice of Present Perfect Simple and Continuous.

The reading text is about a man who is trying to sell his own brand of cigarettes. He is a determined smoker, and defends the rights of smokers to continue with their habit. This raises a lot of issues about people's rights, and about the use and abuse of drugs. We hesitated for a long time about whether we should put such material in an English coursebook, but then persuaded ourselves that controversy should not always be skirted.

Language aims

Grammar
Present Perfect Continuous

The Present Perfect Continuous is often taught idiomatically at the pre-intermediate level. The tense has been used throughout *New Headway Intermediate*, but it is most unlikely that your students are using it correctly, if at all. It is time to increase students' understanding of one of the hardest tenses for foreign learners to grasp, made more difficult because there are two aspects to understand, the perfect aspect and the continuous aspect.

We saw in Unit 7 why students make so many mistakes with the Present Perfect. The form of auxiliary verb *have* + past participle exists in many other European languages, but its use is different. To refer to definite time, English uses the Past Simple, not the Present Perfect, and English has a way of looking at past-joined-to-present which other languages don't have. We say *I live here, I have lived here for ten years*, and not the more logical **I live here, I ~~live~~ here for ten years*. The Present Perfect joins past and present.

It can take learners years to perceive when to use the Present Perfect. The Present Perfect Continuous presents another difficult element for them to grasp, since the continuous aspect probably doesn't exist in their language either. The *Test your grammar* section aims to start students thinking about the continuous aspect. The extra grammar in the Workbook is an explanation of continuous verb forms with some exercises, so you might like to do these in class.

Time expressions

Ways of referring to points in time and periods of time are presented and practised. *How long are you here for?* and *How long have you been here?* are examined. They are always confused by students, for obvious reasons.

Vocabulary

The focus is on compound nouns, an area which students generally like. Perhaps this is due to the pleasure of putting two known elements together to make a third meaning.

PostScript

The PostScript introduces and revises some expressions of quantity, and practises them in the situation of complaining in a restaurant.

Workbook

- Extra grammar – the continuous aspect
- Vocabulary – suffixes and prefixes
- Pronunciation – diphthongs
- Prepositions of time

Notes on the unit

Test your grammar (SB page 96)

1 Read the instructions together. Students work in pairs or small groups to match a line in **A** with a line or picture in **B**. Students can generally do this relatively easily.

Get feedback as a class, and encourage others to comment and correct.

Answers
a What do you do for a living?
   What are you doing on your hands and knees?
b She smokes twenty cigarettes a day.
   She's smoking a Russian cigarette.
c He has a lot of money.
   He's having a bath. He can't come to the phone.
d You're stupid. You always are.
   You're being stupid. You aren't usually.

e Someone fired a gun. Bang!
   Someone was firing a gun. Bang! Bang! Bang!
f The cat drowned. It was terribly sad.
   The cat was drowning so I jumped into the water and saved it.
g What have you done with my headphones? I can't find them.
   What have you been doing since I last saw you?
h Who has drunk my beer? (Picture of empty glass)
   Who has been drinking my beer? (Picture of half-full glass)

2 Students can't usually answer this. They are not sufficiently tuned into Continuous tenses to be able to recognize that this is what the second sentences in each pair have in common. You can't ask students *What ideas do Continuous tenses express?* because it is highly unlikely that they have any idea.

Move on to Presentation (1), and maybe after that you could do the extra input in the Workbook on the continuous aspect.

PRESENTATION (1) (SB page 96)
Present Perfect Continuous

1 Students look at the newspaper headline and the photograph. Answer the questions as a class.

Answers
– He's a vicar.
– His driving test.
– They show other drivers that you're a learner.
– He's tearing up his L-plates because he has just passed his driving test.
– Lessons in a church are short readings from the Bible. *Endeth* is old English for *ends*, and *Here endeth the lesson* is what vicars can say at the end of a church service. But here, the lessons are driving lessons.

2 **T.68** Students read and listen to the newspaper article. In pairs they answer the questions. Get feedback as a class before you give the answers, and ask the others if they agree.

Answers
– Because he has just passed his driving test.
– No, it wasn't.
– He started to drive an automatic, instead of a car with a manual gear change.
– He drove into a ten-foot hedge.
– He confused the clutch and the brake.
– Their hair has turned grey because they have been so frightened by Peter's driving.
– He hasn't been able to get to them.

NB In this exercise and in the ones that follow, there is a lot of practice of the Present Perfect Simple as well as the Continuous. This is deliberate. Students need a lot of revision of the Simple, and they need to see when the Continuous is not possible. So, keep reminding students of the Present Perfect Simple.

3 Read the instruction as a class. Students work in pairs to write the questions. Remember, students often have problems forming questions, so monitor carefully.

Get feedback, and encourage the others to comment. You could get question and answer practice in open pairs across the room.

T.69 Students listen and check their answers. You could ask them to look at the tapescript and tell you which are Simple and which are Continuous.

Grammar questions

Answer the questions as a class. Be prepared to help a lot.

> **Answers**
> – **Present Perfect Simple**
>
> | | |
> |---|---|
> | has finally passed | have been answered (passive) |
> | has had | have turned |
> | has spent | haven't seen |
> | has crashed | haven't been |
>
> – **Present Perfect Continuous**
>
> | | |
> |---|---|
> | has been learning | has been celebrating |
> | have been praying | have been visiting |
> | have been telling | |
>
> – It is unlikely that you will get much response to this question. If students manage *Present Perfect Simple for completed actions, Present Perfect Continuous for longer actions*, that's fine.
>
> – The Present Perfect Simple describes completed actions.
>
> – The Present Perfect Continuous describes an activity over a period of time.

PRACTICE (SB page 97)

1 Questions and answers

NB These four exercises may seem to wander off in strange directions, one about driving, another about living in the country and playing tennis, but they are all trying to make points about the Present Perfect Simple and Continuous. The first exercise practises very naturally several uses of the Present Perfect Simple ('How long have you had your car?' 'How many kilometres has it done?' 'Have you ever had an accident?'), and these contrast with questions in the Past Simple that refer to definite time ('How much did you pay for it?' 'Whose fault was it?').

1 **T.70** Students listen to the conversation and complete the questions. They ask and answer the same questions across the class. Correct mistakes very carefully. Ask *What tense is that? Why is it used here?* to make the point about Present Perfect Simple and Continuous and the Past Simple.

You could have the questions directed at four or five students. For some reason, students often like talking about their cars. If the class is inspired to ask more questions, for example about an accident, let this go on.

2 Students write questions with *How long ...?* The aim of this exercise is to say that if we can use the Continuous in English, we prefer to; and also to highlight the verbs that don't usually go into the Continuous.

> **Answers**
> a How long have you been living ...?
> b How long have you been playing ...?
> c How long have you known ...?
> d How long have you been working ...?
> e How long have you had ...?

3 In pairs, students ask and answer similar questions about themselves.

4 Students write another question in the Past Simple. Again, this is to reinforce the point that when definite time is talked about, we must use the Past Simple, not the Present Perfect.

> **Answers**
> a When **did you** move there?
> b How old **were you** when **you** started **playing tennis**?
> c Where **did you** meet **Jack**?
> d Why **did you** decide **to work in Prague**?
> e How much **did you** pay **for it**?

2 Dialogues

T.71 Students read the instructions and listen to the example on tape. In pairs, they have similar dialogues. Get some feedback as a class, and encourage students to correct each other.

> **Answers**
> a **A** You're covered in paint – what have you been doing?
> **B** I've been decorating the bathroom.
> **A** Have you finished yet?
> **B** I've painted the door, but I haven't put the wallpaper up yet.
> b **A** You've got oil on your face – what have you been doing?
> **B** I've been servicing the car.
> **A** Have you done it yet?
> **B** I've mended the lights, but I haven't changed the oil yet.

c **A** You've got dirty hands – what have you been doing?
  B I'm filthy. I've been working in the garden.
  A Have you finished now?
  B I've cut the grass, but I haven't watered the flowers yet.
d **A** Your eyes are red – what have you been doing?
  B I'm exhausted. I've been revising for my exams.
  A Have you finished yet?
  B I've done my chemistry and history, but I haven't done any English yet.

3 Discussing grammar

Students discuss what is wrong with the sentences. Get feedback and invite comment before you give the answers.

Answers

a With the Continuous, it sounds as though the person cut their finger again and again. In the Simple, the suggestion is that it was one accidental cut.

b *War and Peace* is a very long book and could not be read in an afternoon.

c It would be unusual to expect students to understand why this is wrong. *I've swum* is an unlikely sentence in any situation. Swimming by definition takes time. We need the Continuous to emphasize the activity, with the result in the present.

d The Continuous suggests that the action took place again and again, not just once.

e The answer here is the same as for c. We need the Continuous to suggest activity over a period of time.

ADDITIONAL MATERIAL

Workbook Unit 10
Exercises 1 & 2 Present Perfect Simple and Continuous
Exercises 3 & 4 Continuous aspect

PRESENTATION (2) (SB page 98)

Time expressions

The aim of this presentation is not only to present and practise various ways of referring to time in the past, but also to reinforce Present Perfect (Simple and Continuous) to refer to the indefinite past, and Past Simple and Past Continuous to refer to definite past.

1 Students read about Joanna Hardy. The best way to do this is perhaps for you or one of the class to read the chart of the events in her life out loud. That way, you can check vocabulary.

Students work in pairs to answer the questions. The aim of questions **a–h** is to practise Present Perfect Simple and Continuous. Get feedback as a class and encourage comment and correction before you give the answers.

Answers

a She has written poetry, novels, TV programmes and an autobiography. She has been married twice. She has been to France, Germany, Italy, India, and the Far East.

b Since she was six.

c She's written short stories, poetry, novels, TV programmes and an autobiography.

d She has written four novels.

e Yes, she has. She won the *Times Literary Award* for best fiction in 1975, and she won the *Whitbread Trophy* for literary merit in 1990.

f She's been married to Jack since 1988.

g She's been married twice.

h She's been writing her autobiography since 1996.

2 The aim of this exercise is to practise various time expressions, some conjunctions, some prepositions.

Students work in pairs to complete the sentences. As always, get feedback as a class and encourage comment and correction before you give the answers.

Answers

a at the age of six
b After the publication
c between 1968 and 1971
d while she was at university
e two years after she got married
f while she was making
g until she married Jack
h since she married Jack

PRACTICE (SB page 99)

> **SUGGESTION**
> There is an extra exercise on prepositions of time on page 133 of this Teacher's Book that you might want to photocopy and use before moving on to the Practice ideas.

1 Questions and answers

This exercise practises question formation and time expressions. There are several ways of expressing the time reference in the answer, so encourage students to explore these. Don't just settle for one answer, try to get several. On the tape, there is just one time expression, but you can explore others.

Students work in pairs to ask and answer questions. Get feedback as a class. Be very careful with correction. This is a tricky exercise if you want students to get everything right.

PROBLEMS

Students always have problems with dates.
They make mistakes such as the following:
*on third June   *on three June

Don't let such mistakes go by uncorrected. This is one of the main aims of this activity. They must remember to use *the* and *of*, and get the ordinal numbers correct.
on the third of June   on June the third

Answers

a When was she born? In 1950.

b When was her collection of poems published?
When she was eight/In 1958/In April 1958/Before she went to France and Germany.

c When did her mother die? On 16 September 1961/In 1961/Before she went to Italy.

d When did she get married for the first time?
In spring, 1970/In 1970/while she was at university/during her second year at university.

e When did she graduate? On 20 June 1971/In 1971/Just before the publication of her first novel.

f When was her daughter born? In 1972/On 14 June 1972/The year after she left university.

g When did she go to India and the Far East?
After her divorce/After she got divorced/In 1979.

h When did she get married for the second time?
At 10.30 on 3 August, 1988/In August, 1988.

i How long did her first marriage last? Nine years.

j How long has she been living in Paris?
Since she got married/Since 1988.

T.72 Students listen and check their answers. Note that only one time expression is given on the tape, but the above are also possible.

2 *How long are you here for?*

NB *The aim is to present and practise some more time expressions: 'in a few days' time', 'the day before yesterday', 'the day after tomorrow' and 'this time last week'. It also presents the two questions 'How long are you here for?' and 'How long have you been here?' Both questions are commonly asked of people who are away from home, studying or working, and foreign learners always confuse them because they are so similar. You can expect confusion when you do this exercise, so be ready to help. Use L1 if you can.*

1 Students look at Joanna's itinerary. Point out that she is in Kansas City, and it is Monday.

2 Read the instructions. Ask students in pairs to answer the questions. You can expect mistakes.

T.73 Students listen to the answers. Teach the difference between the first two questions. You might want the class to read the Grammar Reference section, or you can explain it yourself.

3 Students write their own itinerary. In pairs they ask and answer questions. Monitor this very carefully.

3 Discussing grammar

Remember not to do all the Practice activities one after the other. Students need some freer work, too.

1 In pairs, students find the mistakes.
Get some feedback as a class, and encourage the others to comment and correct.

Answers

a What time did you go to bed last night?

b What did you do last weekend?

c What are you doing tonight?

d When did this lesson begin?

e When does this lesson end?
When will this lesson end?
When is this lesson going to end?

f Are you going to study English next month?

g When were you born?

h What's the date today?/What's today's date?

2 In pairs, students ask and answer the questions.

LANGUAGE REVIEW (SB page 99)
Present Perfect Continuous
Time expressions

Read the Language Review together in class, and/or ask students to read it at home. If you have a monolingual class, you could use L1 and ask students to translate some of the sentences. Encourage questions and queries at this point. Don't expect students to have mastered the Present Perfect Simple and Continuous at this stage. They will continue to make mistakes for years, unfortunately.

Ask students to read the Grammar Reference section at home.

ADDITIONAL MATERIAL

Workbook Unit 10
Exercise 5 Time expressions

> **SUGGESTION**
> There is an extra cued dialogue on page 135 of this Teacher's Book for you to photocopy and use.

READING (SB page 100)

Attitudes to smoking have changed a lot in Britain and the States over recent years, and there are now many public places where smoking is banned. You can expect the smokers in your class to feel uncomfortable during this reading exercise!

Pre-reading task

1 Do this as a class discussion. There is no real answer. You can expect the smokers to be defensive!

2 Again, do this as a class.

> **Answers**
> a This is a medical view.
> b This is humorous.
> c This is an adult's view, or a sociological view.
> d This is humorous.
> e This is the cost of caring for smokers when they are ill.

3 Answer all these questions together as a class.

4 Students look at the pictures of B J Cunningham and read the facts about him, and then discuss the questions in pairs. Get feedback as a class.

Reading

Students read the text to see if their ideas about B J Cunningham were correct. Discuss the two questions when you think students have had enough time to get to the end of the text.

Before doing the Comprehension check questions, you might like to go through the text again as a class, with either you or the students taking it in turns to read aloud. This might appeal to you and it might not! You might prefer to have students reading silently.

Comprehension check

NB *Multiple choice questions are an interesting way of checking understanding, because by their very nature they make students doubt themselves. The distracters are sometimes so possible that they make students wonder if they are right, but this process enforces clear thinking. You can expect some debate as the class tries to argue that one answer is 'more right' than another. Don't give the right answer straight away – let the debate go on. Equally don't let frustration build up. Get your timing right.*

Ask students to answer the questions in small groups. Get feedback as a class, and invite discussion of the answers. Ask *Why do you think that's right? Why isn't **a** the answer?*

> **Answers**
> 1 a   2 c   3 a   4 b

5 a (He says his cigarettes are for people who want to admit they are killing themselves, so that's being honest; they are also for people who speak aggressively.)

6 c (He says he is there to remind people that smoking and death are linked.)

7 c   8 a   9 a

Language work

Students work in pairs to write the questions. Get some feedback as a class.

> **Answers**
> 1 How long has B J Cunningham been smoking?
> 2 How many cigarettes does he smoke a day?
> 3 Has he ever given up/tried to give up?
> 4 How long has he been riding Harley-Davidson motorbikes?
> 5 How many motorbikes has he had?
> 6 When did he start the ETC?
> 7 How much has the ETC been losing?
> 8 How many cigarettes did he smoke during the interview?

Discussion

Students discuss the three questions first in small groups, then as a class. There are many issues to discuss here. If your class is interested, the discussion could go on for quite a while. On the other hand, they might be tired after the reading, and a change of topic might be needed.

VOCABULARY AND PRONUNCIATION
(SB page 103)

Compound nouns

1 Students go back to the beginning of the unit and find the words for the meanings.

> **Answers**
> a a driving licence   e a chain smoker
> b a driving test   f a business partner
> c wallpaper   g an ashtray
> d a press conference

2 Read the explanation of compound nouns.

T.74 Students listen to the words, and identify the stress. The stress is on the first part of the compound.

Ask students to practise saying the words. They are usually reluctant to stress the first part, as many languages are not as dependent on stress as English, so really push them to get the stress right.

3 Students work in pairs to complete the boxes. This is a fun way of teaching the words. Students have to think laterally to fill the boxes. If they can't do one, tell them to move on. They will probably have to check spelling often, and you can expect students to get frustrated at the illogicality of the spelling.

Answers

a	toothache toothbrush toothpaste	i	air-conditioning airmail airport
b	dining-room living-room changing room	j	teacup teaspoon teapot
c	traffic-lights traffic warden traffic jam	k	sun-glasses sunbathing sunset
d	motorway motor racing motorbike	l	newsagent travel agent estate agent
e	cookery book telephone book notebook	m	wrapping paper writing paper toilet paper
f	fire-engine fireplace fireworks	n	chairman fireman dustman
g	birthday card credit card get-well card	o	shopping centre shopping basket shopping spree
h	hairdresser hairbrush haircut	p	bookcase bookshop bookworm

Ask three of four students to say the words, so you can check pronunciation, especially stress.

4 Students work in pairs to devise a similar exercise themselves. They can swap their exercises.

LISTENING AND SPEAKING (SB page 104)

Collectors

Pre-listening task

Answer the two questions as a class. You could ask them why people collect things, but we personally don't know what the answer is!

Listening

Ask students to look at the pictures and say what they can see. In Margaret Tyler's house you can see a lot of things that are, in fact, compound nouns. Ask students to identify some.

Sample answers

Margaret Tyler – royal souvenirs: national flags, teapots, milk jugs, coffee mugs, pictures, crowns, biscuit tins.

Ted Hewitt – model buses.

Students divide into two groups. You will need two tape recorders, and ideally two rooms.

T.75a This group listens to Margaret Tyler.

T.75b This group listens to Ted Hewitt.

Students often like to listen two, three or even four times, making sure they have all the information.

When they are ready, they find a partner from the other group and compare and swap information. This should generate a lot of discussion.

There is usually no need for you to check comprehension because students do it all between them. However, you may want to ask a few questions. Students might want to hear the other tape.

Answers

Group A – Margaret Tyler
1 She lives alone in Wembley, North London.
2 She works for a children's charity.
3 She has over four thousand royal souvenirs.
4 She's been collecting for eighteen years.
5 In every room in the house. All the rooms downstairs, all four bedrooms and in the attic, too.
6 A letter from Diana's Lady-in-Waiting.
7 She can't remember how much, but she doesn't think she has spent much.
8 It comes from all over the place. There are lots of other people who collect. There are conventions where they swap things. There are specialist magazines and shops and jumble sales.
9 Yes, lots.
10 She'd love to meet Princess Diana.

Group B – Ted Hewitt
1 He lives with his wife and three children in Chorleywood, a village between London and Oxford.
2 He owns a coach business.
3 At least five hundred.
4 He's been collecting since he was five or six years old.
5 Most of the collection is in one room, but there are others in other rooms of the house, and in the attic, too.
6 A tin-plate double-decker bus made in the late thirties or early forties.
7 He has never paid more than fifty or sixty pounds.
8 There are lots of other people who collect, and there are specialist shops. There are also 'swapmeets' where people go to swap buses.
9 Yes, lots.
10 If he found a model of a full-size bus that he owned, he would have to buy it.

Guessing game

Tell individual students what they collect, and the others must ask questions to find out what it is. The class can then ask some of the other questions. Here are some suggestions.

postcards   *miniature trains*   *beer mats*
old newspapers   *antique books*   *dolls' houses*
vinyl records   *sports programmes*
autographs   *clothes belonging to pop stars*

WRITING (SB page 105)

Beginning and ending letters

There are many conventions and formulaic expressions with letter writing that simply have to be learned and reproduced.

1 Students match the beginning and ending to a letter.

> **Answers**
> **c + 1** asks for information
> **e + 2** says that money has been received
> **a + 4** invites
> **d + 5** accepts an invitation
> **b + 3** gives news

2 In pairs, students decide which line continues each letter. Get feedback as a class and encourage the others to comment before you give the answers.

> **Answers**
> a comes between c and 1
> b comes between b and 3
> c comes between e and 2
> d comes between a and 4
> e comes between d and 5

3 Read the information as a class. Encourage students to ask questions.

NB 'Dear + Name'... always ends 'Yours sincerely'
'Dear Madam/Sir'... always ends 'Yours faithfully'

4 Students write a letter for homework. You could ask students to swap their homework before they hand it in, to see if they can help each other to find mistakes.

PostScript (SB page 106)

Complaining

1 Students often make mistakes with the words in the box. They are small areas of the language that are annoying to teach, and annoying to learn. Be prepared to do some sorting out.

NB 'Enough' comes before a noun and after an adjective, as in 'enough money', 'hot enough'

Students work in pairs to fill the gaps. Get some feedback as a class, and invite the others to comment before you give the answers.

> **Answers**
> a '**How many** cigarettes do you smoke a day?'
>   'Forty.'
>   'That's **too many**. You shouldn't smoke any at all.'
> b '**How much** alcohol do you drink?'
>   'About a bottle of wine a day.'
>   'That's **too much**. You shouldn't drink **as much as** that.'
> c '**How much** do you weigh?'
>   'Sixteen and a half stone.'
>   'That's **too much**. You should try to lose **some/ a little** weight.'
> d '**How much** do you earn?'
>   'Not **enough** money to pay all my bills!'
> e '**How many** people are there in your class?'
>   'Forty.'
>   'I think that's **too many**.'
> f '**How many** aspirins do you take when you have a headache?'
>   'About ten or twelve.'
>   'That's **too many**. You mustn't take **as many as** that!'
> g 'How old are you?'
>   'Seventeen. I'm old **enough** to get married, but I'm not old **enough** to vote!'
> h 'When did you last go to the cinema?'
>   'Quite recently. Just **a few** days ago.'
> i 'Do you take sugar in your coffee?'
>   'Just **a little**.'

2 In pairs, students ask and answer the same questions. Monitor carefully. Ask two or three couples to repeat their dialogues again in front of the class listening. Ask for comments and corrections.

3 Students write a dialogue of complaint, then act it out. It could be fun! Think of props they might need.

Don't forget!

Workbook Unit 10
Exercise 6 Vocabulary – suffixes and prefixes
Exercise 7 Prepositions – prepositions of time
Exercise 8 Pronunciation – diphthongs

Wordlist This is on page 164 of this Teacher's Book for you to photocopy and give to your students.

Video *Wide Open Spaces* Episode 5: Maddy's company commission a piece of music from Nick. He had been expecting a quiet day…

11

Tell me about it!

Indirect questions
Question tags
Informal language

Profile

Student's Book

Language
- indirect questions
- question tags

Pronunciation
- question tags with rising or falling intonation

Vocabulary and everyday English
- parts of the body
- idioms from verb/noun collocations
- polite questions
- informal/slang words/exclamations

Workbook

- extra grammar – questions ending with prepositions
- vocabulary – animal idioms
- pronunciation – a poem and onomatopoeic words
- common multi-word verbs

Video

- Report 6 *WOMAD*, the World of Music and Dance festival

Photocopiable materials for this unit
- **TB page 134** Information for the Speaking activity on SB page 108.
- **TB page 135** Dialogues for the Conversations activity on SB page 110.
- **TB page 133** An extra vocabulary exercise for the Reading on SB page 112.

Introduction to the unit

The theme is asking for and giving information. The reading text is a question and answer section from a science magazine. These sections are becoming common in the British press. The listening exercise is a radio programme about people who suffer from forgetfulness, and suggests ways of improving your memory.

There are two focuses on informal language, with work on idioms in the Vocabulary section, and words such as *quid* and *cuppa* and exclamations such as *Wow!* and *No way!* in the PostScript.

Language aims

Grammar

Indirect questions

These are similar in form to reported questions, dealt with in Unit 12. Problems students encounter with indirect questions will be to do with form not concept.

> **COMMON MISTAKES**
> *I don't know where does she live.*
> *I don't know what's the time?*

It is difficult to get students to use *do/does/did* in direct questions. Now you have to show them that in indirect questions they shouldn't use *do/does/did*.

Question tags

Question tags are extremely common in spoken English. For the foreign learner they represent the same problem as short answers – the learner needs to analyse which auxiliary verb to use, whether it should be positive or negative, and whether the intonation should go up or down, by which time it is too late. Interestingly, English-speaking children acquire question tags relatively early and easily, perhaps because they are a way of engaging people around them in conversation.

It would be most unusual if your students started to use question tags accurately and appropriately by the end of this unit. It is more realistic to think that they need a lot of exposure to them, so that ultimately they might produce them spontaneously. The aim of this work on question tags is, therefore, recognition more than production. Students need to become aware of them as a system, and as a part of spoken English. They seem to have an instinctive reluctance to produce question tags until much later in their language learning career.

Vocabulary

There are several parts to the vocabulary work in this unit. Firstly, parts of the body are brainstormed, then verb/noun collocations are explored (*kick/feet*; *scratch/nails*). Finally there is some work on idioms formed with the words practised already, for example, *to kick the habit*.

PostScript

Learners are often very interested in informal language, slang, colloquial English and idioms. This is perhaps because they feel they represent real English as used by real English speakers, but it is probably safer to steer students away from trying to produce informal English at this level. There are too many potential problems. The slightest mistake of pronunciation, stress, word order or anything can make the foreign learner incomprehensible. It is almost as though native speakers don't expect idiomatic usage from a low-level speaker. It is also difficult for students to learn in which situations informal language is appropriate, and when it is safer to keep to neutral forms. Nevertheless, it is worth pointing out some informal language for recognition purposes.

Workbook

- Extra grammar – questions with prepositions at the end (*What are you looking at?*)
- Vocabulary – animal idioms
- Pronunciation – phonetic script and onomatopoeic words (*snore, roar*)
- Multi-word verbs – common multi-word verbs

Notes on the unit

Test your grammar   (SB page 107)

This *Test your grammar* is in the form of a joke – students might or might not get it! It isn't that funny.

Ask students to look at the picture and tell you what they can see. You will probably have to teach the word *tramp*.

1   **T.76**   Students listen and read at the same time.

NB There are two different ways of asking the time in English, and it is very easy to confuse them – 'What's the time?' 'What time is it?'

2   Students work in pairs to correct the two sentences.

> **Answers**
> I wonder if you could tell me **what time it is**.
> I don't know **what the time is**.

It is enough at this stage if students can correct the mistakes. It would be unwise to ask *Why?* because this would lead into a discussion on indirect questions, thus pre-empting the presentation which is about to come.

PRESENTATION (1)   (SB page 107)
Indirect questions

1   Ask students to look at the picture, and ask some questions, such as *Where is the woman? What does she want? Is she in her own country? Is she on holiday?*

   T.77   Read the introduction as a class. Students listen and look at the list of information she wants. Ask a few more comprehension questions, such as *What's she looking for? Which hotel is recommended? When do the banks close? How old is the town?*

   Ask students to try to remember Rosie's indirect questions, then play the tape to check; or you could play the tape and use it as a sort of dictation, stopping the tape after each indirect question for students to write in the answers.

> **SUGGESTION**
> Practise the five indirect questions around the class. Make sure that word order is right.

● Grammar questions

Do these as a class.

> **Answers**
> – In indirect questions we use the same word order (subject + verb) as statements, for example *I wonder if **you would help** me*.
> – Do/does/did are not used in indirect questions.
> – We use *if*.

Now, go back to the direct and indirect questions in exercise 1 and ask students to compare them.

2   Do this as a class activity first. Ask a pair of students to practise the same conversation. Prompt the pair with the first lines (*Good afternoon. Hello. I wonder if you could help me.*) and when they can't remember what comes next.

Be careful with correction. Don't try to correct every mistake or they might just stop trying, but you will want to correct mistakes in indirect questions.

Now ask the class to do the same in pairs.

3 Students work in pairs. Get feedback, and encourage the rest of the class to comment and correct.

> **Answers**
> a Could you tell me **when the town was founded**?
> b Do you know **what the population of the town is**?
> c I'd like to know **where I can change some money**.
> d Do you happen to know **what the exchange rate is today**?
> e I wonder **if there's a dry cleaner's near here**.
> f Have you any idea **where there is a cheap place to eat**?
> g Can you tell me **how long it takes to get to the centre of town from here**?
> h Do you remember **if it rained here yesterday**?

NB *Students might have problems with the answer to question g – 'It takes (me) three hours to ...' is a strange construction. They might also have problems with the answer to question d – 'There are eight francs thirty to the pound', or 'There are two marks twenty to the pound'.*

4 You could do this exercise as a class first so you can monitor the language before students do it in pairs.

PRACTICE (SB page 108)

1 *We can't hear what she's saying!*

1 **T.78** This is a tricky exercise for students – there is a lot of manipulation, and potential problems of word order and missing *do/does/did*.

Read the introduction as a class. Play the first couple of news stories without asking students to make sentences so that they get the idea of the radio with bad reception.

Play the tape again from the beginning, stopping after each bit of missing information. Ask a student to form an indirect question, then drill this round the class, correcting mistakes carefully. Do this for the first three stories. Play the last two stories, again stopping the tape after each bit of missing information, but students form the indirect questions in pairs.

Get the feedback.

2 Students ask you the direct questions. Again, expect problems, and be prepared to help and explain.

NB *The fifth question is a subject question, so there is no 'did' in the question. In the sixth question – students often want to say* *'How many money ...' which is wrong.*

> **Answers**
> – What time did the train crash happen?
>   Three o'clock this morning.
> – Where was the train going to?
>   It was going to Liverpool.
> – Where is she from?
>   She's from Bristol.
> – Who was she found by?
>   She was found by her father.
> – How many men went into the bank?
>   Six.
> – How much did they steal?
>   Four thousand pounds.
> – How did they escape?/What did they escape in?
>   A stolen car.
> – What was the final score?
>   Liverpool 3, Real Madrid 2.
> – Who did he beat?
>   Billy Connors.
> – What did he say after the fight?
>   He said he always knew he would be world champion one day.

> **SUGGESTION**
> You could get further practice of indirect questions using a current news story. Choose one where there are unknown elements, so students could genuinely say *I wonder where ...*, *I'd love to know how much ...*, etc.

2 Speaking

1 Ask students what they know about *Madame Tussaud's Waxworks* in London. Some might have been there and know a lot, others will know nothing.

Students work in pairs to make statements using the prompts **a–i**. Get feedback and correct carefully.

> **Answers**
> I wonder/I'd love to know/Does anybody know ...?
> a ... where Madame Tussaud **came** from.
> b ... when **she was** alive.
> c ... how **she learned** to make things in wax.
> d ... which countries **she lived** in.
> e ... **if she ever married/ever got married**.
> f ... **if she had any** children.
> g ... why **she went/came** to England.
> h ... when the Waxworks **opened** in London.
> i ... how many people a year **visit** the Waxworks.

2 You will need to photocopy the Student **A** and Student **B** information on page 134 of this Teacher's Book.

Read the instructions and the example carefully. Give out the information, and tell students not to look at each other's information!

This exercise is long and taxing, so allow enough time for it. Go round monitoring carefully. Expect mistakes as students have the choice of making direct or indirect questions and they will confuse them.

Get some feedback, and correct carefully.

3 Asking polite questions

This exercise practises *what* and *which* + noun, and *how* + adjective/adverb, *many* and *much*. It should be fun since students make polite questions about silly things like favourite ice-cream!

1 Students work in pairs to form the questions.

Get feedback, and invite the others to comment and correct. Drill the questions around the room.

NB *Students might wonder about the difference between 'what' and 'which'. Explain that they are often both possible – 'What/Which is the best hotel in town?' 'What/Which is your favourite colour?'*

We prefer 'which' when there is limited choice: 'We have brown bread or white – which do you want?'

When the speaker doesn't have a limited number of choices in mind, we use 'what' – 'What language do they speak in Switzerland?'

> **Answers**
> What/which football team do you support?
> What/which newspaper do you read?
> What colour eyes have you got?
> How long does it take you to get ready in the morning?
> What size shoes do you take?
> What flavour ice-cream is your favourite?
> How far is it to the station from here?
> What sort of car have you got?
> How much time do you spend watching TV?
> How many times have you been on a plane?

2 Read the introduction. Students work in pairs to ask and answer indirect questions. Get feedback with open pair practice across the room – it could be funny!

> **Answers**
> Could you tell me/Would you mind telling me/I wonder if you could tell me ...
> ... what/which football team you support?
> ... what/which newspaper you read?
> ... what colour eyes you've got?
> ... how long it takes you to get ready in the morning?
> ... what size shoes you take?
> ... what flavour ice-cream is your favourite?
> ... how far it is to the station from here?
> ... what sort of car you've got?
> ... how much time you spend watching TV?
> ... how many times you've been on a plane?

ADDITIONAL MATERIAL

Workbook Unit 11

Exercises 1–5 All these practise direct and indirect questions. Here are the factual answers to the questions in exercises 1 and 2.

> **Answers to the quizzes in exercises 1 and 2 of Workbook Unit 11**
>
> **Quiz 1**
> a Is the town of Timbuktu in Africa? **Yes, it is.**
> b Do all birds lay eggs? **Yes, they do.**
> c Did dinosaurs lay eggs? **Yes, they did.**
> d Was John F. Kennedy the youngest American president? **No, he wasn't. Theodore Roosevelt was the youngest at 42.**
> e Has there ever been a female president of the USA? **No, there hasn't.**
> f Have the Olympic Games ever been held in the same city more than once? **Yes, in London in 1908 and 1948.**
> g Does Switzerland have a president? **Yes. He or she is elected yearly.**
> h Did William Shakespeare ever live in London? **Yes, he did.**
>
> **Quiz 2**
> a Where does the word *alphabet* come from? **From Greek.**
> b What kind of weather does the Beaufort Scale measure? **The wind.**
> c How many European countries does the Danube flow through? **Nine. Germany, Austria, Slovakia, Hungary, Croatia, Serbia, Bulgaria, Romania and Ukraine.**
> d Who was the first man in space? **Yuri Gagarin.**
> e What does NASA stand for? **National Aeronautics and Space Administration.**
> f Who did Adolph Hitler marry? **Eva Braun.**
> g When did Margaret Thatcher become prime minister of Britain? **1979.**
> h Which Latin American country did Montezuma II rule in the 16th century? **Mexico.**

PRESENTATION (2)   (SB page 109)

Question tags

As we said in the introduction, don't expect your students to be using question tags accurately and appropriately from now on. It will take a very long time before students even attempt to use them without being prompted. The idea of this presentation and practice is to make students aware of them as a system so that they can begin to recognize them and see how important they are in spoken English.

1 **T.79** Students read and listen to the dialogue between Jessie and her mother. Note that here all the question tags fall.

Play the dialogue again, pausing after Jessie's lines that contain a question tag. Drill these sentences around the class, paying particular attention to pronunciation and falling intonation.

● Grammar questions

Answer these as a class. They are quite difficult questions, so don't be surprised if your students don't know the answers. Be prepared to help and nudge.

> **Answers**
> – Jessie is trying to make her mother have a conversation with her. She wants some attention.
> – We repeat the auxiliary verb. If there is no auxiliary verb, we use *do/does/did*. A positive sentence has a negative tag; a negative sentence has a positive tag.

2 In pairs, students look at the dialogue between Caroline Bailey (C) and her secretary and fill the gaps with a question tag.

Get some feedback. Encourage the others to comment and correct.

T.80 Students listen and check their answers. Note that here all the question tags rise.

● Grammar questions

Do these as a class. These questions are a little easier. If students can't remember Jessie's question tags, play a part of **T.79** again.

> **Answers**
> – Jessie's question tags went down; Caroline's went up.
> – Caroline's use of question tags means 'I'm not sure so I'm checking'. Jessie's use of question tags means 'Please talk to me'.

> **SUGGESTION**
> Ask students in pairs to practise the two dialogues. First, ask the class the close their books. Indicate two students who must try to remember the dialogues as much as they can. The first one is quite easy to remember, but you will need to give some prompts for the second. Then students do the same in pairs. Occasionally, asking students to memorize something is good practice.

PRACTICE (SB page 110)

1 Grammar and intonation

1 In pairs, students add tags to the sentences. They will need to do this on a separate piece of paper.

Don't get any feedback until you've played the tape to check the answers. This is because students first need to know if the tags fall or rise. Notice that the answers are given in the tapescript.

2 **T.81a** Students listen and check their answers, and put an arrow to show rising or falling intonation.

Now you need to practise them. Drill the sentences round the class. Foreign learners are usually very reluctant to stretch their voice range so really try to encourage wide intonation.

3 In pairs, students match a response with a line in exercise 1.

Get feedback in open pairs across the room.

T.81b Students listen and check their answers. In pairs they practise the dialogues.

2 Conversations

This practice activity is deliberately controlled. Students are restricted in the sentences they are asked to make question tags for. This is because the use of question tags is very subtle and difficult to explain. If students were asked to make their own dialogues with question tags, they might put them everywhere and make horrendous mistakes. For example:

*I'm going to the shops, aren't I? Do you want anything, don't you?

*Yes, I need a newspaper, don't I? I'll give you some money, won't I?

You need to photocopy the dialogues on page 135 of this Teacher's Book. Decide how many of the dialogues you want to give to each pair.

1 Give out the dialogues. In pairs, students decide where the tags can go, and what the tags should be. You might want to use one dialogue as an example to show where the tags can't go, to give them the idea that they can't go just anywhere.

2 Pairs of students take it in turns to act out their dialogue. If there are mistakes, correct them carefully.

3 **T.82** Students listen and check their answers. There are occasions when more tags could be used than are in the sample answers, so do be careful when accepting or rejecting students' suggestions.

LANGUAGE REVIEW (SB page 110)

Indirect questions
Question tags

Read the Language Review together in class, and/or ask students to read it at home. If you have a monolingual class, you could use L1 and ask students to translate some of the sentences. Encourage questions and queries.

Ask students to read the Grammar Reference section at home.

ADDITIONAL MATERIAL

Workbook Unit 11
Exercise 7–9 These all practise question tags.

● VOCABULARY AND IDIOMS
(SB page 110)

Do you know what your body can do?

1 You could draw the outline of a body on the board and ask students to write the words in the right place. Careful! This could get out of hand if too many words are covered, so make sure you stop it before the class drowns under new words.

2 Students work in pairs to say which verb goes with which part of the body. Don't try to get a sentence, just ask for *kick–foot*, *bite–teeth*, etc.

Get feedback.

> **Answers**
>
> | | | | |
> |---|---|---|---|
> | hit | – hand, fist | scratch | – nails |
> | climb | – feet, legs | tie | – hands |
> | chew | – jaw, teeth | kneel | – knees |
> | drop | – hand, fingers | think | – brain |
> | hold | – hand, fingers | pat | – hand, back, shoulder |
> | hug | – arms | blow | – mouth, lips |
> | kiss | – lips | clap | – hands |
> | lick | – tongue | stare | – eyes |
> | point | – (index) finger | whistle | – lips |

3 Students work in pairs to match a line in **A** with a line in **B**.

Get feedback.

> **Answers**
>
> whistle a tune
> kiss me on the cheek
> kick a ball
> blow up a balloon
> lick an ice-cream
> tie a knot
> point a gun at the bank clerk
> stare out of the window
> climb a ladder

> pat me on the back
> scratch your head
> kneel to pray
> drop a pile of books
> chew a toffee
> hit a nail with a hammer
> hug your grandmother
> think about home
> bite into an apple
> clap in time with the music
> hold me in your arms

4 Students check the idioms in their dictionaries.

5 Students complete the sentences. This exercise is difficult so we've given the first letter of each missing word. Even so, you will probably have to help quite a lot. You need to pay special attention to the actual meaning of the idioms. Use L1 if you can.

> **Answers**
>
> a hold your breath
> b hit the roof
> c kick the habit
> d think the world of
> e kiss my own car goodbye
> f blowing his own trumpet
> g Drop me a line

● READING AND SPEAKING (SB page 111)

How well do you know your world?
Pre-reading task

1 Students work in small groups to see how many of the questions they can answer.

2 Read the instructions as a class. Students work alone.

Get feedback. Correct mistakes.

3 Discuss the questions and answers as a class.

Reading

You ask ... we answer!

Students read the questions and answers.

Comprehension check

Students work in small groups to answer the questions. Get feedback before you give the answers.

> **Answers**
>
> 1 a The world's biggest office. <u>it</u> = the Pentagon.
>   b Man-made things on earth. <u>What</u> = the only man-made object visible from outer space.
>   c Dolphins. <u>they</u> = dolphins.
>   d Horseshoes. <u>its</u> = the horseshoe's position.

e Driving on the left.   this = driving on the left.

f Walking under ladders.   this superstition = walking under ladders.

g New English words.   these = new words that enter the English language.

h Mayday.   the expression = Mayday.

i Women live longer than men.   they = men.

Answers to the questions

a During World War II.

b It isn't true that the only man-made object visible from orbit is the Great Wall of China.

c No. They automatically rescue anything which is about the same size as themselves.

d It must point up like a cup so that the luck can't fall out.

e Because Napoleon insisted that his armies marched on the right.

f Walking under a ladder brings bad luck because someone on the ladder might drop something on you.

g Because no list is kept.

h Mayday comes from the French *m'aidez*.

i Because men are generally more aggressive, especially when driving, and they have more dangerous jobs.

2 The Oxford English Dictionary accepts about 4,000 new words every year.

The Pentagon is designed to hold up to 40,000 people.

50 countries drive on the left.

Spaceships orbit the earth at about 200 kilometres up.

Until 1783 criminals climbed a ladder to the gallows with a rope round their neck.

In 1927 Mayday became the international word meaning *Help*.

In 1700 Henri Misson visited Britain.

17,000 meals a day are served in the Pentagon.

In Japan the average age that women live to is 82. For men it is 76.

It took just 16 months to build the Pentagon.

SUGGESTION

There is an extra vocabulary exercise on page 133 of this Teacher's Book for you to photocopy and use.

Producing a class poster

This kind of activity cannot be done half-heartedly! It needs careful instructions from you and a lot of encouragement to keep students working at it. However, the rewards are worth it, and students will have visual proof of their hard work that others will read and learn from.

● LISTENING AND SPEAKING
(SB page 114)

The forgetful generation

Pre-listening task

1 **T.83a** Read and listen to the introduction as a class.

2 Discuss the questions in small groups.

Listening

1 **T.83b** Students listen and take notes about Ellen, Josh and Fiona on a separate piece of paper.

Let students discuss their answers in pairs before you get feedback as a class.

Answers

	What did they forget?	What did they do?
Ellen	She forgot that she had finished university and had a job.	She didn't go to work. She got the bus to the university for a lecture, went to the lecture room and wondered why she didn't know anybody.
Josh	He forgot that his parents had moved to a different town when he was ten.	He caught a train to Newcastle instead of Plymouth, because he thought that his parents still lived in Newcastle.
Fiona	She forgot to put on her shoes.	She left her house to catch the bus to work still wearing her slippers.

2 **T.83c** Students listen to the rest of the programme. In pairs they answer the questions.

Get feedback before you give the answers.

Answers

a He's a neuro-psychologist.

b Companies have far fewer employees, so one person does several jobs.

c She began sentences but then couldn't remember what she was talking about.

d She had a new job, she travelled a lot, she had a home and family to think about, and she had recently moved house.

e Alan Buchan helped her to recognize the problem. They talked about her stressful lifestyle, and she realized that she wasn't going crazy and was able to help herself.

f No, he doesn't.

g A notebook and a pencil. He advises this because it is a very good feeling when you can cross something off the list.

h She pretends that she has forgotten the professor's name.

What do you think?

Answer the questions as a class.

● WRITING (SB page 114)

For and against

1 Students discuss the three questions as a class. Perhaps there are things happening in your town now that are relevant – new buildings, new roads, new shopping precincts, etc.

2 Students read the text.

3 Students discuss the two questions in pairs or small groups. Get feedback before you give the answers.

> **Answers**
> a The first paragraph describes the advantages of living in the city. The second describes the disadvantages of city life. The third gives the writer's personal opinion on the topic.
>
> b <u>advantages and disadvantages</u> = pros and cons
> <u>On the plus side</u> = one advantage is that
> <u>For example</u> = for instance
> <u>What is more</u> = another point is that/moreover
> <u>All in all</u> = to sum up
> <u>For one thing</u> = one disadvantage is that
> <u>particularly</u> = especially
> <u>Last of all</u> = finally
> <u>despite</u> = in spite of
> <u>In conclusion</u> = all things considered
> <u>I think that</u> = in my opinion

4 Students write notes and compare them.

5 Students write three paragraphs for homework.

PostScript (SB page 115)

Informal language

See the notes at the beginning of this unit regarding students' interest in informal language and the need to steer them away from trying to use it. The aim is that students learn to recognize these items but not to produce them.

1 Read the introduction and example as a class. Use the example of *bloke* and *guy* to refer to a *man* informally. There are no doubt equivalents in students' own languages.

Students work in pairs to choose the words that fit best. This is more difficult than it might appear.

Students might want to know what some of the informal words, are for example *cuppa* and *fag*.

T.84 Students listen and check their answers.

2 Go over the dialogues again in more detail. You will need to sort out any problems.

> **Answers**
> a *I'm dying for a cuppa* = I want a cup of tea very much.
> b *My old man* = my father
>   *What's he on about?* = What's he talking about?
>   *What's up with him?* = What's the matter with him?
>   *Yuk!* is an interjection we use to express disgust or bad taste.
> c *fag* = cigarette
>   *loads* = lots
>   *Ta!* = Thanks.
> d *Gimme* = give me
>   *No way!* = certainly not
> e *Kind of* = In one way yes, and in another way no.
>   *What's on tonight?* = What's on television?
>   *Dunno* = I don't know
> f *that stuff* = it – a word we use when we forget what something is called.
>   *Oh!* is used to express a variety of emotions, for example surprise, fear, happiness. Here it means 'I understand'.
>   *Wow!* expresses astonishment and wonder.

Don't encourage your students to use these items. There are too many potential problems.

Don't forget!

Workbook Unit 11

Exercise 6 Extra grammar – questions with a preposition at the end

Exercise 10 Vocabulary – animal idioms

Exercises 11 & 12 Pronunciation – phonetic script and onomatopoeic words

Exercise 13 Multi-word verbs

Wordlist This is on page 165 of this Teacher's Book for you to photocopy and give to your students.

Video Report 6: WOMAD, the World of Music and Dance festival.

12 Two weddings, a birth and a funeral

Reported speech
Saying sorry

Profile

Student's Book

Language
- reported statements
- reported questions
- reported commands, requests, etc.
- reporting verbs
- apologizing

Pronunciation
- *had/would*
- stress and intonation
- recognizing phonetic script

Vocabulary and everyday English
- birth, marriage, death
- apologizing

Workbook
- extra grammar – *ask* and *tell*, *talk* and *speak*
- vocabulary – birth, marriage, death
- pronunciation – word stress and *had/would*
- multi-word verbs with two particles

Video
- *Wide Open Spaces* Episode 6

Introduction to the unit

This last unit of *New Headway Intermediate* deals with reported speech not only as an aim in itself, but also because it is a useful way to pull together and revise many aspects of the tense system. The theme of weddings, births and funerals has been chosen as an appropriate one with which to conclude a course because it brings together basic themes of life itself! The tone of the presentation sections is not meant to be serious – they comprise humorous scenes to do with weddings and marriage.

In the skills work we incorporate judiciously selected examples of English literature.

Some teachers are cautious about the use of literature in their language courses, but we feel that there is such a wealth of very well-known writers past and present in English that it is a shame not to reflect this to some extent in language coursebooks. Moreover, if the literary extracts are carefully selected and handled, they can be of great interest to students, and give them a tremendous sense of achievement and perhaps even the confidence and motivation to try and read more.

Language aims

Grammar
Reported speech

NB *The previous unit, Unit 11, dealt with indirect questions and focused on the problems of word order connected with this. The same word order problems apply to reported questions but with the added complication of 'one tense back'.*

Direct speech:	*'Where is she going?'*
	'What did they see?'
Indirect question:	*I wonder where she is going.*
	I wonder what they saw.
Reported question:	*He asked where she was going.*
	He asked what they had seen.

Tense usage in reported speech is quite straightforward and logical. The 'one tense back' rule is the same in many languages. There are three main areas of reported speech: statements, questions and commands. These are divided up in the following way in this unit.

Presentation (1) covers reported statements and questions in all tenses. It focuses on *say*, *tell* and *ask* as reporting verbs.

Presentation (2) deals with reported commands and introduces other verbs which can be used as reporting verbs.

COMMON MISTAKES

Students tend to have problems with form rather than concept.

1 Confusing the forms of *say* and *tell*.
  *She ~~said me~~ that she lived in Paris.
  *She ~~told~~ that she lived in Paris.
  *He ~~said~~ me to sit down.

2 Word order in reported questions.
  *He asked where was I going.
  *She asked me what ~~did I want~~.
  *He asked ~~do I smoke~~.

3 Transferring forms with *that*, which report commands in L1, to reported commands in English.
  *He told ~~that I~~ come early.
  *She asked ~~that I close~~ the window.
  *He ordered ~~that they went~~.

Vocabulary

The vocabulary fits the theme of the unit with a word sort on birth, marriage and death. The activity also introduces some of the words needed for the reading texts, which are extracts from Charles Dickens' *David Copperfield* about the day that David Copperfield was born, and also a poem by W H Auden called *Funeral Blues*. (This is the poem that features in the funeral scene of the film *Four Weddings and a Funeral*.)

There is also continued work on phonetic script in the form of a crossword.

PostScript

This focuses on different ways of saying sorry. Students often confuse *Sorry* and *Excuse me*, so we try to sort this out in this section with discriminatory exercises. Various expressions are practised via social situations.

Workbook

• Exercise 5 This highlights and practises the different forms when *ask* can be used to report both questions and commands, and *tell* can be used to report both statements and commands.

• Exercise 7 This illustrates and practises the difference between *talk* and *speak*.

• Exercise 8 Vocabulary – This explores parts of speech to do with birth, marriage and death.

• Exercise 9 Multi-word verbs with two particles, as in *They couldn't **put up with** the noise.*

• Exercise 11 Pronunciation – This contrasts *had* and *would* in an exercise which involves recognizing phonetic script. There is also an exercise on word stress, using some of the words from the unit.

Notes on the unit

Test your grammar (SB page 116)

The report of this proposal of marriage sounds very stilted and strange, but it is meant to be funny. The conversation between John and Moira highlights the notion of what reported speech is because it is *not* reported naturally but literally.

1 Try to set the scene for the humorous tone of the first parts of the unit. Ask your students if any of them have ever received a proposal of marriage. Who from? Where? When? Then ask them to comment on the picture. Either ask them to read about John and Moira, or exaggerate the unnaturalness of the story by reading it aloud yourself to your students.

Ask students to work out the exact conversation in pairs. Give them about five minutes to do this.

NB *The students are not actually required to convert any of the reported speech into direct speech. They simply have to complete endings of each line of the conversation. This is purely a recognition exercise – they are not being asked to produce at this stage.*

Now ask some of the pairs to act out the marriage proposal to the rest of the class. Encourage them to exaggerate the humour of it, and hopefully thereby you will get some good stress and intonation practice!

Answer
John 'Hello, Moira. How **are you**?'
Moira 'I'm **fine. How are you**?'
John 'I feel **wonderful** because we **are together again.** It's been **a long time since our holiday in Paris.**'
Moira 'I loved **every minute in Paris.** I'll never **forget it. Can we go back there next spring**?'
John 'I **love you**, Moira. Will you **marry me and come to Paris with me for our honeymoon**?'
Moira 'Oh, yes, yes, **I will. I love you too.**'

2 Ask the whole class this question. It is a very easy one!

> **Answer**
> The story is reported speech. The conversation is direct speech.

3 **T.85** Play the tape and ask if they notice any differences. You could get them to act it out one more time, after hearing the stress and intonation on the tape.

PRESENTATION (1) (SB page 116)

Reported statements and questions

1 First ask students to look quickly at the pictures and the lines of conversation. Ask *Where are Adam and Beatrice? Who are they? What has just happened?*

> **Answers**
> Adam and Beatrice are at a wedding reception. They are both friends of the people who have just got married.

Now ask students to work in pairs to match the lines.

> **Answers**
> a **A** Are you on your own?
>   **B** No, I'm not. I'm with my husband.
> b **A** How do you know John and Moira?
>   **B** I was at university with Moira.
> c **A** Do you like big weddings?
>   **B** I prefer smaller ones.
> d **A** Where did you meet your husband, then?
>   **B** Actually, I met him at a wedding.
> e **A** Why aren't you drinking?
>   **B** Because I'm driving.
> f **A** Have you travelled far to get here?
>   **B** Yes, we have. We flew in from New York yesterday.
> g **A** Why aren't you wearing a hat?
>   **B** I never wear hats.
> h **A** Where are you staying tonight?
>   **B** We're at the *Red Lion*.
> i **A** Can you give me a lift there?
>   **B** Yes, we can. Are you staying at the *Red Lion*, too?
> j **A** Yes, I am. Will there be enough room in your car?
>   **B** Oh, yes, lots. There won't be a problem.

2 **T.86a** Play tape for students to listen and check their answers.

NB This conversation has been specially written to include examples of a variety of tenses. Thus, when it is reported (as it is in the following exercise when Beatrice tells her husband about her conversation with Adam) it illustrates fully the 'one tense back' rule in reported speech.

3 This is Beatrice reporting her conversation with Adam to her husband. Read aloud to your students what she says and then move straight on to do the grammar questions.

● Grammar questions

Ask a student to read aloud the first pair of sentences to the class. Ask another student to read aloud the second pair. Read aloud the questions yourself, and discuss the answers with the whole class.

> **Answers**
> – The basic rule is 'one tense back'. This is illustrated by *I'm/I am* (Present Simple) becomes *she was* (Past Simple) and *I was* (Past Simple) becomes *she had been* (Past Perfect). Also note that *I* becomes *she*.
> – *tell* must be used with a direct object: *she told **him**. say* does not have a direct object *she said*. It can be used with an indirect object *she said **to him**.*

NB Also, point out to your students 'that' is optional. This is why it is in brackets in the sentences.

Repeat the procedure with the next pairs of sentences.

> **Answers**
> – Not only is the 'one tense back' rule followed, but the word order changes to that of a statement. Thus, *Are you* becomes *I was*, and *do you know* becomes *I knew*. Also *you* becomes *I*.
> – *If* is used when there is no question word.

PRACTICE (SB page 117)

1 Reporting a conversation

Ask students to work in pairs and look again at the conversation between Adam and Beatrice on page 116 and continue to report it. Go round the class and help them as they do this. There will be lots of little differences in the reporting, especially in the use of *say* and *tell*, so be flexible, as long as they use it correctly.

> **Sample answer**
> Then he asked me if I liked big weddings, and I said that I preferred smaller ones.
> He asked me where I'd met you and I told him that we'd met at a wedding. Then he asked me why I wasn't drinking, and I said that it was because I was driving. He asked me if we'd travelled far to get here, so I said that we'd flown from New York yesterday (the day before).
> Then he asked me why I wasn't wearing a hat, so I said that I never wore hats.

He then asked where we were staying tonight (that night), and I told him we were at the *Red Lion*. He asked me if we could give him a lift there, and I said that we could. I asked him if he was staying at the *Red Lion* too, and he said he was. He asked if there would be enough room in our car, and I told him that there was lots and that it wouldn't be a problem.

NB *'Yesterday' and 'tonight' can become 'the day before' or 'that night' according to the immediacy of the reporting.*
You will need to point out that both the Present Perfect and the Past Simple become the Past Perfect in reported speech.

T.86b Play the tape and ask students to note any little differences and additions to the conversation. They could read the tapescript on page 141 at the same time or immediately afterwards.

Practise saying some of the sentences from the tape to give very controlled practice of the target language, particularly those sentences which contain the Past Perfect in contracted form. Remind your students that *'d* is *had*. The following sentences could be good for repetition.

He asked me where I'd met you and I told him we'd met at a wedding.
He asked me if we'd travelled far … so I said that we'd flown in from New York.

2 Grammar

1 This is a necessary, but purely manipulative, exercise. It could be set as homework but it is worthwhile doing it in class to provide immediate consolidation of the grammar. You could go through it with the whole class so as to ensure that they have really understood, or you could ask them to do it in pairs. Only you can judge what is best for your students.

Answers
a He said (that) he was exhausted.
b She asked me if I was leaving on Friday (or the following Friday.)
c They said (that) they hadn't seen Jack for a long time.
d They said (that) they'd flown to Madrid.
e I asked them which airport they'd flown from.
f The announcement said (that) the flight had been cancelled.
g They told us (that) their flight had been delayed by five hours. (Careful! This is a passive sentence.)
h She asked what time it had taken off.
i He said he would help me unpack.
j He told the teacher (that) he couldn't do the exercise.

2 This exercise is to raise awareness of the changes in meaning because different tenses are used. Put students into pairs to discuss the three pairs of sentences, then conduct a discussion with the whole class. Be flexible about how your students express the different meanings – just satisfy yourself that they are on the right lines. You could accept answers in L1 in a monolingual class. However, do make sure that they tell you what the people actually said in direct speech in English.

Answers
a The first sentence means that Beatrice still lives in New York. (Direct speech = *I live in New York*) The second sentence means that she doesn't live there now but lived there some time in the past. (Direct speech = *I lived* or *I've lived in New York*.)
b In the first sentence *she* = Moira's mother, and *'d* = the contracted form of *would*. Moira's actual words to her mother were *You'll love John*. In the second sentence *she* = Moira, and Moira's actual words to her mother were *I love John*.
c In the first sentence, *'d* is the contracted form of *would*. Adam's direct question was *How **will** you travel* … He is asking about a future event. In the second sentence, *'d* is the contracted form of *had*. Adam's direct question was *How **did** you travel?* He is asking about a past event.

3 Stress and intonation

1 The aim of this activity is controlled oral practice with emphasis on good stress and intonation. **B** is very upset when she learns about George's lies from **A**.

Practise the example sentence in open pairs across the class. Put the students into pairs to do the exercise. Don't worry too much at this stage about good pronunciation, let them focus on getting the responses right.

Answers
(● signifies the main stressed syllables in B's response.)
a But he told me he hated it!
b But he told me that he was moving to Australia!
c But he told me that he'd left her!
d But he told me he'd be twenty-one!
e But he told me he'd gone to Barbados!
  or
  But he told me he'd been to Barbados!
f But he told me that he'd given up three years ago!
g But he told me he'd been given promotion!
h But he told me that he'd fallen in love with me!

2 **T.87** Ask students to listen and check their answers, then to practise the dialogues again, but this time really working on good stress and intonation.

Tell them that **B** is very upset at George's lies – that their stress and intonation must reflect this. Round the activity off with some open pair practice of some of the sentences across the class.

ADDITIONAL MATERIAL

Workbook Unit 12

Exercise 1–4 These exercises give further practice of reported statements and questions to use as homework or to supplement classroom work.

PRESENTATION (2) (SB page 118)

Reported commands

1 The newspaper article provides the context for examples of reported commands. First ask your students to read only the title and the opening paragraph.

Ask them some questions: *What does the title mean? Is it a good or a bad marriage? Why did the judge send Patrick and Pauline to prison? What is another word for 'rowing'?* (= 'arguing', 'quarrelling'). You could teach your students *to have a row*, taking care that they pronounce 'row' correctly: /raʊ/.

Now ask your students to read the article.

NB It is a good idea to check your students' general understanding of the article with some quick comprehension questions, such as:
'How long have Patrick and Pauline been married?'
'Why did the neighbours complain?'
'Why did Mr and Mrs Fish complain?'
'Why did they ring the police?'
'Why were Patrick and Pauline arguing?'
'Did the judge think they were telling the truth?'
'Is this the first time the police have been called?'
'Why did the judge send them to prison?'
'What is a 'marriage guidance counsellor'?'

2 Ask students to work on this in pairs and then conduct a full class feedback where you highlight the differences between the direct and reported speech. Some are reported commands, others illustrate the use of other verbs to report speech.

Answers
a Judge Margaret Pickles.
   She **ordered them** to spend fourteen days in prison.
b The neighbours.
   Neighbours **complained** that they could hear them shouting from the bus stop.
c Mrs Iris Fish.
   I **asked them nicely to stop** because my baby couldn't get to sleep.
d Mr Fish.
   My husband **told them to stop** (making a noise).
e Mr and Mrs Fish.
   We **asked them to come** immediately.
f Mr and Mrs Peters.
   Mr and Mrs Peters **admitted** they had been arguing.
g Mrs Peters.
   Mrs Peters said she **had accused** Mr Peters of wasting their money on drink and gambling.
h Mr and Mrs Peters.
   They **denied** throwing the chair.
i The judge.
   She **reminded** them that they had already had two previous warnings from the police.
j The judge.
   She **told** them that they would soon cool down in prison.
k The judge.
   She **advised them to talk** to a marriage guidance counsellor.

● Grammar questions

Go through these with the whole class. Read them aloud and encourage suggestions after each one.

Answers
– a, c, d and e are commands or requests.
  (a and d = commands; c and e = requests)
  a is reported with the verb *order*; d with *tell*;
  c and e with *ask*.
  They are all formed in the same way:
  verb + object + infinitive with *to*
  ask   someone *to do* something.
  tell   someone *to do* something.
  order someone *to do* something

– *My husband told them to stop.*
  (reported command)
  She told them that they would soon cool down in prison. (reported statement)

– *I asked them to stop making a noise* is a reported request.
  She asked me if I knew the time is a reported question.

– *order, complain, admit, accuse, deny, remind, advise.*

Go through the form of each of the sentences with these.

PRACTICE (SB page 119)

1 Other reporting verbs

These exercises introduce students to other reporting verbs which follow the same pattern as *ask someone to do something*.

They could be set for homework, but it is worthwhile doing them in class to provide immediate consolidation.

1 Go through this first part with the whole class. Check that they understand all the words.

> **Answers**
>
> tell – **c** order – **j** remind – **b** beg – **d** advise – **i**
> ask – **a** invite – **e** warn – **g** refuse – **h** offer – **f**

2 Ask your students to do this in pairs.

> **Answers**
>
> a Maria asked Mark to translate the sentence for her.
> b Mary reminded her son to send Aunt Maud a birthday card.
> c The postman told me to sign on the dotted line.
> d John begged Moira to marry him.
> e John invited his boss to the wedding.
> f Mark offered to pay for the next round.
> g Mary warned her children not to run round the edge of the swimming pool.
>
> NB *This one could be a little difficult because students might not know the verb 'to warn'. Also, this is a negative sentence: 'warn somebody not to do something'.*
>
> h Bobby refused to go to bed.
> i Ben advised Bill to talk to his solicitor.
> j The teacher ordered Jo to take the chewing gum out of his/her mouth immediately.

ADDITIONAL MATERIAL

Workbook Unit 12

Exercise 6 This provides further practice of other reporting verbs.

2 Listening and speaking

Remind students of the newspaper article about the rowing couple. Ask them to give you a very quick recap of the characters – *Who are they?* and the story – *What happened?*

1 **T.88a** and **T.88b** Divide the class into two groups. Tell them to imagine that they are all policemen on the case. Group **A** will listen to Pauline Peters' statement and take some notes. Group **B** will listen to the neighbour, Iris Fish, and take some notes. The idea is that students from the two groups report back to each other on what the women have said, thereby (hopefully!) getting freer practice of reported speech.

NB *If possible, put the groups next to separate tape recorders in different parts of the classroom to do the listening simultaneously. Alternatively, you could have the groups come to the front of the class and listen one after the other to their tape. The tapes are short, but they may still need to listen more than once.*

2 Ask students to find someone from the other group and report and compare the stories. Go round and listen and encourage them as they do this; they may well be reluctant to use the variety of reporting verbs unless nudged a little by you.

> **Sample answers** (The differences are underlined.)
> **Group A**
> Pauline admitted that they sometimes argued. She said that they sometimes argued about money because they were both unemployed, but they didn't argue often, and usually just watched TV quietly in the evenings. She told me that she got upset when Patrick gambled and drank, especially because he had promised to stop. She admitted shouting at Iris but denied throwing the chair – she said it had fallen out of the window. She apologized for waking the baby and said she liked babies. She offered to babysit for Mr and Mrs Fish.
>
> **Group B**
> Iris complained that they argued every night. She said that she and Mr Fish could hear every word, but that it was not so bad during the day because Mr and Mrs Peters were at work. She told me that usually they argued about the television programmes and then Mr Peters went out to the pub. She said that last night he had come back really drunk and he had been shouting and swearing outside. He ordered his wife to open the door but she had refused to – she had opened the window and thrown a plant at him and tonight she had thrown a chair at Mr Fish. She said that they were selfish and didn't care about the baby.

3 Students could work in their groups to produce a written group report for the classroom notice-board (if you have one) or for the other group to read. Alternatively, they could do it for homework.

The contents of the report should be similar to the sample answers above.

ADDITIONAL MATERIAL

Workbook Unit 12

Exercise 4–6 These exercises give further practice of reported commands and requests. In Exercise 6 they are contrasted with statements. They can be used as homework or to supplement classroom work.

LANGUAGE REVIEW (SB page 119)

Reported statements
Reported questions
Reported commands

This is a lengthy review.

Read the relevant sections to your students after each presentation, or do it as a final summary. They could be encouraged to translate some of the sentences into their own language, especially in a monolingual class.

Ask them to read the Grammar Reference section for homework and whilst they are doing some of the exercises in the Workbook.

● VOCABULARY AND PRONUNCIATION
(SB page 120)

Birth, marriage and death

It is important to do this vocabulary activity before the reading because it covers many of the words needed in the readings. It also helps set the scene for the texts.

1   Students could do this in pairs or small groups, drawing columns on a separate piece of paper. Encourage them to use their dictionaries.

> **ALTERNATIVE SUGGESTION**
> Draw three columns on the board and invite individual students to come up to the board and write in the words, whilst the others to comment.

> **Answers**
>
> | Birth | Marriage | Death |
> |---|---|---|
> | cot | wedding | grave |
> | nappy | bouquet | grief |
> | pram | reception | wreath |
> | pregnant | *widow | to bury |
> | bonnet | honeymoon | mourners |
> | godmother | to get engaged | coffin |
> | christening | best man | funeral |
> | to have a baby | bridegroom | cemetery |
> | maternity leave | to get divorced | *widow |
> | | to exchange rings | sympathy |
>
> *widow fits both the marriage and death sections.

2   Ask students to work in pairs. Remind them that they can check the phonetic chart on the back page.

> **Answers**

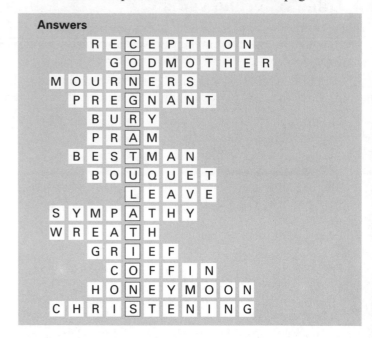

3   Encourage some discussion to round off this activity. Ask generally and also about specific occasions in your students' families, but be *very* sensitive on the subject of funerals.

ADDITIONAL MATERIAL

Workbook Unit 12

Exercise 8 Vocabulary This explores parts of speech to do with birth, marriage and death.

● READING AND LISTENING (SB page 120)

A birth and a death

Both texts about the birth and the death are taken from English literature.

The birth is the birth of David Copperfield from the novel of the same name by Charles Dickens. The death is someone expressing their grief at the death of a loved one in the poem *Funeral Blues* by W H Auden.

NB There is such a wealth of very well-known writers past and present in English that it is a shame not to reflect this to some extent in language coursebooks. If the literature extracts are carefully selected and handled, they can be of great interest to students, and give them a tremendous sense of achievement, and perhaps even the confidence and motivation to try and read more.

We have chosen well-known writers and well-known texts. 'David Copperfield' is one of Dickens' most famous works and the extract from it is both sad and humorous. The W H Auden poem is the one read aloud in the funeral scene of the film 'Four Weddings and a Funeral'. We have chosen to have the texts on tape as an additional aid to understanding and to help create the appropriate atmosphere.

Pre-reading task

Put students into small groups.

1   The aim of this is to set the scene in a personalized fashion. Launch it by telling your class what you know about the day you were born. Encourage students to share more interesting stories with the whole class.

2   Now introduce your students to the writer and the novel, asking them what they know.

NB **CHARLES DICKENS**
Born 1812. Died 1870. One of the greatest novelists of Victorian England. His best known novels are: 'David Copperfield', 'Oliver Twist', 'The Pickwick Papers', 'Great Expectations', 'Nicholas Nickleby' and 'A Christmas Carol' (about the miser Scrooge.) He was unusual for his time because he wrote about social injustice. One of his greatest talents was his ability to describe people in very comical and colourful ways. His portrayal of Betsey Trotwood in 'David Copperfield' is an example.

Reading and listening (1)

A birth

T.89a   Read the introduction and ask students to identify the mother and aunt in the picture. Check that your students understand the meaning of *widow* and *widowed*. Now ask them to read and listen to Part 1. Tell them not to worry at this point about understanding every word, just to try to form an opinion of what the two women are like.

I AM BORN (Part I)

NB Although the language is at times old-fashioned and literary, the content and vocabulary is such that students should easily be able to get an impression of the situation and the characters.

Answers
David's aunt, Betsey Trotwood, seems to have a very strong, confident personality. She is quite a frightening character.

David's mother, Mrs Copperfield, on the other hand, seems very shy, unconfident and unhappy.

They have not met before because Betsey says 'You have *heard* of me, I dare say.' It is clear that they have not seen each other before from the conversation.

Comprehension check

Ask students to work in pairs to go through the questions. You could give feedback on question 1 before they continue with the rest, because this follows on well from the initial discussion about the characters of the women.

Answers
1   **Betsey Trotwood** – forceful, confident, strong, impatient, bossy, insensitive, severe.
    Mrs Copperfield – shy, frightened, weak, miserable, flustered, meek.
    'Motherly' does not describe either of them. Mrs Copperfield is about to become a mother, but seems very frightened at the idea of having a baby and being too young to look after it.
2   'Posthumous' means that David was born after the death of his father. His father had died six months before. His father's name was also David Copperfield. We know this because Betsey Trotwood addresses the mother as Mrs David Copperfield.
3   Because it is the day of David's birth.
4   This refers to the trial of giving birth. David's mother is afraid that she will die while having her baby. (It is interesting to note the vague language used to describe pregnancy and childbirth in these puritanical Victorian times.)
5   Because his mother was so frightened at Betsey Trotwood's visit that she went into labour and had the baby on that very Friday.
6   Because she looks so young. 'You are a very baby!' (line 25)
7   She is sad and frightened because: she is a very young widow; she is about to have a baby and she thinks she might die giving birth; Betsey Trotwood is a frightening character.
8   She is absolutely certain that the baby will be a girl.

What do you think?

Discuss these as a class. It may be a very brief discussion. Don't worry if your students can't offer many ideas, fill in with your own.

Suggested answers

1 Betsey Trotwood wants the baby to be a girl so badly that it seems that she has no time for boys and men. Perhaps this is because she has been badly treated by a man. There might be a particular reason why she has never married.

2 The baby will be born and it will be a boy. David's mother may die. Betsey might bring up the baby, etc.

I AM BORN (Part II)

T.89b Repeat the procedure. Ask questions about the pictures before students listen and read. The man in the picture is Mr Chillip. Ask your students who they think he is. They may guess that he is the doctor.

Comprehension check

Ask students to work on the questions in pairs and then go through them as a class.

Answers

1 She clearly thinks that he is stupid. It seems she doesn't like men! He is clearly very frightened of her. She treats him very sternly.

2 Betsey is talking about the baby when she asks 'How is *she*?' Mr Chillip thinks that she is talking about the mother.

3 No, she doesn't because she is so angry that it is a boy.

4 She hits him with her hat/bonnet because she is so furious when he explains that the baby is a boy.

5 She is not interested in a boy baby. She is used to getting her own way, and this has not happened.

What do you think?

Suggested answers

– Betsey's behaviour is very strange, and insensitive to David's poor mother. She acts like a spoilt child, who has not got her own way.

– Probably, or why else would she be in Chapter 1! In fact, later in his life David does live with his aunt. She turns out to have a heart of gold.

NB Your students may want to know how the story continues: His weak mother does not die giving birth to David. She gets married again to a cruel man, Mr Murdstone, and dies having his child. Mr Murdstone hates David and sends him away to school where he is treated badly. He leaves when he is still very young and gets a miserable job in London. There he meets the kind, optimistic but always poor Mr Micawber and his family. Finally, penniless, he walks from London to Dover (about 60 miles) to his aunt Betsey Trotwood's home. Despite her behaviour at his birth, she is very pleased to see him and offers him a home with her,

which she shares with a friendly and harmless madman called Mr Dick. David has many more adventures and meets many more very colourful characters, including a lovely, intelligent girl called Agnes Wickfield. David fails to notice Agnes' love for him, and marries a weak, pretty, but silly girl called Dora. She, like his mother, dies young and David finally marries Agnes.

If time is short, both the vocabulary and the language work exercises could be set for homework.

Vocabulary

Students could do this in pairs.

Answers

1 **Part I**
shy – **timid** (line 6), uncertain – **doubtful** (line 7), was used to – **was accustomed to** (line 16), hat – **cap** (line 24), crying – **sobbing** (line 28)

2 **Part II**
gentle – **mild** (line 1), most humble – **meekest** (line 2), strictness – **severity** (line 6), hat – **bonnet** (line 24), hit – **aimed a blow** (line 25), disappeared – **vanished** (line 26)

Language work

This returns to the theme of the unit, reported speech.

Students work it in pairs or work alone, and then check with a partner. It is important to make clear that each verb can only be used once, and they will probably have to do the exercise by a process of elimination.

Answers

1 introduced	5 asked	9 added
2 said	6 didn't answer	10 suggested
3 told	7 expressed	11 told
4 exclaimed	8 invited	12 begged

Reading and listening (2)

A death

Pre-reading task

1 Tell your students that they are going to read a modern love poem by a famous English poet called W H Auden. The poem is called *Funeral Blues*.

NB It is not very likely that the class will know anything about the poet, but they may have heard the poem if they have seen the film 'Four Weddings and a Funeral'.

T.90 Don't ask them to open their books at this stage. Tell them that you want them to listen to the poem first, before they read it, to see how much they can follow. Ask everyone to relax and close their eyes, and then play the tape. Ask a few general questions.

Answers

What has happened? – The poet's loved one has died.

How does the writer feel about the world? –
He can't understand how the world continues to go on.
It all seems meaningless.

2 It can be fun to try to build this poem using any words
   or phrases your students can remember – many of the
   words seem to be quite memorable. Write them on the
   board. (All our students remembered the line: *He was
   my North, my South*, etc.)

Reading

Now they can open their books. Play the tape again and
ask your students to read and listen at the same time.
Ask them to answer the questions in pairs.

Answers

1 He wants the rest of the world to stop because he
   feels so grief-stricken.

2 The lines of the first verse describe things that could
   possibly happen. The lines of the second and last
   verses describe impossible things.

3 Verse three.

4 This means that quite ordinary things look different.
   The whole world looks beautiful even if it is really
   not. The weather is sunny even if it is raining;
   everyone you meet seems happy; buildings,
   countryside are beautiful, etc. Nothing can make
   you feel unhappy. The poem describes the opposite
   of this when you lose the person you love, nothing
   looks good and everything makes you feel unhappy.
   You cannot find a reason for living, and you wonder
   how anyone can.

Learning by heart

This is not very fashionable but it is immensely satisfying
if it is done appropriately and occasionally.

1 Ask your students to learn their favourite verse.

2 See if all the verses have been learnt by someone.
   If not, you fill in. Invite students to say their chosen
   verse. You could ask them to the front of the class.

● WRITING (SB page 124)

Correcting mistakes

This could be homework, but spend time doing this in
class – it has revision from the whole book.

1 Read the introduction aloud. Ask your students to
   mark the text where they find mistakes.

Answer (includes answers to 1 and 2)

Szerens u. 43
Budapest   1125
Hungary
Friday 6 September

Dear Mr and Mrs Bennett

I **have been** home now **for** two weeks but I **had** to start
work immediately, so this is the first time **that it** is
possible for me to write. How are you all? Are you
busy as usual? **Is** Andrew still **working** hard for his
exam next month? I ~~am~~ miss you a lot and also all my
friends from my English class. Yesterday I ~~'ve~~ received
a letter from my **Greek** friend, Christina and she told
me about some of the other students. She **said** that
Etsuko and Yukiko **are going to** write **to** me from
Japan. I am lucky because I made so many good
friends **while** I was in England. It was really interesting
for me to meet people from so many different
countries. I think that we not only improved our
English (I hope **so**!) but we also **got to know** people
from all over the world and this is important.

My family are fine. They had a good summer **holiday**
by the lake. We are all very **excited** because my
brother **Is getting/Is going to get** married just before
Christmas and we like his girlfriend **very much**. They
have **been looking** for a flat near the city centre but it
is **not** easy to find one. If they **don't** find one soon they
will have to stay here with us.

Please can you check something for me? I can't find
my red scarf. I think I **might** have **left** it in the
cupboard in my bedroom.

Please write soon. My family send best wishes to you
all. I hope I can come back next year. **Staying** with you
was a **really** wonderful experience for me. Thank you
for **everything** and excuse my mistakes. I **have** already
forgotten so **many** words.

Love
Kati

PS I hope you like the photo. It's nice, isn't it?

2 Students work in pairs to produce a correct version.
   Go round the class and check their work.

3 Ask when and where your students have stayed with
   other people. They could write the letter for
   homework, and bring it back to class for other
   students to help correct.

PostScript (SB page 125)

Saying sorry

1 Students often confuse these expressions. You could write some on the board and explain them: *Sorry* – an apology and a regret; *Excuse me* – is to attract someone's attention; *Pardon?* – (polite) when you can't hear someone clearly; *What?* – (not polite) when you can't hear someone clearly.

Ask them to work with a partner to do the exercise and to practise the conversations as they do it.

Answers

a '**Excuse me**, can you tell where the post office is?'
'**I'm sorry**, I'm a stranger here myself.'

b 'Ouch! That's my foot!'
'**Sorry**. I wasn't looking where I was going.'

c '**Excuse me**, what's that creature called?'
'It's a Diplodocus.'
'**Pardon**?'
'A Diplodocus. D-I-P-L-O-D-O-C-U-S.'
'Thank you very much.'

d 'I failed my driving test for the sixth time!'
'**I *am* sorry**.'

e '**Excuse me**, we need to get past. My little boy isn't feeling well.'

f 'Do you want your hearing aid, Grandma?'
'**Pardon**?'
'I said: *Do you want your hearing aid*?'
'**What**?'
'DO YOU WANT YOUR HEARING AID?!'
'**I'm sorry**, I can't hear you. I need my hearing aid.'

2 **T.91a** Play the tape for your students to listen and check their answers. Then ask them to act out the conversations with good stress and intonation.

3 Ask students to work in pairs. If you don't have much time, you could divide the situations between the pairs, and then get them to act them in front of the class.

Sample answers

a Hello, Elana? Hello, again! I don't know what happened. I think we must have been cut off. I'm sorry about that. Never mind. Now, where were we?

b Excuse me! Hello! Excuse me! Excuse me, please! Hi! Yes, please! Can we have another large bottle of fizzy mineral water, please? Thanks.

c Oh, I *am* sorry to hear about that. Of course I understand. We'll go out another time.

d What! You want to go where? And with a bottle of whisky? How old do you think you are? You can think again!

e Excuse me! I wonder if you could help me. I thought this jumper was medium, but when I got home I saw it was the wrong size. Can I change it?

f Pardon? Could you say that again, please. I didn't understand.

g Excuse me, please! Thank you. Excuse me. I'm getting off at the next stop. Excuse me. Sorry.

h Oh, no! Of course, you're vegetarian! I *am* sorry! How awful of me. Don't worry, there are lots of other things for you to eat.

Don't forget!

Workbook Unit 12

Exercise 7 *talk/speak*.

Exercise 9 Multi-word verbs with two particles, as in *They couldn't **put up with** the noise*.

Exercises 10 & 11 Pronunciation Exercise 10 contrasts *had* and *would*. Exercise 11 is an exercise on word stress using some of the words from the unit.

Wordlist This is on page 166 of this Teacher's Book for you to photocopy and give to your students.

Video *Wide Open Spaces* Episode 6: Maddy and Nick hear that their old London flat is up for sale.

Stop and check There is a Stop and check revision section for use after each quarter of the Student's Book.

Stop and check 4 for Units 10–12 is on pages 142–3 of this Teacher's Book. You need to photocopy it. The key is on page 152.

> ### SUGGESTION
>
> You can use the Stop and check any way you want, but here is one way:
>
> • Give it to your students to do for homework, preferably when they have enough time, for example, over a weekend.
>
> • In class, ask them to go over the test again in groups of five or six people. They should try to agree on definitive answers. If they can't agree, they should ask you.
>
> • You provide the answers and any necessary explanations.

Progress tests There are Progress tests at the end of Unit 6 and Unit 12.

Progress test 2 for Units 7–12 is on pages 147–9 of this Teacher's Book. You need to photocopy it. The key is on page 153.

These Progress tests serve the same function as Stop and check tests, but teachers sometimes like to have their own checks of progress.

Photocopiable Material

Unit 1 5 Speaking (SB page 9)

Student A

Charles Hendrickson was born in … (*When?*). He went to school in Paris and Geneva, and then went to … University (*Which?*), where he studied history.

After university he went to … (*Where?*), and spent two years travelling around the Far East. Then he decided to … (*What?*), and he went to work for the Guardian newspaper in Manchester. He stayed there for … years (*How many?*).

While he was working in Manchester he met his wife, Susan. They got married in … (*When?*), and they have four children.

Charles started working for the Times in … (*When?*). Since then he has been to Russia, Vietnam, Argentina, and South Africa. In 1992 he won … (*What?*) for his reporting of the situation in South Africa.

He lives with his wife, their four children, four cats, and a dog … (*Where?*)

Student A

Charles Hendrickson was born in … (*When?*). He went to school in Paris and Geneva, and then went to … University (*Which?*), where he studied hlstory.

After university he went to … (*Where?*), and spent two years travelling around the Far East. Then he decided to … (*What?*), and he went to work for the Guardian newspaper in Manchester. He stayed there for … years (*How many?*).

While he was working in Manchester he met his wife, Susan. They got married in … (*When?*), and they have four children.

Charles started working for the Times in … (*When?*). Since then he has been to Russia, Vietnam, Argentina, and South Africa. In 1992 he won … (*What?*) for his reporting of the situation in South Africa.

He lives with his wife, their four children, four cats, and a dog … (*Where?*)

Student B

Charles Hendrickson was born in 1940. He went to school in … (*Where?*), and then went to Oxford University, where he studied … (*What?*).

After university he went to India, and spent … (*How long?*) travelling around the Far East. Then he decided to apply for a job in journalism, and he went to work for … (*Which newspaper?*) in Manchester. He stayed there for eight years.

While he was working in Manchester he met … (*Who?*). They got married in 1964, and they have … children (*How many?*).

Charles started working for the Times in 1968. Since then he has been to … (*Which countries?*). In 1992 he won a prize for his reporting of the situation in South Africa.

He lives with … (*Who?*) on a boat on the River Thames in London.

Student B

Charles Hendrickson was born in 1940. He went to school in … (*Where?*), and then went to Oxford University, where he studied … (*What?*).

After university he went to India, and spent … (*How long?*) travelling around the Far East. Then he decided to apply for a job in journalism, and he went to work for … (*Which newspaper?*) in Manchester. He stayed there for eight years.

While he was working in Manchester he met … (*Who?*). They got married in 1964, and they have … children (*How many?*).

Charles started working for the Times in 1968. Since then he has been to … (*Which countries?*). In 1992 he won a prize for his reporting of the situation in South Africa.

He lives with … (*Who?*) on a boat on the River Thames in London.

© Oxford University Press Photocopiable

Unit 2 **Suggestion** (TB page 23)

Find sentences in the text about Sister Wendy which mean the same as the following.

a She lives totally alone.

b She describes the art treasures from her own point of view.

c She uses simple language, not the complicated language of experts.

d I am a useless human being.

e I am not very sociable.

f She loves considering what she is going to eat.

g I hate watching myself on television.

Unit 3 **Suggestion** (TB page 33)

Group A

1 She was <u>painfully</u> shy so she hated going to parties.

2 When his wife died he was <u>grief-stricken</u>.

3 She died because she swallowed <u>poison</u>.

4 He lost his job, then his wife left him and he was so upset that he <u>suffered a nervous breakdown</u>.

5 He felt angry and <u>bitter</u> when he lost his job to a much younger man.

6 <u>Archaeologists</u> found ancient jewellery at the <u>excavations</u> in Rome.

Group B

1 I like to <u>breathe</u> the fresh air in the countryside.

2 That tree was <u>blown</u> down in the wind.

3 His <u>doting</u> parents gave him everything that he wanted. He was <u>thoroughly spoilt</u>.

4 There are a lot of <u>pigeons</u> in Trafalgar Square.

5 <u>Triangles</u> and <u>squares</u> are <u>geometrical shapes</u>.

6 Oh no! I've <u>spilt</u> my coffee on your new carpet!

Group C

1 Fred Astaire was a very famous <u>tap</u> dancer. I always <u>tap</u> my feet when I see him dance.

2 A <u>slave</u> works for no money at all.

3 I have had this bag for many years. It's old and <u>battered</u> now but I still use it.

4 Our town has a busy, <u>bustling</u> market every Wednesday.

5 Al Capone was a famous <u>gangster</u> and a <u>gambler</u>.

6 He was always fighting. He was a <u>rough</u>, <u>tough</u> man who used his <u>fists</u> a lot.

Unit 4 **Suggestion** (TB page 45)

Here is a reading and speaking activity on etiquette in Britain. There is usually more than one possibility, as the answer is usually 'It depends'. Nevertheless, there is always at least one suggestion that is definitely wrong.

Imagine you are in Britain. A friend of a similar age and background to yourself has invited you home for a meal.

Choose the best answer, a, b, c, or d about how you should behave. There is not necessarily one best answer.

1 When you go to their house, should you …
a take some flowers?
b take some wine?
c take a special gift from your country?
d ask them before what they would like you to bring?

2 When you arrive and meet the other guests, should you …
a introduce yourself to the other guests?
b shake hands with all the other guests?
c wait to be introduced to the other guests by your hosts?
d announce in a loud voice your name, job, and position in your company?

3 You would like to look round their house. Should you …
a wait to be invited?
b ask if you can look round?
c go and look round without asking?
d pretend that you want the toilet and nose around on your own?

4 Some food is served that you really don't like. Should you say …
a 'I'll just have a little bit of that, please'?
b 'I'd rather not have any of that, thank you'?
c 'I'm awfully sorry. I don't like that'?
d nothing, and just eat it?

5 In the days after the invitation, should you …
a write your hosts a thank-you letter?
b phone them to say thank you?
c invite them to your house or to a restaurant?
d not get in touch at all?

© Oxford University Press **Photocopiable**

Student A1

You are Peter Hobday's secretary. Mr Hobday owns several hotels.

It is 10.00 in the morning. Someone phones, trying to get hold of Mr Hobday. Here is his diary for today. Deal with the phone call. Begin by picking up the phone and saying,
'Hello. Mr Hobday's office. Can I help you?'

9.00 –11.00	In a meeting with the marketing director
11.00 –12.00	Dentist
12.30 – 2.00	Lunch with his accountant
2.00 – 3.00	Visiting the Savoy Hotel
3.00 – 3.30	Talking to the head chef at the Savoy
4.00 – 6.00	Back in the office

Student B1

You are a business person called Robin Freshwater. You want to get in touch with Peter Hobday, the owner of several hotels.

It is 10.00 in the morning. Phone Mr Hobday's office. When the phone is answered, say 'Good morning. Can I speak to Peter Hobday, please?'

If he isn't there, try to find out when he's free, so you can try again later.

Student A2

You are Andrew Smith's secretary. Mr Smith manufactures mobile phones.

It is 10.00 in the morning. Someone phones, trying to get hold of Mr Smith. Here is his diary for today. Deal with the phone call.

Begin by picking up the phone and saying,
'Hello. Mr Smith's office. Can I help you?'

10.00 –12.00	Having a meeting with his sales team
12.00 – 2.00	Going shopping for his wife's birthday present
2.00 – 3.00	Seeing his bank manager
4.00 – 5.30	In the office

Student B2

You are Peter Lent, a businessman.

You want to get hold of Andrew Smith, the manufacturer of mobile phones.

It is 10.00 in the morning. Phone Mr Smith's office. When the phone is answered, say, 'Good morning. Can I speak to Andrew Smith, please?'

If he isn't there, try to find out when he's free, so you can try again later.

Student A3

You are Lady Alice Cooper's secretary. Lady Alice doesn't work.

It is 10.00 in the morning. Someone phones, trying to get hold of Lady Alice.

Here is her diary for today. Deal with the phone call. Begin by picking up the phone and saying,
'Hello. Lady Alice Cooper's office. Can I help you?'

10.00 –12.00	Having her hair done
12.00 – 2.00	Having lunch at the Hilton
2.00 – 4.00	Going round an art exhibition
4.00 – 7.30	At home

Student B3

You are Tina Brown, a journalist.

You want to get hold of Lady Alice Cooper because you want to have an interview with her for your magazine.

It is 10.00 in the morning. Phone Lady Alice's office. When the phone is answered, say, 'Good morning. Can I speak to Lady Alice Cooper, please?'

If she isn't there, try to find out when she's free, so you can try again later.

Map of the British Isles

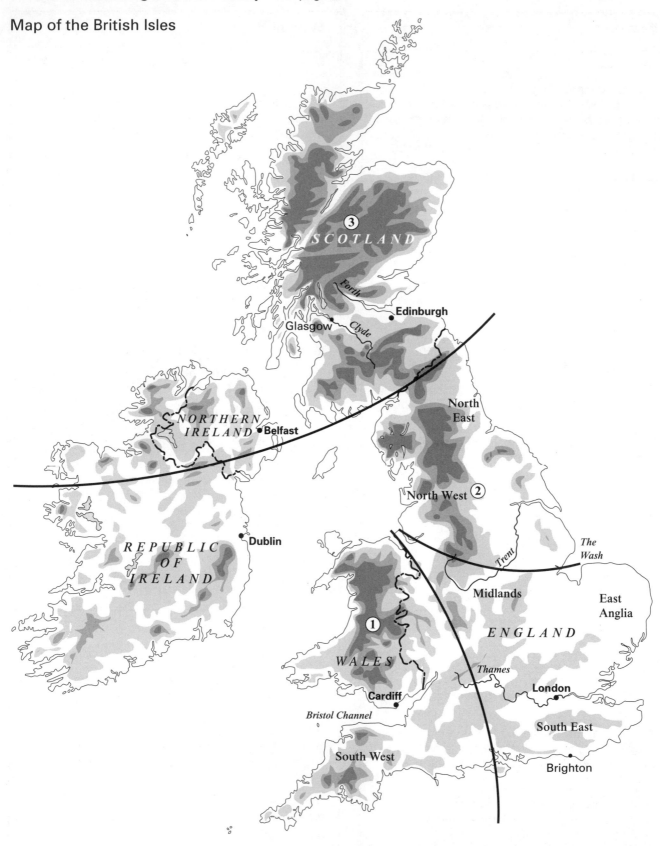

© **Oxford University Press**   Photocopiable

Student A1

You want to speak to Mr James in the Service Department at Ford Garages.

You want your car serviced. If Mr James isn't there, be prepared to leave a message and give your phone number. Say how long you'll be on that number.

Student B1

You work for Ford Garages. Someone phones for Mr James from the Service Department, but he's not there at the moment.

Explain the situation, and offer to take a message. Get all the information you need.

Remember! You answer the phone. Begin by saying, 'Hello. Ford Garages. Can I help you?'

Student A2

You want to book two nights at the Palace Hotel. Decide which dates you want, and what sort of room you want. You need to know the price of the room and what is included. Does the hotel need a deposit? Can you pay by credit card?

Be prepared to give your name, address, and details of your credit card.

Student B2

First you are the telephonist at the Palace Hotel. Answer the phone and say, 'Hello. Palace Hotel. How can I help you?' Put the caller through to Reservations.

Now you work in Reservations! Answer the phone and say, 'Hello. Reservations. Can I help you?' Someone wants to book a room. Ask the dates, and what sort of room is required.

Remember to get the person's name, address, and details of their credit card.

Student A3

You need a plumber desperately! Your washing machine is pouring water all over the floor.

You phone Chris, a local plumber. He's probably out at work, so you might have to leave a message on his answer phone.

Be prepared to leave a message, giving your name and number, and explaining the situation. Ask him to get in touch as soon as possible.

Student B3

Your name is Chris, and you're a plumber. Decide what message to record onto your answer phone. Remember that customers might be phoning, so you must tell them when you'll phone back.

When the phone rings, deliver your recorded message.

Student A4

You phone your friend Jo to invite her to go to the cinema. You, Mary, and Steve have arranged to meet outside the cinema at 7.00. Would Jo like to join you?

Jo will probably be out, so be prepared to leave a message on her answer phone.

Student B4

Your name is Jo. Decide what message to record onto your answer phone at home.

When the phone rings, deliver your recorded message!

Student A5

You phone the International School of English for a brochure. When the phone rings, ask for the Admissions Department. You want to know course dates and fees. You also want to know when the next course starts.

Be ready to give your name and address.

Student B5

First you are the telephonist at the International School of English. Answer the phone and say, 'Good morning! International School of English'. Put the caller through to the Admissions Department.

Now you work in the Admissions Department! Answer the phone and say 'Hello. Admissions. How can I help you?'

The caller wants information from you about course dates and fees. Be ready to give the information about your school.

The caller also wants a brochure, so you'll have to get their name and address.

Suggestion (TB page 71)

Here are some answers about Amanda, Giles and Hugo in the text about *The modern servant*. Write the questions.

1 _____ ?

Yes, she has. She finished it last month.

2 _____ ?

Yes, she has. She's applied for the post of nanny to twins.

3 _____ ?

For three years.

4 _____ ?

For over three hundred years.

5 _____ ?

For four years.

6 _____ ?

No, he hasn't. But perhaps he will by the time he is forty.

You want to try to keep your win a secret from the world. But what about your family? Are you going to tell your relatives?

~

No.
go to

Yes.
go to

You have received your cheque at a big press conference, after which your name and photograph appeared in all the newspapers. As a result you get thousands of letters begging for money. What are you going to do?

~

Give all of them £10.
go to

Give some money to the people who sound genuine, but nothing to the crazy ones.
go to

Give nothing to anyone.
go to

Your relatives find out that you've won a lot of money, and they feel very upset that you didn't tell them. Can things ever be the same again?

Anyway, you have to make another big decision. Are you going to carry on in your old job, or are you going to give up work? After all, you don't need the money any more.

~

If you're going to carry on working,
go to

If you're going to stop working,
go to

You have a reputation for being kind and generous, so you feel you're handling your new wealth quite well.

Meanwhile, you have to make another big decision. Are you going to carry on in your old job, or are you going to give up work? After all, you don't need the money any more.

~

If you're going to carry on working,
go to

If you're going to stop working,
go to

You tell your relatives, and they're all very pleased, especially when you give them all £1,000 each. They're a little bit jealous, but you were generous, so that's all right.

Anyway, you have to make another big decision. Are you going to carry on in your old job, or are you going to give up work? After all, you don't need the money any more.

~

If you're going to carry on working,
go to

If you're going to stop working,
go to

8

The press keeps asking people about you. They don't write about the people you have given to, but they write article after article about the people you didn't give to. You don't feel that you're handling your new wealth very well.

Anyway, you have to make another big decision. Are you going to carry on in your old job, or are you going to give up work? After all, you don't need the money any more.

If you're going to carry on working,
go to

If you're going to stop working,
go to

© **Oxford University Press** Photocopiable

11

The press keep asking people about you and what you're doing with all your money. When they find out that you have not given a penny to anyone, they write horrible things about you.
As a result you feel awful.
You aren't handling this new wealth at all well.

Meanwhile, you have to make another big decision. Are you going to carry on in your old job, or are you going to give up work? After all, you don't need the money any more.

If you're going to carry on working,

go to **7**

If you're going to stop working,

go to **13**

21

You just carry on working as usual. People think you're a little strange, and you're getting a reputation for being a bit of an eccentric. Why, if you've got so much money, do you carry on doing your old job?

~

You could spend a few hundred pounds on one or two things for your flat.

go to **14**

You could go on a shopping spree to New York, and buy presents for everyone you know. For goodness sake, you can afford it, so why not enjoy it?

go to **3**

7

You've decided to carry on in your old job, at least for the time being. Of course, by now everyone at work knows you're a multi-millionaire. What are you going to do?

~

Throw a huge party for all your work colleagues.

go to **9**

Just carry on working and ignore everyone's comments.

go to **21**

14

You spend a tiny percentage of your money, and invest the rest in the bank.

This new wealth isn't doing very much for you. It certainly isn't making you very happy.

~

Why don't you give it all away to a charity, or to someone who might do something more creative with it?

go to **17**

Why not just carry on working? If that's what you want to do, then do it.

go to **19**

9

You have a huge party, and everyone has a wonderful time. All your work colleagues think you're a great person, and love you very much. That's what they all said at the end of the party, anyway, after the champagne had been flowing all night.

You carry on working for another six months, and you've still got all this money in the bank. You can't just ignore it. You've got to do something with it.

You could spend a few hundred pounds on one or two things for your flat.

go to **14**

You could go on a shopping spree to New York, and buy presents for everyone you know. For goodness sake, you can afford it, so why not enjoy it?

go to **3**

3

You go to New York and have a great time. Everyone loves their presents.

You've still got loads of money. What are you going to do with it?

~

Give a lot to various charities, both at home and in other countries.

go to **16**

Give up work now. You'd like a new challenge.

go to **6**

Carry on working, doing the same old thing.

go to **4**

© Oxford University Press Photocopiable

33

You try to fight your drug addiction alone, but you can't do it. You keep falling back into bad habits.

There is one last thing you can try. You can go to the Betty Ford Clinic in California, where they have a very good success rate with people like you. Unfortunately it will cost the rest of your money.

What are you going to do?

~

Go to the clinic. What's the point of your money if you haven't got your health?

go to

Keep trying to give up your addiction. If you haven't got any money, how can you buy the drugs you need.

go to **32**

24

You go to the detoxification centre, and six weeks later you are cured of your addictions.

While you're in the centre, you meet some born-again religious fanatics. They say that if you give them all your money, you will be saved.

~

If you want to give them all your money,

go to **36**

If you don't want to give them a penny,

go to **34**

40

You find the meaning of life. You are cured – completely cured, and the world seems a beautiful place again.

Was it worth having so much money? Maybe people just shouldn't have so much more than others?

You could even try to get your old job back!

You have come to the end of the activity.

~

WELL DONE!

36

You give all your money to the religious group and go to live with them in a community in California.

You find true happiness, and live with the group for the rest of your life.

You have come to the end of this activity.

~

WELL DONE!

32

You live a life which is dominated by your drug habit, which you never manage to control. You are an addict for the rest of your life.

Was the money worth it? Weren't you happy when you were just doing your old job, and had friends to go out with on a Friday night? What you would give to be able to go back to those days!

You have come to the end of this activity.

BAD LUCK!

34

You come out of the centre cured. You feel a little disillusioned with life. What is money for? It doesn't seem to bring much happiness.

~

You could invest it in a friend's business. You trust her, and you would be doing something useful with your money.

go to **35**

You could use your money to help homeless people and drug addicts. This would be a constructive thing to do with your money.

go to

© Oxford University Press **Photocopiable**

17

You feel an awful lot better now that you don't have to worry about all that money. You are relieved, and you have found true happiness. Having so much money was quite an experience, but you think that you are probably better off without it.

You have come to the end of the activity.

~

WELL DONE!

16

You're feeling good. You seem to be getting a balance of what to do with your money. Spend some and save some.

One day you get a phone call. It's your Uncle Ernie who you haven't heard from for years. He asks for £100,000 or he will tell the press stories about you from your childhood. What are you going to do?

~

Give him the money.

go to **5**

Not give him the money.

go to **20**

19

Your life grinds on until you die of boredom. Money didn't do much for you, did it? You didn't seem to find much to do with it, either.

You have come to the end of the activity.

~

BAD LUCK!

5

You give Uncle Ernie the money, and this keeps him quiet.

You're getting fed up with the responsibility of having so much money, and so many people keep sending you begging letters. You feel it is time for a major decision in your life.

~

Why not give it all away? It would be the end of all your troubles. You could go back to life as it used to be.

go to **17**

Or you could just decide never, ever to give anyone any money ever again. After all, it's yours to do with what you want.

go to **28**

4

Your life grinds on until you die of boredom. Money didn't do much for you, did it? You didn't seem to find much to do with it, either.

You have come to the end of the activity.

~

BAD LUCK!

20

You decide not to give Uncle Ernie the money he asked for. As a result, he tells stories about you to the press, which are then published.

You're getting fed up with all this attention from the press, and you've had enough of the responsibility of handling so much money.

~

You decide to give it all away.

go to **17**

© Oxford University Press **Photocopiable**

6

You've finally given up work. You've got all this time and all this money. What on earth are you going to do?

~

You could do some charity work at your local hospital. You feel it would do you good to think of other people for a change.

go to **27**

You could invest all your money in a new business that you've read about in the papers. It promises to double your money within six months.

go to **30**

30

You have invested all your money in a new business venture. It goes wrong and you lose it all. Everything. You don't have a penny left.

This is the best thing that could happen to you. Suddenly you don't have a care in the world. All the worries about what to do with so much money have disappeared. You go back to your old job, where you are very happy until you retire.

You have come to the end of this activity.

WELL DONE!

28

You live a rich, miserable existence for the rest of your life.

Maybe you would have been happier without the money. Who knows?

You have come to the end of this activity.

~

BAD LUCK!

13

You've stopped work because you have so much money, and you don't see why you should carry on getting up so early in the morning if you don't have to. So what are you going to do?

~

You could buy your local football team. You've always been interested in football, and the club needs some money urgently. You could be manager!

go to **22**

Buy some fantastic clothes and a Mercedes sports car, and start going to the most fashionable restaurants and night clubs.

go to **25**

Go on a world cruise. Here's your big chance to see the world!

go to **29**

27

You have found true happiness. You have managed to be both rich and happy, which is no easy thing to do. You have balanced wealth with care and concern for other people.

You have come to the end of this activity.

~

WELL DONE!

29

You're on a world cruise. You meet another millionaire on board ship, but this is a multi-multi-multi-millionaire. He/she is also single. If you two got married, you would be rich forever. However, you don't actually love him/her.

~

If you decide to get married,

go to **23**

If you decide it would be crazy to get married,

go to **26**

© Oxford University Press Photocopiable

25

You start to have a great time, going out every night and not getting home till dawn. Suddenly a lot of people seem to like you. Is it because you're the one who pays for everything?

At a night club one evening, a friend of yours shows you some white powder and says, 'Here! Try this!'

What are you going to do?

~

Try it. Why not? A little won't do you any harm.

go to **37**

Don't touch it. You'd be mad.

go to **31**

39

You've invested all your money in risky schemes, and you've lost the lot. You don't have a penny left. Naughty, naughty! You were too greedy, weren't you?

You have come to the end of this activity.

~

BAD LUCK!

Maybe you can get your old job back? Was it worth having so much money?

22

You're the manager of a football team. You're doing well. It is the last game of the season. If you win this match, you will win the championship.

Just to make sure you win, you could offer your opponents a bribe to lose the match. You're pretty sure you could get away with it.

What are you going to do?

~

Offer a bribe.

go to **43**

Play fair.

go to **46**

35

Your friend runs away with all your money. What a friend! With friends like that, who needs enemies?

You're broke. You've lost the lot.

You've come to the end of this activity.

~

BAD LUCK!

Maybe you could get your old job back? Maybe that's when you were happiest in your whole life?

23

You got married with the intention of becoming super rich, but it becomes clear within six months that you don't get on with your new husband/wife. Inevitably you get divorced.

Meanwhile you have more decisions to make. You have spoken to your accountant about what to do with your money. Your accountant has two suggestions.

~

Invest your money in high-risk schemes. You could make another fortune.

go to **39**

Invest your money in low-risk schemes. You won't make a lot, but you won't lose it, either.

go to **42**

38

You have found true happiness and the meaning of life. You have managed to be both rich and happy, which is not easy. You have balanced spending money on yourself and using it to help others.

You have come to the end of this activity.

~

WELL DONE!

© Oxford University Press **Photocopiable**

42

You chose low-risk investments, which provide you with an income for life. Not a fortune, but enough to keep you, your family and friends happy for the rest of your life.

You have come to the end of this activity.

~

WELL DONE!

31

Well done. You resisted the temptation to try the illegal drug. You could have become addicted. Maybe these friends aren't so friendly after all.

You decide to get some financial advice. Your accountant has two suggestions.

~

Invest your money in high-risk schemes. You could make another fortune.

go to **52**

Invest your money in low-risk schemes. You won't make a lot, but you won't lose it, either.

go to **53**

26

Thank goodness you chose not to get married. He/she wasn't a millionaire at all, but a con artist. You nearly lost the lot!

Meanwhile you have more decisions to make. You have spoken to your accountant about what to do with your money. Your accountant has two suggestions.

~

Invest your money in high-risk schemes. You could make another fortune.

go to **39**

Invest your money in low-risk schemes. You won't make a lot, but you won't lose it, either.

go to **53**

43

You bribed the opposition and you won the championship. Everything seems to be going OK.

Unfortunately, there are some rumours about you and your dishonesty going round.

What are you going to do?

~

You can deny everything.

go to **41**

You can come clean and admit that you did wrong.

go to **44**

37

Unfortunately one thing leads to another, and you have started drinking and taking drugs. You are losing control of your life. What are you going to do?

~

Get yourself to a detoxification centre. You need help.

go to **24**

Fight it alone. You've never needed anyone's help before, and anyway you can stop taking drugs whenever you want.

go to **33**

41

You deny all knowledge of any wrong doing. The case goes to court, and you are found guilty. You are sentenced to four years in prison.

While you are in prison, you meet someone who says he knows how to make a fortune, probably not legally. When you get out of prison, what are you going to do?

~

Invest in this man's scheme. You need the money badly.

go to **45**

Go on the straight and narrow. You've learned your lesson.

go to **48**

© **Oxford University Press**   Photocopiable

45

You invest what you have left in the scheme, and you lose the lot. Every penny.

You have come to the end of this activity.

~

BAD LUCK!

Maybe you weren't meant to be a football manager? Maybe you would have been happier just staying in your old job?

47

You invest all your money in a new business venture. It goes wrong and you lose it all. Everything. You don't have a penny left.

This is the best thing that could happen to you. Suddenly you don't have a care in the world. All the worries about what to do with so much money have disappeared. You go back to your old job, where you are very happy until you retire.

You have come to the end of this activity.

WELL DONE!

48

When you come out of prison, you give up on football. There are so many dishonest people in the game.

You decide to ask for your old job back, and you're in luck! You go back to work, and stay there until it's time for your retirement. You live out your days poor, but you are a wise and happy person.

You have come to the end of this activity.

WELL DONE!

49

You carry on with the football team. Things go from bad to worse. You suffer from stress, you start drinking too much alcohol, and your team is relegated to a lower division.

You finally have a heart attack, and you are forced to resign from the club.

You live out your life older, poorer and wiser.

You have come to the end of this activity.

BAD LUCK!

44

You admit that you offered the other team a bribe. You are fined several thousand pounds, and the Board of Directors forgives you.

However, you're going off the idea of being involved in football. The game is full of dishonest people.

What are you going to do?

.

~

Sell the team and do something else with the money.

go to

Carry on with the team. Things have to get better soon.

go to

46

You play fair and resist the temptation to bribe the opposition. You win the championship and become a famous manager.

You are offered the chance of being the manager of your country's football team. What an honour! However, it would mean more work and more stress. Is that the kind of thing you want?

~

If you decide to accept the job,

go to **50**

If you decide not to take it,

go to **51**

© **Oxford University Press** **Photocopiable**

50

You become the manager of your country's football team. Unfortunately after two years your luck runs out. You haven't won a game for nine months, and you are sacked. You are poor and on the street. You have come to the end of this activity.

BAD LUCK!

Was it a good idea to go into football? Was it worth winning all that money? You could have just stayed in your old job. Maybe they would take you back?

52

You invest every penny you have in a high-risk scheme. Unfortunately there is a stock market collapse and you lose the lot. It has all gone.

This is the best thing that could happen to you. Suddenly you don't have a care in the world. All the worries about what to do with so much money have disappeared. You go back to your old job, where you are very happy until you retire.

You have come to the end of this activity.

WELL DONE!

51

You decide not to give yourself all the stress and hard work, and you're happy being the manager of your local team.

You carry on in the job for years. There are ups and downs, but by and large you are happy.

You have come to the end of this activity.

~

WELL DONE!

53

You invest your money in low-risk schemes, but you still make loads of money. You can't stop making money.

What are you going to do?

~

Give half of it away to charity. You don't need it, and you've got enough to live on.

go to **54**

Invest all of it in environmental education to make everyone aware of how we need to take care of the world and its animals.

go to **55**

55

Your ideas work wonderfully, and the world is saved! You are made a Sir or Lady, and you go to Buckingham Palace to receive your award.

Everyone says what a wonderful person you are.

You have come to the end of this activity.

~

WELL DONE!

54

You find true happiness. You have managed to be both rich and happy, and you have balanced spending your money on yourself, and using it to benefit other people.

You have come to the end of this activity.

~

WELL DONE!

© Oxford University Press   Photocopiable

Unit 9 Suggestion (TB page 85)

22 Pitlochrie Drive
Perth
Scotland
19 May

Dear Susie

I am sixteen years old and totally depressed. I'm in love with Danny Darcy, the pop star. I know it's hopeless but I can't get him out of my mind. I sit up in my room, playing his music and just dreaming dreams of meeting him, and being in his arms. I write to him every day but all I get back are photocopied notes from his fan club. My friends think I'm mad, so I don't see them any more. I can't concentrate on my homework and I have exams soon. My mum and dad don't notice what I do because they're both doctors and very busy all of the time. Please, please help me! I'm desperate but I can't help myself.

Yours in misery

Lucy Craig

62 Myrtle Street
Luton
Beds. LU2 7AE
27 April

Dear Susie

I'm almost too tired to write but I have no one to turn to. I've been married for three years and we were hoping to start a family soon. Everything was just fine and then Colin, my husband, lost his job. So now he's depressed because he has nothing to do all day, he just goes to his mother's house. She lives in the next street. The thing is that there is a lot he could do. I'm a staff nurse at our local hospital and I work all hours of the day, and nights, too sometimes, so he could look after our house, but he won't. He says that housework is boring. I think so, too, but someone has to do it, so it's always me. His mother encourages him to go round to her house because she lives on her own, and at least he doesn't drink there. I'm really afraid he's becoming an alcoholic; I found four whisky bottles under the bed this morning, and drinking makes him snore. I'd rather work nights and then I can sleep during the day without listening to him snore.

What can I do? I still love him.

Pam Gurney

Unit 10 Suggestion (TB page 95)

Prepositions of time

For each of the time expressions, put *in*, *at*, *on*, or nothing.

a ____ March
b ____ 1986
c ____ 14 May
d ____ Monday
e ____ last Monday
f ____ summer
g ____ 8 o' clock
h ____ the 1960s
i ____ two days ago
j ____ the weekend
k ____ Christmas
l ____ last year
m ____ the end of April
n ____ the morning
o ____ Monday morning

Unit 11 Suggestion (TB page 106)

Vocabulary and pronunciation

Put in the missing parts of speech. All the missing words are in the texts. Check the pronunciation in your dictionary, particularly where there is a change in stress between the parts of speech.

Noun	Verb
_____	to be born
_____	behave
discovery	_____
approval	_____
record	_____
_____	develop
_____	rescue
_____	explain
_____	rule
belief	_____
_____	paint
protection	_____

Noun	Adjective
aggression	_____
_____	accidental
risk	_____
truth	_____
length	_____
technology	_____
_____	distressing
_____	dangerous
nature	_____
fame	_____
_____	strong
_____	evil

© Oxford University Press Photocopiable

Student A

Marie Tussaud was born in Strasbourg in 1761. Her father died … (*When?*), and her family moved to Switzerland.

Her mother worked for a German … (*Who for?*). The doctor was a kind man who enjoyed making wax models of parts of the human body. He soon got a reputation for making good likenesses of people's heads as well.

He moved to … (*Where?*) because he wanted to earn money by making models of the rich and famous. Soon Marie and her mother joined him in Paris. When she was six years old, the doctor taught her … (*What?*). Her portraits became so popular that by the time she was twenty she was living in the Palace of Versailles because the royal family invited her to live there.

The French Revolution started in … (*When?*), and this was the beginning of hard times for Marie. However, she met and married François Tussaud, who was an … (*What job?*). They had three children, a daughter who died and two sons.

In 1802 she received permission from Napoleon to go to London, because she wanted to … (*What … do in England?*). She went round Britain and Ireland with her four-year-old son, and her shows were a great success. She never saw France or her husband again.

She opened her exhibition centre in London in … (*When?*), and it has been in the same place ever since. Marie died in 1850.

Madame Tussaud's is now London's most popular tourist attraction. About … (*How many?*) million people visit it every year.

Student B

Marie Tussaud was born in Strasbourg in 1761. Her father died two months before she was born, and her family moved to … (*Where?*).

Her mother worked for a German doctor. The doctor was a kind man who enjoyed … (*What … doing?*). He soon got a reputation for making good likenesses of people's heads as well.

He moved to Paris because (*Why?*). Soon Marie and her mother joined him in Paris. When she was six years old, the doctor taught her how to work in wax. Her portraits became so popular that by the time she was twenty she was living in (*Where?*) because the royal family invited her to live there.

The French Revolution started in 1789, and this was the beginning of hard times for Marie. However, she met and married (*Who?*), who was an engineer. They had … (*How many …?*) children.

In 1802 she received permission from Napoleon to go to London, because she wanted to take her waxwork collection to England. She went round Britain and Ireland with … (*Who with?*), and her shows were a great success. She never saw France or her husband again.

She opened her exhibition centre in London in 1835, and it has been in the same place ever since. Marie died in … (*When?*).

Madame Tussaud's is now London's most popular tourist attraction. About 2.2 million people visit it every year.

© Oxford University Press Photocopiable

Unit 10 Suggestion (TB page 96)

Work in pairs. Prepare a phone conversation, then act it out.

Student **A** phones Student **B**. You are old friends, but you haven't heard from each other for a long time because **A** got a new job and moved to another town.

B Answer the phone.

A Say who you are. Ask how **B** is.

B You are surprised and delighted to hear from **A**. Ask for some news about the past and present.

A Give some news of your work and family, past and present. Ask **B** for some news.

B Give some news. Then ask about a mutual friend.

A Answer. Say that you're coming to **B**'s town on business, and that you'd like to meet.

B You are pleased. Invite **A** to your home for a meal.

A Accept the invitation. Suggest a day and a time.

B The day and the time are fine, but does **A** know how to get to your house?

A You don't know. Ask for directions.

B Give directions.

A Check directions. Tell **B** that you're really looking forward to seeing him/her again.

B Respond. Check the day and the date. Say goodbye.

A Say goodbye.

Unit 11 2 Conversations (SB page 110)

1 **A** You broke that vase.
   B Yes, I did. I dropped it. I'm sorry.
   A You'll buy another one.
   B Yes, of course. How much was it?
   A £200.
   B It wasn't £200!
   A Yes, it *was*.

2 **A** It's so romantic.
   B What is?
   A Well, they're really in love.
   B Who are?
   A Paul and Mary.
   B Paul and Mary *aren't* in love.
   A Oh, yes, they are. They're mad about each other.

3 **A** Have you paid the electricity bill?
   B No, *you've* paid it.
   A No, I haven't!
   B But you *always* pay it.
   A No, I don't. I always pay the telephone bill.
   B Oh, yes. Sorry.

4 **A** We love each other.
   B Er – I think so.
   A We don't ever want to part.
   B Well …
   A We'll get married and have six children.
   B What! You haven't bought me a ring.
   A Yes, I have. Diamonds are forever.
   B Oh, dear!

5 **A** Helen didn't win the lottery.
   B Oh, yes, she did. She won two million pounds!
   A She isn't going to give it all away.
   B Oh, yes, she is.
   A She's very kind. Not many people would do that.
   B Well, *you* certainly wouldn't.

6 **A** That isn't a letter from Bertie.
   B Yes, it is. He hasn't written for six months.
   A What does he want?
   B He wants to borrow some money.
   A I'm not lending him another penny!
   B You've already lent him £2,000.
   A I certainly have.

7 **A** You *haven't* forgotten the map.
   B Oh, dear. Yes, I have.
   A But I put it next to your rucksack.
   B I didn't see it.
   A So, how can we find the village?
   B We could ask a policeman.
   A There *aren't* many policemen on this mountain!

8 **A** We can't afford that new car.
   B Are you sure? Haven't we saved a lot of money?
   A Yes, but, we need that money.
   B What for?
   A Our old age.
   B You're joking.
   A Yes, I am. I've just bought it for you!
   B Wow!

Stop and check 1

Units 1–3

General revision

Look at the letter from Claudia, who's a student in England, to her friend, Julie. There are 32 gaps. After some gaps there is a verb in brackets. Put the verb in the correct tense.

Example
Last week I _visited_ (visit) Liverpool.

When there is no verb in brackets, write *one* suitable word – perhaps a preposition, an adverb, an auxiliary verb, an article, etc.

Example
I came _to_ York to learn English.
☐ 32

Dear Julie
I 1 _____ (arrive) in England three days
2 _____. I 3 _____ (stay) with a family in a
village near York. They're really nice. Mr Jones
4 _____ (work) in York. Mrs Jones has just had
a baby, so she 5 _____ (not work) at the
moment. I 6 _____ (not ask) her what she does
yet, but I 7 _____ (think) she's 8 _____
secretary.
I 9 _____ (have) a good time here,
10 _____ everything is very expensive. Yesterday
I 11 _____ (take) the train 12 _____ York to do
some sightseeing. Something really embarrassing
happened 13 _____ I was there. After I
14 _____ (visit) the Viking museum, I 15 _____
(decide) to do some shopping. Earlier in the day, I
16 _____ (see) a beautiful sweater in a
department store, so I 17 _____ (go) back
18 _____ (buy) it. The shop assistant 19 _____
(put) it into a bag when I realized that I
20 _____ (forget) my purse with my credit
cards! So, unfortunately, I couldn't buy 21 _____
after all.
  Anyway, after that I went to York Minster.

I have never seen such a beautiful cathedral!
It 22 _____ built between 1220 and 1470. In
1984 it 23 _____ struck by lightning during a
storm, and there was a terrible fire. But they've
rebuilt it since then.
  While I 24 _____ (walk) back to the station,
I 25 _____ (meet) Frank. Do you remember him?
I haven't heard from him 26 _____ over a year.
When we last 27 _____ (see) him, he 28 _____
(work) in a bank. Now he 29 _____ (learn)
English here at the same school as me! What a
coincidence! Last night we went to 30 _____
cinema together and saw a horror film. Frank was
terrified, but I 31 _____ enjoyed it!
  That's about all the news for now. Write soon
and tell me about your holiday in Portugal. What
was Lisbon 32 _____?

          Love   Claudia

Questions

Read the interview with Gary Kasparov (G), the famous chess player. Write the interviewer's (I) questions.

Example
I How long *have you been playing chess*?
G I've been playing chess since I was 3 or 4.
I Where _____ ?
G I was born in Azerbaijan in the former Soviet Union.
I When _____ ?
G I became an international Grand Master in 1980, when I was 17.
I How long _____ ?
G I've been the world chess champion since 1984.
I How often _____ ?
G I play chess every day – sometimes against a computer!
I What _____ ?
G I'm preparing for a match against Anatoly Karpov.

☐ 10

© Oxford University Press   Photocopiable

Auxiliary verbs

Complete the sentences using the correct auxiliary verb.
Some are affirmative, some are negative.

Example
What _did_ you get up this morning?

1 What _____ you doing when the phone rang?
2 _____ you ever read any Agatha Christie?
3 I'm sorry. I can't drive you to the station because my car _____ being serviced.
4 How long _____ she been learning English?
5 In France they say 'Bon appétit'. But in Britain people _____ usually say anything before they start their meal.
6 _____ you go to work yesterday?
7 'Where _____ BMW cars made?' 'In Germany.'
8 I _____ watch the film last night. Was it good?

8

Vocabulary

1 Do these words and phrases come after *play*, *do*, *make*, *go*, or *have*? Put them in the correct columns.

a meeting	the piano	by ear	on holiday
a shower	aerobics	golf	a statement
sightseeing	athletics	skiing	for a jog
a holiday	a day off	home	the shopping
a mistake	you good	football	
a phone call	a decision	your homework	

play	do	make	go	have
the piano				

22

2 Choose the word that is different from the others, and say why it is different. Think about the meaning and the grammar!

Example
a farmer   a ski instructor   a traffic warden   a secretary
A farmer, a ski instructor, and a traffic warden all work outside. A secretary works inside.

1	want	know	enjoy	agree
2	oil painting	sketch	palette	drawing
3	pop group	composer	orchestra	band
4	lovely	eventually	loudly	immediately
5	newspaper	play	novel	poem
6	good-looking	stupid	boring	mean
7	monastery	castle	hotel	house
8	do	have	make	be

8

Active or passive?

Put the verbs in brackets into the correct tense.
Some are active, some are passive.

11

Reuters News Agency

Martin Webb _has worked_ (work) for the Reuters News Agency for ten years. He describes the company.

'Reuters is one of the world's biggest news agencies. It ¹_____ (supply) news and stock market prices to media and financial institutions all over the world. It ²_____ (start) by Paul Reuter in 1849 – with pigeons! Reuter ³_____ (be born) in 1816 in Germany. During the 1840s he ⁴_____ (employ) as a bank clerk in Berlin. German bankers ⁵_____ (need) to know the prices on the Paris stock exchange, but the French telegraph system only went as far as Belgium. From there the information ⁶_____ (send) to Germany by train. The journey ⁷_____ (take) nine hours. The same information ⁸_____ (carry) by Paul Reuter's pigeons in only two hours!

'Reuters ⁹_____ (change) a lot since those days. Over the past fifty years, we've opened offices in many different countries – and we ¹⁰_____ still _____ (expand). Now, news and stock market prices ¹¹_____ (send) all over the world within seconds.'

Translate

Translate the sentences into your language.
Translate the *ideas*, not word by word.

1 When I arrived, the children were going to bed.
2 When I arrived, the children went to bed.
3 When I arrived, the children had gone to bed.
4 Hamlet was written by William Shakespeare.
5 Champagne is made in France.
6 She's working at home today.
7 Do you know the answer?
8 She works in a bank.
9 What did you think of the film?

9

Total 100

Stop and check 2

Units 4–6

General revision

Look at the letter from Julie to her friend, Claudia, who's a student in England. There are 28 gaps. Sometimes you have to choose the correct verb.

Example
I *must* / *had to* / *could* take the train because there weren't any buses.

When there is a gap, write one suitable word – perhaps an article, a relative pronoun, an adjective, a noun, etc.

Example
I got back *from* Japan last week.

[28]

Dear Claudia

Thanks for your letter. I'm pleased **¹to hear / hearing / hear** that you're having a good time in York. How is the English course going? **²Are you allowed to / Do you have to / Must you** do lots of homework? What's your teacher **³____** ? Is he friendly? You **⁴have to / should / must** write and tell me more!

I had **⁵____** wonderful time in Japan. My friend, Akiko, invited me **⁶stay / to stay / staying** with her family in Kyoto. Do you remember her? She's the girl **⁷____** visited me last summer. They have a house on a hill just outside Kyoto. There was a beautiful **⁸____** of the city from my bedroom window. Akiko's family were incredibly kind and hospitable, and wouldn't let **⁹that I pay / me pay / me to pay** for anything. We ate out a lot. Japanese **¹⁰____** is delicious – lots of vegetables, fish, and rice. The weather was really nice. It was warm and **¹¹____** , except on the last day, when it turned cloudy and chilly. I loved **¹²visit / visiting / to visit** the temples and gardens – the autumn colours were quite spectacular. (**¹³I'll send / I'm going to send / I'm sending** you some photos when I've had them developed.) We went everywhere by train. I think Japan has **¹⁴____** best trains in the world. They're always clean and never late!

I **¹⁵had to / must / could** learn Japanese customs very quickly! In Japan you **¹⁶don't have to / aren't allowed to** wear your shoes in the house – you wear

slippers **¹⁷____** the host provides. And you **¹⁸have to / are allowed to** make a loud noise when you drink tea! (In fact, it's polite if you do!) I caught a cold while I was there, but I **¹⁹couldn't / shouldn't / didn't have to** blow my nose in public as it's considered to be rude.

Tomorrow my mother and father **²⁰will come / are going to come / are coming** to stay for a few days. I **²¹must / can** tidy the house before they arrive! Tomorrow evening **²²we're going / we'll go / we're going to go** to the theatre, and on Wednesday Ann has invited us all **²³go round / going round / to go round** for a meal. Apart from that, I haven't made any plans – perhaps **²⁴I'm taking / I'll take / I'm going to take** them for a drive in the country. Or we could go to Stratford and visit the house **²⁵____** Shakespeare was born.

Anyway, I **²⁶must / can** stop writing now – it's nearly midnight and I've got an early start tomorrow. Write again soon and let me **²⁷know / knowing / to know** how you're getting on. Give my love to Frank when you see him.

Hope **²⁸see / seeing / to see** you soon!

Love

Julie

Future forms

Complete Harry and Kate's conversation using the verb in brackets in the correct form (*will* or *going to*).

Harry ___Are___ you ___going___ (go) on holiday at Easter?

Kate Yes, but we haven't booked it yet.

Harry Where are you thinking of going?

Kate Oh, I don't know … In the summer we **¹_____** (visit) friends in Italy, so I think perhaps we **²_____** (stay) in this country at Easter. What about you?

Harry We **³_____** (rent) a cottage near Edinburgh. It **⁴_____** (be) our first visit to Scotland. Jane **⁵_____** (have) a baby in the summer, so we can't do anything too adventurous or tiring.

Kate Scotland – What a good idea! Maybe we **⁶_____** (do) the same.

[6]

© Oxford University Press **Photocopiable**

can, must, and should

Read the following extract from a guidebook to Thailand.
Fill in the gaps with *can*, *can't*, *must*, *mustn't*, *should*, or *shouldn't*. (Sometimes more than one answer is correct.)

Visas

UK visitors_____*must*_____ apply for a visa.
You **1**_____ enter the country without one.

Customs Regulations

- You **2**_____ bring in up to 200 cigarettes.
- You **3**_____ bring in guns or drugs.
- You **4**_____ bring in one litre of wine or spirits.
- Cars **5**_____ be brought into Thailand for personal use,
  but you **6**_____ have a valid Driving Licence.
- You **7**_____ have at least US $250 with you. If you don't
  you **8**_____ enter the country.

Advice to travellers

- It's usually very hot in Thailand, so you **9**_____ bring
  summer clothes.
- You **10**_____ drink tap water. (It's not always
  dangerous, but it's safer to buy bottled drinking water.)
- Traveller's cheques get a better exchange rate than cash,
  so you **11**_____ bring traveller's cheques with you.
- You **12**_____ tip taxi drivers. They don't expect tips,
  and they might be embarrassed.
- You **13**_____ make international phone calls from hotels
  as they are very expensive. You **14**_____
  use the government telephone offices.
- You **15**_____ have medical insurance. | 15 |

Vocabulary

| 1 Match a word in **A** with its opposite in **B**. | 15 | | 2 Find the connection. Match a word in **A** with a word in **B** | 14 |

A	B
young	humorous
hard-working	delicious
polluted	reserved
disgusting	rude
punctual	lazy
serious	agricultural
polite	cloudy
tasty	elderly
outgoing	poor
industrial	talkative
sunny	boiling
formal	late
hospitable	tasteless
freezing	clean
wealthy	unfriendly
quiet (people)	casual

A	B
etiquette	weather
shake hands	part-time
employment	marriage
address	bow /baʊ/
gift-wrap	chilly
forecast	holiday
sightseeing	food
receptionist	meeting
buffet car	hobbies
recipe	hotel
kettle	postcode
interests	present
climate	phone
honeymoon	train
code	tea

like

Read the answers. Write questions with *like*.

Example
What does she look like? | 7 |
She's quite tall and slim, and she wears
glasses.

1 _____ ?
She's fairly reserved, but very friendly when
you get to know her.

2 _____ ?
He's short, with dark brown hair.

3 _____ ?
A disaster! It rained on Saturday, and we sat
in a traffic jam most of Sunday!

4 _____ ?
They're very keen on gardening, and they
like going skiing in winter.

5 _____ ?
I don't know. We could go to the cinema.

6 _____ ?
He doesn't have many hobbies. He spends
most of the time playing with his computer.

7 _____ ?
He's really nice. Very outgoing and easy to
talk to.

Translate

Translate the sentences into your language.
Translate the *ideas*, not word by word.

1 Passengers must have a valid ticket.
2 You mustn't steal from other people.
3 Nurses have to wear a uniform.
4 Do you have to go to college tomorrow?
5 You should eat more fruit.
6 Teenagers don't have to go out to work.
7 Would you mind opening the window?
8 Your shoes will be ready next Thursday.
9 I'll phone you tonight.
10 She's going to study maths at university
   next year.
11 I'm having lunch with my mother
   tomorrow.
12 What's London like?
13 What does Peter look like?
14 How are your parents?
15 I don't mind waiting. | 15 |

| Total | 100 |

Stop and check 3
Units 7–9

General revision

1 Look at the letter from Alberto, who's staying in Bristol in England, to his friend, Paul. There are 33 gaps. After some gaps there is a verb in brackets. Put the verb in the correct tense.

Example I __haven't visited__ (not visit) Scotland yet.

When there is no verb in brackets, write *one* suitable word – perhaps a modal verb, an auxiliary verb, a conjunction, an adverb, etc.

Example I'll write again __when__ I have time. | 33 |

Dear Paul

My stay in England is coming to an end. In ten days' time I 1_____ (be) back in Italy. I can hardly believe that I 2_____ (be) in Bristol for three months. The time 3_____ (go) so quickly! Yesterday I 4_____ (take) my final exams. As soon as I 5_____ (get) the results, I 6_____ (let) you know.

I'd really like to have a holiday 7_____ the course finishes, but I have to go straight back to Italy. If I 8_____ (have) more time, I 9_____ visit Scotland. Unfortunately I 10_____ (not see) much of Britain – I 11_____ even _____ (not be) to London yet!

I really like England. The people are friendly, the countryside's lovely, and the food's actually quite good. My friend, Pablo, loves it here. He even says he wouldn't 12_____ living here. But for me the problem is the weather. I think I'd 13_____ live somewhere warmer and drier. Recently it's been 14_____ terrible – raining every day.

My host family 15_____ (be) really nice to me. They have looked 16_____ me very well. I shall miss them. But I'm looking 17_____ to seeing my family again. My parents were planning to move to Rome. They might 18_____ moved already. I 19_____ (not hear) from them for a while. My brother 20_____ (be made) redundant, so now he 21_____ (look for) a new job. It 22_____ be very worrying for him and his wife. He says he 23_____ have to move to another town where there are more jobs, but he's not sure.

Yesterday I 24_____ (go) to the cinema with Pablo to see Aliens. It's the fifth time Pablo 25_____ (see) it! He 26_____ really like it. Well, 27_____ do I, but I wouldn't want to see it that many times!

I 28_____ (apply) for lots of jobs recently. Yesterday I 29_____ (apply) for one with the EU in Brussels. It 30_____ be great if I 31_____ (get) it, but I haven't got a very good chance. They want someone with fluent English and French, and my French isn't very good any more.

Anyway, I haven't booked my plane ticket 32_____ , so I must go into town now and do that. See you next week. I'll give you a ring 33_____ I arrive home.

Take care. Best wishes,
Alberto

Present Perfect: active and passive

Complete the text with verbs from the box.
Put them into the Present Perfect active or passive.

~~die~~	find	block	be	bury	advise
speak	hear	crash	kill	discover	

Here is the news. Lord Kimpton, who was Prime Minister for 4 years in the 1960s, __has died__ . Lord Kimpton was 79. Politicians from both the Labour and Conservative Parties 1_____ warmly of his achievements.

Gale-force winds are causing chaos in southern England. Many roads 2_____ by fallen trees and there 3_____ a number of serious motorway accidents involving lorries and coaches. The police 4_____ motorists to stay at home unless their journey is absolutely necessary.

Three men who went missing yesterday while climbing in Scotland 5_____ safe and well.

Archaeologists 6_____ the tomb of a Pharaoh near Cairo. The tomb 7_____ in the sand for over 4,000 years.

And some late news. We 8_____ just _____ that a plane 9_____ at Prague Airport. First reports say that over 50 people 10_____ . We'll bring you more news of this disaster as soon as we have it. | 10 |

© Oxford University Press Photocopiable

Conditionals and time clauses

Join a phrase in **A** with a conjunction in **B** and a phrase in **C** to make eight sentences. Use each conjunction twice. [8]

A	B	C
I'd buy a new house		you go to work in the morning?
I'll tidy the house		
I'll call you	when	you see her.
If you want a ticket, you should phone the theatre	if	he gets the job?
		my guests arrive.
What will he do	before	I won the lottery.
I'm watching TV right now, but I promise I'll help you	as soon as	dinner is ready.
You'll recognize her		the ticket office opens.
Do you have breakfast		this programme finishes.

Vocabulary

1 Complete the story with multi-word verbs from the box. If the verb has an object, make sure it is in the correct position.

Example [20]
He gave me a form and I _filled it in_ (it).

look for	go back	bring back	take back	sort out
make up	be in	give back	try on	be away

Last week I went to a clothes shop. I said to the assistant, 'I ¹_____ (a sweater) for my boyfriend. I like the blue one and the red one in the window, but I can't ²_____ (my mind) which one to buy.'
'Never mind,' said the assistant. 'Take them both and ask your boyfriend to ³_____ (them). Then you can ⁴_____ (the one that he doesn't want) and I'll ⁵_____ you (your money).'
Well, my boyfriend chose the blue one, so I ⁶_____ (the red one) to the shop. There was a different shop assistant. She said, 'I'm sorry. The assistant you spoke to made a mistake. We can't give you your money back.' I asked to see the manager.
'I'm afraid she ⁷_____ on holiday,' said the assistant.
'Well, can I see the assistant manager?'
'No, he ⁸_____ not _____ today, either. But he'll be here tomorrow and he can ⁹_____ (your problem) then.'
I ¹⁰_____ the next day and the assistant manager apologized and allowed me to return the red sweater.

2 Make a chart. Put the adjectives in the correct columns – Base and Strong.

~~tired~~	surprised	difficult	tasty
cold	astonished	beautiful	clever
funny	impossible	brilliant	filthy
pretty	frightened	delicious	terrified
dirty	~~exhausted~~	hilarious	freezing

Base adjective	Strong adjective
tired	exhausted

[9]

3 Complete the sentences with adjectives from Exercise 2. [8]

Example Jack told a very _funny_ joke last night. We couldn't stop laughing!

1 Put the fire on. It's absolutely _____ in here!

2 I was very _____ to see him. I thought he was in Australia!

3 'How was your exam?'
'It was quite _____ , but I managed to answer all the questions.'

4 We walked 20 kilometres. I was absolutely _____ when we got home!

5 'How was the meal?' 'It was very _____ . I really enjoyed it.'

6 'What's the weather like?'
'It's quite _____ , so put a coat on.'

7 Albert Einstein was an absolutely _____ scientist.

8 The windows were very _____ so I washed them.

Translate

Translate these sentences into your own language. [12]
Translate the ideas, not word by word.

1 He has lived in London for ten years.
2 If I won the lottery, I'd travel around the world.
3 When I get home, I'll have a bath.
4 She might have gone out.
5 I saw the film yesterday.
6 If it's a nice day on Sunday, we'll have a picnic.

Total [100]

Stop and check 4

Units 10–12

General revision

Look at the letter from Mary to her friend, Ann, who lives in France. There are 25 gaps. After some gaps there is a verb in brackets. Put the verb in the correct tense.

Example
I *have been learning* (learn) English for two years.

When there is no verb in brackets, write one suitable word – perhaps a preposition, an auxiliary verb, a conjunction, an adverb, etc.

Example   I last saw her *in* 1993. | 25 |

Dear Ann
Thanks for your letter. It was great to ¹_____ from you.
So, what ²_____ I _____ (do) recently? Well,
my friend, Bev, ³_____ (stay) with me for the past two
weeks. I don't think you've met Bev, ⁴_____ you?
I ⁵_____ (know) her since we were at university
together. She's the one that ⁶_____ (try) to
get a job in Africa since she ⁷_____ (graduate)
last year. Without success, I'm afraid.
    Anyway, we are having a great time. The weather
⁸_____ (be) wonderful for weeks now, so we
⁹_____ (drive) round the countryside. I wonder
¹⁰_____ you are having such good weather in France.
We have visited quite a few of the little villages around
Oxford. I didn't know there ¹¹_____ (be) so many nice
places to see round here. Then, Bev said she ¹²_____
never _____ (be) to Stonehenge, so we went there,
too. ¹³_____ Saturday, Harry ¹⁴_____ (invite) Bev
and me to dinner. He cooked a lovely meal. But I'm a bit
worried about him – he ¹⁵_____ (drink) too
much recently. He ¹⁶_____ (drink) two bottles of wine
¹⁷_____ we were there on Saturday. He said he
¹⁸_____ (be) under a lot of pressure at work since his
promotion. But alcohol won't help, ¹⁹_____ it?
    Bev ²⁰_____ (go back) to London the day
²¹_____ tomorrow. She's asked me ²²_____ go with
her. I'd love to, but unfortunately I haven't got ²³_____
time. I have more visitors arriving ²⁴_____ the end
of the week! I've no ²⁵_____ when I'm next coming to
France, but I hope it won't be too long. Take care.
                                    Love, Mary

Indirect questions

Complete the answers. | 6 |

    Example   Has Pam gone to bed?
              I don't know *if she's gone to bed* .
1 Where does James live?
   I've no idea _____
2 Do you want to go out tonight?
   I'm not sure _____
3 Have I passed the exam?
   I'm sorry. I can't tell you _____
4 How many languages are there in the world?
   I haven't a clue _____
5 Who's that woman over there?
   I can't remember _____
6 Did Ben buy some more sugar?
   I don't know _____

Reported statements and questions

Turn the direct speech into reported speech. | 12 |

    Example
    Jim How are you? Jim asked Sue *how she was.*
    Sue I'm fine, thanks. Sue replied *that she was fine.*

Jim I haven't seen you for ages. What have you been doing?
Jim said _____
and asked her _____

Sue I've been abroad. I spent a year in France.
Sue replied _____
She said _____

Jim What do you think of France?
Jim asked her _____

Sue The people are very friendly and the food is great.
Sue said _____
and that _____

Jim Are you going to stay in this country now?
Jim asked her _____

Sue I'll probably stay for a while. Are you driving back to London today?
Sue said _____
Then she asked Jim _____

Jim Yes I am.
Jim said _____

Sue Can you give me a lift?
Sue asked him _____

© Oxford University Press   Photocopiable

Reported commands

Choose the verb that can be used to report the direct speech. Tick (✔) the correct box.

1 'Would you like to spend the weekend with us?'

They [ ] encouraged / [ ] invited / [ ] told her to spend the weekend with them.

2 'Could you open the window, please?'

She [ ] invited / [ ] ordered / [ ] asked him to open the window.

3 'Go to bed immediately!'

Kate's mother [ ] begged / [ ] asked / [ ] ordered her to go to bed immediately.

4 'Don't forget to post the letter!'

He [ ] asked / [ ] reminded / [ ] warned me to post the letter.

5 'Park the car behind the lorry.'

The instructor [ ] warned / [ ] told / [ ] advised him to park behind the van.

6 'Please, please, turn down the music!'

Dick's sister [ ] begged / [ ] advised / [ ] warned him to turn down the music.

7 'Don't play with matches. They're very dangerous.'

He [ ] encouraged / [ ] reminded / [ ] warned the children not to play with matches.

8 'I'll give you a lift to the station.'

She [ ] refused / [ ] offered / [ ] begged to give him a lift to the station.

9 'I won't lend you any more money.'

Jeff [ ] warned / [ ] offered / [ ] refused to lend me any more money.

10 'Please, don't touch it.'

She [ ] asked / [ ] ordered / [ ] told us not to touch the painting.

[10]

Vocabulary

1 In which order do these events *usually* happen in a relationship? [10]

a [ ] to get engaged   f [ ] to have a baby
b [ ] to have a christening   g [ ] to get married
c [ ] to have a reception   h [ ] to get divorced
d [ ] to go on honeymoon   i [ ] to get pregnant
e [ ] to have maternity leave   j [ ] to fall in love

2 Match a word in **A** with a word in **B** to make compound nouns. [20]

A	B	A	B
driving	paper	easy	loving
shopping	glasses	absent	dressed
traffic	card	grief	hearted
air	licence	hard	minded
birthday	lights	well	natured
motor	agent	self	going
hair	port	light	stricken
wrapping	dresser	good	handed
sun	way	fun	employed
estate	basket	right	working

3 Complete the sentences with compound nouns from Exercise 2.

Example The _traffic lights_ were green, so we drove on.

1 Ben caught the plane at Heathrow _____ .

2 The _____ showed us around the new house.

3 The police officer asked me to show him my _____ .

4 She was _____ when her dog died.

5 I wear _____ to protect my eyes.

6 He saw her putting the chocolate in her _____ .

7 The car was travelling at 120 km/h along the _____ .

8 I need to wrap Cathy's birthday present.
Have you got any _____ ? [8]

Translate

Translate these sentences into your own language. Translate the *ideas*, not word by word. [9]

1 I've been learning English for three years.
2 How long have you known your teacher?
3 She speaks good English, doesn't she?
4 They told me that I had to go home.
5 She told him to do his homework carefully.
6 He said he'd been married before.
7 How long are you here for?
8 I don't know where she lives.
9 I'm sorry, I can't help you.

Total [100]

Progress test 1 Units 1–6

Exercise 1 Tenses

Put the verb in brackets in the correct tense. The tenses used are Present Simple, Present Continuous, Past Simple, Past Continuous, Past Perfect, and *will*. There are also examples of the infinitive.

Example
Yesterday I __went__ (go) to London. I wanted __to do__ (do) some shopping.

Mrs Hay ¹_____ (drive) along a small country road when she ²_____ (see) a man at the side of the road. He ³_____ (wave) and pointing at his car. Mrs Hay ⁴_____ (stop) and

⁵_____ (ask) the man if he was all right.
'My car's broken down,' said the man.

'Where do you want ⁶_____ (go)?' asked Mrs Hay.

'London,' replied the man.

'Well, I ⁷_____ (not go) to London, but I

⁸_____ (give) you a lift to the station, if you like.' On the way to the station they chatted.

⁹_____ you _____ (work) in London?' asked Mrs Hay.

'No, I don't. I ¹⁰_____ (run) my own business in ✗

Oxford. But today I ¹¹_____ (have) lunch with a ✗

friend in London – we always ¹²_____ (have) lunch together on Fridays. I promised

¹³_____ (meet) her at one o'clock.'

'There's a train at 11.30. I don't think you

¹⁴_____ (be) late for your appointment.'
When they arrived at the station, a train

¹⁵_____ (stand) at the platform.

'That's your train,' said Mrs Hay.

'You ¹⁶_____ (catch) it if you're quick.' After the man ¹⁷ _had got out_ (get out) of the car, Mrs Hay

¹⁸_____ (drove away). A few minutes later she realized that she ¹⁹_____ ✗ (make) a mistake: it was the wrong train. She went back to the station, but the train wasn't there: it ²⁰_____ already

_____ (leave)! She went into the station and asked at the information desk where the train was going. 'Edinburgh,' the information clerk told her. 'Where does it stop next?' asked Mrs Hay. 'It's the express service,' the clerk told her. 'It doesn't stop until it gets to Edinburgh.'

[20]

Exercise 2 Auxiliary verbs

Complete the sentences with the correct form of *be*, *do*, or *have* in the positive or negative.

1 That's Peter over there. He _____ wearing a red jacket.

2 '_____ you ever been to Spain?' 'Yes, I went there in 1992.'

3 'Where _____ you live?' 'I live in London.'

4 She's not allowed to drive. She _____ passed her driving test yet.

5 Tea _____ grown in India and China.

6 Who _____ you play tennis with yesterday?

7 When I arrived, they _____ having dinner.

8 She _____ usually go shopping on Saturdays. She prefers to go during the week.

[8]

Exercise 3 Irregular past tenses

What is the past tense of the following irregular verbs?

1 become_____   6 lose _____

2 catch _____   7 think _____

3 fall _____   8 wear _____

4 fly _____   9 write _____

5 grow _____

[9]

© Oxford University Press Photocopiable

Exercise 4 Question formation

Look at the chart.

	Pierre	**Donna and Mike**
Nationality	French	Canadian
Occupation	Teacher	Students
City	Paris	Toronto
Holiday last year	2 weeks in Germany	A month in the USA
Next holiday	3 weeks in Italy	2 weeks in Greece, visiting ancient ruins

Using the information in the chart, write an appropriate question.

Example
Where do Donna and Mike come from?
They come from Canada.

1 _____
   He comes from France.

2 _____
   He lives in Paris.

3 _____
   Germany.

4 _____
   Three weeks.

5 _____
   They're students.

6 _____
   A month.

7 _____
   Because they're very interested in the ancient ruins.

[7]

Exercise 5 Verb patterns

Choose the correct verb form.
1 He invited me *stay / to stay / staying* at his house.
2 I can't stand *cook / to cook / cooking*.
3 Write soon and let me *know / to know / knowing* what your plans are.
4 Joe forgot *post / to post / posting* the letter.
5 I don't mind *cook / to cook / cooking*, as long as I don't have to do the shopping.
6 The climb was very long and tiring, so we often stopped *have / to have / having a rest*.
7 He's a very funny person. He always makes me *laugh / to laugh / laughing*.
8 His mother told Ben *wash / to wash / washing* his hands before the meal.

[8]

Exercise 6 Correct the sentences

There is one mistake in each of the following sentences. Find it and write the corrected sentence below.

1 Where are you born?

   _____

2 On weekdays they're usually getting up at six thirty.

   _____

3 'Where's James?' 'He does the washing up in the kitchen.'

   _____

4 During I was on holiday I read six novels.

   _____

5 I no could swim until I was 12.

   _____

6 You mustn't to take photographs in the theatre.

   _____

7 We didn't allowed to wear jewellery at school.

   _____

8 You mustn't pay in cash. You can also pay by credit card.

   _____

9 Bob's a policeman. He have to wear a uniform.

   _____

10 Student to teacher: 'Must I finish this exercise tonight?'

   _____

11 I don't think you must hitch-hike. It could be dangerous.

   _____

12 'We haven't got any milk left.' 'Haven't we? I'm going to the shops to buy some then.'

   _____

[12]

Exercise 7 Numbers

Match the numbers and words.

1	1934	a	nineteen pounds thirty four
2	19.34%	b	nineteen and three-quarters
3	193.4	c	nineteen point three four percent
4	£19.34	d	nineteen thirty-four
5	19 ¾	e	a hundred and ninety-three point four

[5]

Exercise 8 Word order

Put the words in the correct order.

1 watching while TV I rang was phone the

_____

2 do what you get have time up to ?

_____

3 in we school aren't smoke to allowed

_____

4 she been Russia has to ever ?

_____

5 to our with friends us invited stay them

_____

6 think win I England the don't will match

_____

7 Paris is husband in next my to year going work

_____

8 phone had couldn't she lost him number she his because

_____

8

Exercise 9 Word formation

Write the nouns.

1 discuss _____

2 foreign _____

3 advise _____

4 strange _____

5 behave _____

Write the adjectives.

6 cloud _____

7 fog _____

8 sunshine _____

9 wind _____

10 rain _____

10

Exercise 10 Everyday English

What would you say in these situations?

1 You are in a bar. Offer to buy your friend a drink.

_____

2 You arrive late for a meeting. Apologize and say why you are late.

_____

3 Your brother has just come home from the cinema. Ask him for his opinion of the film.

_____

4 You are on a bus. Politely ask the passenger next to the window to open the window.

_____

5 Somebody asks you, 'What does your teacher look like?' What do you say?

_____

6 You are in a clothes shop. You are looking at some sweaters but you don't want to buy anything. The shop assistant comes up to you and says, 'Can I help you?' What do you reply?

_____

7 You are in a hotel at reception. Ask the receptionist to order you a taxi to go to the station.

_____

7

Exercise 11 Vocabulary

Complete the sentences.

1 'Are you v_____?' 'Yes, I am. I never eat meat.'

2 The English painter, Thomas Gainsborough, painted many p_____ of wealthy people.

3 The air in the city centre is very p_____. You can hardly breathe when the traffic's heavy!

4 Germany has produced many famous c_____, for example Bach, Beethoven, and Brahms.

5 'These vegetables are delicious. Did you get them at the supermarket?' 'No, they're h_____.'

6 I've just finished reading a b_____ of Charles Dickens. He had an interesting life.

6

Score   Total 100

Progress test 2 Units 7–12

Exercise 1 Tenses and verb forms

Put the verb in brackets in the correct tense. Some verbs are passive, and there are also examples of the Second Conditional, indirect questions, infinitives, gerunds, and reported statements and requests.

Example
I _started_ (start) teaching five years ago. I really like _teaching_ (teach) children.

An interview with Sarah Jenkins
Sarah Jenkins is an English teacher. She ¹_____ (work) in a language school in London. She

²_____ (teach) English since she ³_____ (leave) university five years ago. I asked her first if she

⁴_____ (enjoy) teaching English.
'Yes, I do,' she replied. 'It's hard work, but it's very rewarding.'

'⁵_____ you ever _____ (work) abroad?'

'Yes,' replied Sarah, 'I ⁶_____ (spend) two years in Madrid. But the school soon closed and I

⁷_____ (make) redundant. Luckily, some of my students asked me if I ⁸_____ (continue) to teach them privately, so I stayed in Madrid.

'And how long ⁹_____ you _____ (teach) in London?' I asked.
'Since I came back from Madrid, three years ago.'
I then asked Sarah what the most memorable moment of her career was.

'Well, a funny thing ¹⁰_____(happen) while I

¹¹_____(work) at the school in Madrid. I had a student called Gloria. On some days she was the best student in the class. But on other days she performed

really badly. I tried very hard ¹²_____ (help) her, but things got worse. Then, one day, I met Gloria in the street and asked her about her boyfriend.

(The day before she ¹³_____ (tell) me a sad story about him.) She looked surprised and told me that her

name ¹⁴_____ (be) Victoria, not Gloria.

She continued, "My twin sister and I ¹⁵_____ (alternate) in your classes since September – two for the price of one!" After that it was much easier to teach them. At the beginning of each class I simply asked, "Are you Gloria or Victoria today?"'
Finally I asked Sarah about her plans for the future.
'Well, I'm very interested in teaching young children,

so next September I ¹⁶_____ (do) a special training course.'
'And are you going to stay in Britain, or would you like to work abroad again?'

'I ¹⁷_____ (promote) recently. I'm now Director of Studies. So I think I ¹⁸_____ (stay) here for a few more years. Of course, if someone ¹⁹_____ (offer) me a well-paid job in Italy or Greece, I ²⁰_____ (take) it, but that's not very likely!'

| 20 |

Exercise 2 Conditionals

Using the prompts, write a sentence in either the first or the second conditional.

1 'Are you coming to town with me this afternoon?'
 'Perhaps. If I / finish / decorating the living room, I / come / with you.'

 _____

2 'I haven't got any money. If I / have / some money, I / buy / you a drink.'

 _____

3 'I always go to Italy for my holidays. If the weather in Britain / be / better, I / take / my holidays / there.'

 _____

4 'I've got so much work to do!'
 'I'm sorry. I have a lot of work, too. If I / have / more time, I / help / you.'

 _____

5 'I'm a teacher. If I / be / the Minister for Education, I / spend / more money on schools.'

 _____

6 'I've lost my address book.'
 'If I / find it, I / bring it to you.'

 _____

| 6 |

Exercise 3   Passives

Make these active sentences passive.

1   Do they still build ships in Scotland?

   Are _____

2   Do you think aliens will ever visit Earth?

   Do you think Earth_____

3   The Chinese invented printing.

   Printing _____

4   You mustn't take photographs in the museum.

   Photographs_____

5   They have recently discovered oil near the Falkland Islands.

   Oil_____

6   They're planning a big celebration to mark the end of the millennium.

   A big celebration_____

7   The police think that someone might have murdered him.

   The police think he _____

8   They didn't know the bones were human until they had carried out a number of tests.

   They didn't know the bones were human until a number of tests _____

9   In some countries they are going to make soft drugs legal.

   In some countries soft drugs _____

10 If the car is fitted with an alarm, they can't steal it.

   If the car is fitted with an alarm, it _____

   _____

   | 10 |

Exercise 4   Modals

Finish each sentence (b) so that it means the same as sentence (a).

Example
   (a) I'm sure he's not Swedish. He has black hair and brown eyes.
   (b) *He can't be Swedish.* He has black hair and brown eyes.

1 (a) The dog's barking. I'm sure he's hungry.

   (b) The dog's barking. He must _____

2 (a) There's no food in his bowl. I'm certain he hasn't eaten anything since this morning.

   (b) There's no food in his bowl. He can't _____

   _____

3 (a) Sally hasn't got in touch with me. Perhaps she phoned while I was out.

   (b) Sally hasn't got in touch with me. She could ____

   _____

4 (a) Ah, the phone's ringing. Perhaps it's Sally.

   (b) Ah, the phone's ringing. It could _____

   _____

5 (a) Why did the car crash? Perhaps the driver didn't see the red light.

   (b) Why did the car crash? The driver might _____

   _____

6 (a) I'm sure it was Tom I saw at the theatre last night.

   (b) It must _____

7 (a) Why is that man standing at the side of the road? Perhaps he's trying to hitch a lift.

   (b) Why is that man standing at the side of the road?

   He might _____

   | 7 |

Exercise 5   Time expressions

Complete the sentences with *in, at, on, ago, for, since,* or nothing.

1   I left college _____ 1982.

2   What are you doing _____ next Thursday?

3   I like to relax _____ weekends.

4   He came to live here four years _____ .

5   He'd been painting _____ many years before he sold his first picture.

6   Shakespeare was born _____ 23 April, 1564.

7   Spring begins _____ March.

8   We always eat turkey _____ Christmas.

9   _____ you left, there have been many changes.

10 I started my new job _____ last Monday.

   | 10 |

© Oxford University Press   Photocopiable

Exercise 6
Reported statements and questions

Put the direct speech into reported speech.

1 'I always play football on Saturdays,' he said.

_____

2 'We've been waiting since six o'clock,' she said.

_____

3 'Where did you go last night?' she asked me.

_____

4 'Will you stay in a hotel?' I asked him.

_____

5 'I'm really looking forward to the holiday,' he said.

_____

[5]

Exercise 7   Reported commands

Use the verbs to put the direct speech into reported speech. Not all the verbs are used.

| ask | beg | refuse | offer |
| remind | advise | order | invite |

1 'Don't forget to take all your belongings with you,' said the driver to the passengers as they left the coach.

As the passengers left the coach, the driver _____

_____

2 'If I were you, I wouldn't visit the Bronx,' said the travel agent to the young couple.

The travel agent _____

_____

3 'Would you like to stay at my house?' said Peter to James.

Peter _____

4 'I won't eat my vegetables!' said Timmy.

Timmy _____

5 'I'll give you a lift into town,' said Ray to Mary.

Ray _____

[5]

Exercise 8   Correct these sentences

There is one mistake in each of the following sentences. Find it and write the corrected sentence below.

1 How long do you live in London?

_____

2 Yesterday evening I have seen a really good film.

_____

3 I'll phone you as soon as I'll arrive.

_____

4 If I won a million pounds, I'll buy a Rolls Royce.

_____

5 I work in this office since 1992.

_____

6 'I went to Canada last year.' 'So have I.'

_____

7 If you have a headache you ought take an aspirin.

_____

8 'What's the matter?' 'I've just been seeing a road accident.'

_____

9 Could you tell me how much does this cost?

_____

10 She said me that she was hungry.

_____

[10]

Exercise 9 Everyday English

What would you say in these situations?

1 Somebody telephones your house and wants to speak to your son, but he isn't at home. Tell the caller where your son is and offer to take a message.

_____

_____

_____

2 You phone the travel agent to inquire about flights to the USA. The office is closed so you leave a message on the answer phone. Introduce yourself, say why you are phoning, ask the travel agent to call you back, leave your number, and end the call.

_____

_____

_____

3 Your friend says she has a headache. Make helpful suggestions.

_____

_____

_____

4 Your brother rings you and says he's just won £100,000 on the National Lottery. Suggest things he could do with the money.

_____

_____

_____

5 You have arranged to go to the cinema with your friend. But on that day your sister has an accident and is taken to hospital. You want to visit her in the evening and have to cancel the appointment with your friend. What will you say to him?

_____

_____

_____

6 Your friend tells you he has just failed to get a place at university, and that he has to stay at school for another year.

_____

_____

_____

Total 12

Exercise 10 Phrasal verbs

Match a verb from **A** with an adverb/preposition from **B** to complete the sentences. Put the verbs in the correct form.

A	turn	look	bring	take	get
B	over	up	on	after	off

1 Quick! _____ the television – the film's about to start.

2 We _____ from Heathrow Airport at 1 pm and landed in Paris an hour later.

3 My grandparents were very poor. I don't know how they managed to _____ six children.

4 He found it very difficult to _____ his mother's death.

5 We can get a baby-sitter to _____ the children while we're out.

[5]

Exercise 11 Adjectives

Use *un-*, *in-*, or *im-* to make these adjectives negative.

1 tidy _____

2 possible _____

3 sensitive _____

4 patient _____

5 sociable _____

[5]

Exercise 12 Compound nouns

Complete the sentences with a compound noun formed with either *traffic*, *motor* or *driving*.

1 Sorry I'm late. I got stuck in a _____ in the town centre for half an hour.

2 A new _____ has just been built between London and Birmingham.

3 The policewoman stopped the car and asked the driver to show her his _____ .

4 'Are you going to watch the Formula 1 Grand Prix on television?'

   'No. I don't like _____ .'

5 'Why are you angry?'

   'I parked outside the bank. A _____ saw me and gave me a parking ticket! I have to pay a £32 fine!'

[5]

Score

Total [100]

© Oxford University Press Photocopiable

Key to Stop and checks

Stop and check 1 Units 1–3

General revision

1	arrived	17	went
2	ago	18	to buy
3	'm staying	19	was putting
4	works	20	'd forgotten
5	isn't working	21	it
6	haven't asked	22	was
7	think	23	was
8	a	24	was walking
9	'm having	25	met
10	although/but	26	for
11	took	27	saw
12	to	28	was working
13	while	29	's learning
14	'd visited	30	the
15	decided	31	really
16	saw/had seen	32	like

Total 32

Questions

Where were you born?

When did you become an international Grand Master?

How long have you been the world chess champion?

How often do you play chess?

What are you doing now/at the moment?

Total 10

Auxiliary verbs

1	were	5	don't
2	Have	6	Did
3	is	7	are
4	has	8	didn't

Total 8

Vocabulary

Exercise 1

play – the piano, by ear, golf, football

do – aerobics, athletics, you good, your homework, the shopping,

make – a mistake, a phone call, a decision, a statement

go – sightseeing, skiing, home, on holiday, for a jog

have – a meeting, a shower, a holiday, a day off

Total 22

Exercise 2

1 enjoy (others not used with '-ing')

2 palette (others are works of art)

3 composer (others are groups of players)

4 lovely (an adjective; others are adverbs)

5 newspaper (not fiction)

6 good-looking (the only positive one)

7 monastery (others are for all people), or house (others are for a lot of people)

8 make (a full verb; others are auxiliaries)

Total 8

Active or passive?

1	supplies	7	took
2	was started	8	was carried
3	was born	9	has changed
4	was employed	10	are … expanding
5	needed	11	are sent
6	was sent		

Total 11

Translate (self check) **Total 9**

Stop and check 2 Units 4–6

General revision

1	to hear	15	had to
2	Do you have to	16	aren't allowed to
3	like	17	which
4	must	18	are allowed to
5	a	19	couldn't
6	to stay	20	are coming
7	who	21	must
8	view	22	we're going
9	me pay	23	to go round
10	food	24	I'll take
11	sunny	25	where
12	visiting	26	must
13	I'll send	27	know
14	the	28	to see

Total 28

Future forms

1	're going to visit	4	'll be
2	'll stay	5	is going to have
3	're going to rent	6	'll do

Total 6

can, must, and should

1	can't	7	must	13	shouldn't
2	can	8	can't	14	should
3	mustn't	9	should	15	should/must
4	can	10	shouldn't		
5	can	11	should		
6	must	12	mustn't/shouldn't		

Total 15

Vocabulary

Exercise 1

A	B
young	elderly
hard-working	lazy
polluted	clean
disgusting	delicious
punctual	late
serious	humorous
polite	rude
tasty	tasteless
outgoing	reserved
industrial	agricultural
sunny	cloudy
formal	casual
hospitable	unfriendly
freezing	boiling
wealthy	poor
quiet	talkative

Total 15

Exercise 2

A	B
etiquette	bow
shake hands	meeting
employment	part-time
address	postcode
gift-wrap	present
forecast	weather
sightseeing	holiday
receptionist	hotel
buffet car	train
recipe	food
kettle	tea
interests	hobbies
climate	chilly
honeymoon	marriage
code	phone

Total 14

like

1 What's she like?

2 What does he look like?

3 What was the weekend like?

4 What do they like doing?

5 What would you like to do?

6 What does he like doing?

7 What's he like?

Total 7

Translate (self check) **Total 15**

Stop and check 3 Units 7–9

General revision

1 'll be	18 have
2 've been	19 haven't heard
3 has gone	20 was made
4 took	21 's looking for
5 get	22 must
6 'll let	23 may/might
7 when	24 went
8 had	25 has seen
9 'd	26 must
10 haven't seen	27 so
11 haven't … been	28 've applied
12 mind	29 applied
13 rather	30 would
14 absolutely/really	31 got
15 has been	32 yet
16 after	33 when/as soon as
17 forward	

Total 33

Present Perfect: active and passive

1 have spoken
2 have been blocked
3 have been
4 have advised
5 have been found
6 have discovered
7 has been buried
8 have … heard
9 has crashed
10 have been killed

Total 10

Conditionals and time clauses

I'd buy a new house if I won the lottery.

I'll tidy the house before my guests arrive.

I'll call you when dinner is ready.

If you want a ticket, you should phone the theatre as soon as the ticket office opens.

What will he do if he gets the job?

I'm watching TV right now, but I promise I'll help you as soon as this programme finishes.

You'll recognize her when you see her.

Do you have breakfast before you go to work in the morning?

Total 8

Vocabulary

Exercise 1

1 'm looking for a sweater
2 make up my mind
3 try them on
4 bring back the one that he doesn't want
5 give you your money back/back your money
6 took the red one back/back the red one
7 's away
8 's not in/isn't in
9 sort out your problem/your problem out
10 went back

Total 20

Exercise 2

Base	Strong
cold	freezing
funny	hilarious
pretty	beautiful
dirty	filthy
surprised	astonished
frightened	terrified
difficult	impossible
tasty	delicious
clever	brilliant

Total 9

Exercise 3

1 freezing		5 tasty	
2 surprised		6 cold	
3 difficult		7 brilliant	
4 exhausted		8 dirty	

Total 8

Translate (self check) **Total 12**

Stop and check 4 Units 10–12

General revision

1 hear	14 invited
2 have … been doing	15 's been drinking
3 has been staying	16 drank
4 have	17 while
5 've known	18 's been
6 has been trying	19 will
7 graduated	20 is going back
8 has been	21 after
9 've been driving	22 to
10 if	23 the/enough
11 were	24 at
12 had … been	25 idea
13 On	

Total 25

Indirect questions

1 I've no idea where James lives.
2 I'm not sure if I want to go out tonight.
3 I'm sorry. I can't tell you if you've passed the exam.
4 I haven't a clue how many languages there are in the world.
5 I can't remember who that woman over there is.
6 I don't know if Ben bought some more sugar.

Total 6

Reported statements and questions

Jim said (that) he hadn't seen Sue for ages and asked her what she'd been doing.

Sue replied (that) she'd been abroad. She said (that) she'd spent a year in France.

Jim asked her what she thought of France.

Sue said (that) the people were very friendly and (that) the food was great.

Jim asked her if she was going to stay in this country now.

Sue said (that) she'd probably stay for a while. Then she asked Jim if he was driving back to London that day.

Jim said (that) he was.

Sue asked him if he could give her a lift.

Total 12

Reported commands

1 invited		6 begged	
2 asked		7 warned	
3 ordered		8 offered	
4 reminded		9 refused	
5 told		10 asked	

Total 10

Vocabulary

Exercise 1

a – 2	b – 9	c – 4	d – 5	e – 7
f – 8	g – 3	h – 10	i – 6	j – 1

Total 10

Exercise 2

driving-licence	easy-going
shopping basket	absent-minded
traffic lights	grief-stricken
airport	hard-working
birthday card	well-dressed
motorway	self-employed
hairdresser	light-hearted
wrapping paper	good-natured
sunglasses	fun-loving
estate agent	right-handed

Total 20

Exercise 3

1 airport		5 sunglasses	
2 estate agent		6 shopping basket	
3 driving-licence		7 motorway	
4 grief-stricken		8 wrapping paper	

Total 8

Translate (self check) **Total 9**

Key to Progress tests

Exercise 1

1	was driving	11	'm having
2	saw	12	have
3	was waving	13	to meet
4	stopped	14	'll be
5	asked	15	was standing
6	to go	16	'll catch
7	'm not going	17	had got out
8	'll give	18	drove away
9	Do … work	19	had made
10	run	20	had … left

Total 20

Exercise 2

1	's	5	is
2	Have	6	did
3	do	7	were
4	hasn't	8	doesn't

Total 8

Exercise 3

1	became	6	lost
2	caught	7	thought
3	fell	8	wore
4	flew	9	wrote
5	grew		

Total 9

Exercise 4

1 Where does Pierre come from?
2 Where does Pierre live?
3 Where did Pierre go for his holiday last year?
4 How long is Pierre going to spend in Italy?
5 What do Donna and Mike do?
6 How long did Donna and Mike spend in the USA?
7 Why are Donna and Mike going to visit Greece?

Total 7

Exercise 5

1	to stay	5	cooking
2	cooking	6	to have
3	know	7	laugh
4	to post	8	to wash

Total 8

Exercise 6

1 Where were you born?
2 On weekdays they usually get up at six thirty.
3 'Where's James?' 'He's doing the washing up in the kitchen.'
4 While I was on holiday I read six novels.
5 I couldn't swim until I was 12.
6 You mustn't take photographs in the theatre.
7 We weren't allowed to wear jewellery at school.
8 You don't have to pay in cash. You can also pay by credit card.
9 Bob's a policeman. He has to wear a uniform.
10 Student to teacher: 'Do I have to finish this exercise tonight?'
11 I don't think you should hitch-hike. It could be dangerous.
12 'Haven't we? I'll go to the shops to buy some then.'

Total 12

Exercise 7

1 d 2 c 3 e 4 a 5 b

Total 5

Exercise 8

1 While I was watching TV, the phone rang.
2 What time do you have to get up?
3 We aren't allowed to smoke in school.
4 Has she ever been to Russia?
5 Our friends invited us to stay with them.
6 I don't think England will win the match.
7 My husband is going to work in Paris next year.
8 She couldn't phone him because she had lost his number.

Total 8

Exercise 9

1	discussion	6	cloudy
2	foreigner	7	foggy
3	advice	8	sunny
4	stranger	9	windy
5	behaviour	10	rainy

Total 10

Exercise 10

(These are model answers. Variations are possible.)
1 Can I/Let me buy you a drink.
2 Sorry I'm late. I got held up in the traffic.
3 What did you think of the film?
4 Would you mind opening the window, please?
5 She's short with long dark hair.
6 No, I'm just looking, thank you.
7 Could you order me a taxi to go to the station, please?

Total 7

Exercise 11

1 vegetarian
2 portraits
3 polluted
4 composers
5 homegrown
6 biography

Total 6

Test 2 Units 7–12

Exercise 1
1 works
2 has been teaching
3 left
4 enjoyed
5 Have … worked
6 spent
7 was made
8 would continue
9 have … been teaching
10 happened
11 was working
12 to help
13 had told
14 was
15 have been alternating
16 'm doing / 'm going to do
17 was promoted
18 'll stay
19 offered (*or* offers)
20 'd take (*or* 'll take)

Total 20

Exercise 2
1 'If I finish decorating the living room, I'll come with you.'
2 'If I had some money, I'd buy you a drink.'
3 'If the weather in Britain were better, I'd take my holidays there.'
4 'If I had more time, I'd help you.'
5 'If I were the Minister for Education, I'd spend more money on schools.'
6 'If I find it, I'll bring it to you.'

Total 6

Exercise 3
1 Are ships still built in Scotland?
2 Do you think Earth will ever be visited by aliens?
3 Printing was invented by the Chinese.
4 Photographs mustn't be taken in the museum.
5 Oil has recently been discovered near the Falkland Islands.
6 A big celebration is being planned to mark the end of the millennium.
7 The police think that he might have been murdered.
8 They didn't know the bones were human until a number of tests had been carried out.
9 In some countries soft drugs are going to be made legal.
10 If the car is fitted with an alarm, it can't be stolen.

Exercise 4
1 He must be hungry.
2 He can't have eaten anything since this morning.
3 She could have phoned while I was out.
4 It could be Sally now.
5 The driver might not have seen the red light.
6 It must have been Tom I saw at the theatre last night.
7 He might be trying to hitch a lift.

Total 7

Exercise 5
1 in
2 (nothing)
3 at
4 ago
5 for
6 on
7 in
8 at
9 Since
10 (nothing)

Total 10

Exercise 6
1 He said that he always played football on Saturdays.
2 She said that they had been waiting since six o'clock.
3 She asked me where I had gone last night.
4 I asked him whether/if he would stay in a hotel.
5 He said he was really looking forward to the holiday.

Total 5

Exercise 7
1 As the passengers left the coach, the driver reminded them to take all their belongings with them.
2 The travel agent advised the young couple not to visit the Bronx.
3 Peter invited James to stay at his house.
4 Timmy refused to eat his vegetables.
5 Ray offered (to give) Mary a lift to the station.

Total 5

Exercise 8
1 How long have you lived / have you been living in London?
2 Yesterday evening I saw a really good film.
3 I'll phone you as soon as I arrive.
4 If I won a million pounds, I'd buy a Rolls Royce.
5 I have worked in this office since 1992.
6 'I went to Canada last year.'
   'So did I.'

7 If you have a headache you ought to take an aspirin.
8 'What's the matter?'
   'I've just seen a road accident.'
9 Could you tell me how much this costs?
10 She told me that she was hungry.

Total 10

Exercise 9
(These are model answers. Variations are possible.)
1 I'm sorry, he isn't in. He's just gone out to the shops. Can I take a message?
2 Hello my name is Bill Smith. I'm ringing to inquire about flights to the USA. Could you ring me back, please? My phone number is 241605. Thank you. Good-bye.
3 You'd better take an aspirin. And I think you should go and lie down for a while.
4 Why don't you buy a new car? / If I were you, I wouldn't spend it, I'd invest it.
5 I'm terribly sorry, but I'm afraid I can't come to the cinema tonight. Fiona's had an accident and is in hospital, and I really want to visit her this evening.
6 I am sorry. But I'm sure you'll get a place next year.

Total 12

Exercise 10
1 turn on
2 took off
3 bring up
4 get over
5 look after

Total 5

Exercise 11
1 untidy
2 impossible
3 insensitive
4 impatient
5 unsociable

Total 5

Exercise 12
1 traffic jam
2 motorway
3 driving-licence
4 motor racing
5 traffic warden

Total 5

Wordlist

Here is a list of words that appear unit by unit in *New Headway Intermediate*. Photocopy the word list for each unit as you go through the book and give it to your students. It is probably best given towards the end of the unit as an aid to revision.

Encourage them to write in the translation if they feel it is necessary. Most of the new words are here, but if we feel a word isn't very useful or very common, we have omitted it. Some very useful words are repeated if they appear in a later unit; it is a good idea to revise them.

Abbreviations

adj	=	adjective
adv	=	adverb
conj	=	conjunction
det	=	determiner
n	=	noun
pl n	=	plural noun
pp	=	past participle
prep	=	preposition
pron	=	pronoun
(r)	=	an 'r' heard when the word is followed by a vowel sound
v	=	verb

Unit 1

achievement *n* /ə'tʃi:vmənt/
amazing *adj* /ə'meɪzɪŋ/
ancient *adj* /'eɪnʃənt/
assassinate *v* /ə'sæsɪneɪt/
attack *n, v* /ə'tæk/
benefit *n, v* /'benɪfɪt/
break (from work) *n* /breɪk/
builder *n* /'bɪldə(r)/
butterfly *n* /'bʌtəflaɪ/
century *n* /'sentʃəri/
communicate *v* /kə'mju:nɪkeɪt/
computer *n* /kəm'pju:'tə(r)/
contemplate *v* /'kɒntəmpleɪt/
convenient *adj* /kən'vi:niənt/
corn *n* /kɔ:n/
create *v* /kri:'eɪt/
dare *n, v* /deə(r)/
definitely *adv* /'defɪnətli/
depressing *adj* /dɪ'presɪŋ/
destroy *v* /dɪ'strɔɪ/
editor *n* /'edɪtə(r)/
editorial *n* /ˌedɪ'tɔ:riəl/
enable *v* /ɪ'neɪbl/
extend *v* /ɪk'stend/
fail *n* /feɪl/
famine *n* /'fæmɪn/
fax machine *n* /'fæks məˌʃi:n/
fear *n* /fɪə(r)/
feed *v* /fi:d/
fed up (with sb/sth) /ˌfed'ʌp (wɪð ...)/
fill *v* /fɪl/
freedom *n* /'fri:dəm/
giant *adj, n* /'dʒaɪənt/
go out with sb *v* /ˌgəʊ 'aʊt wɪð .../
greed *n* /gri:d/
hang on (= wait; *informal*) *v* /ˌhæŋ 'ɒn/
held up (in the traffic) *pp* /ˌheld 'ʌp/
huge *adj* /hju:dʒ/
humble *adj* /'hʌmbl/
impressed *adj* /ɪm'prest/
impressive *adj* /ɪm'presɪv/
include *v* /ɪn'klu:d/
inconceivable *adj* /ˌɪnkən'si:vəbl/
incredible *adj* /ɪn'kredəbl/
influential *adj* /ˌɪnflu:'enʃl/
invention *n* /ɪn'venʃn/
jog *n, v* /dʒɒg/
keep in touch *v* /ˌki:p ɪn 'tʌtʃ/
knock *n, v* /nɒk/
knowledge *n* /'nɒlɪdʒ/
leap *n, v* /li:p/
leave sb **alone** *v* /ˌli:v ... ə'ləʊn/
lighthouse *n* /'laɪthaʊs/
long for sth *v* /'lɒŋ fə(r) .../
loo (*informal*) *n* /lu:/

mankind *n* /ˌmæn'kaɪnd/
man-made *adj* /ˌmæn'meɪd/
marvellous *adj* /'mɑ:vələs/
medal *n* /'medl/
microchip *n* /'maɪkrəʊtʃɪp/
musical instrument *n* /ˌmju:zɪkl 'ɪnstrəmənt/
noodle *n* /'nu:dl/
obsessed *adj* /əb'sest/
obvious *adj* /'ɒbviəs/
operation *n* /ˌɒpə'reɪʃn/
oversleep *v* /ˌəʊvə'sli:p/
owe (money) *v* /əʊ/
palace *n* /'pælɪs/
pear *n* /peə(r)/
pet *n* /pet/
philosophical *adj* /ˌfɪlə'sɒfɪkl/
play (in a theatre) *n* /pleɪ/
pleasure *n* /'pleʒə(r)/
point (in a discussion) *n* /pɔɪnt/
print *n, v* /prɪnt/
product *n* /'prɒdʌkt/
race (of people) *n* /reɪs/
raw *adj* /rɔ:/
ray (the sun's rays) *n* /reɪ/
reputation *n* /ˌrepjʊ'teɪʃn/
reputable *adj* /'repjʊtəbl/
research *n* /rɪ'sɜ:tʃ/
revolutionize *v* /ˌrevə'lu:ʃənaɪz/
rise *v* /raɪz/
risk *n, v* /rɪsk/
round (of drinks) *n* /raʊnd/
save (a life) *v* /seɪv/
silk *n* /sɪlk/
slightly *adv* /'slaɪtli/
stand for sth *v* /ˌstænd fə(r) '.../
statue *n* /'stætʃu:/
step *n, v* /step/
stone *n* /stəʊn/
sunny *adj* /'sʌni/
surgeon *n* /'sɜ:dʒən/
swimming costume *n* /'swɪmɪŋ ˌkɒstju:m/
take part *v* /ˌteɪk 'pɑ:t/
tomb *n* /tu:m/
tradition *n* /trə'dɪʃn/
unprecedented *adj* /ʌn'presɪdentɪd/
vegan *n* /'vi:gən/
warring *v* /'wɔ:rɪŋ/
washing machine *n* /'wɒʃɪŋ məˌʃi:n/
wing *n* /wɪŋ/
wonder *n* /'wʌndə(r)/
worship *v* /'wɜ:ʃɪp/

Unit 2

accountant *n* /əˈkaʊntənt/
aerobics *pl n* /eəˈrəʊbɪks/
affect *v* /əˈfekt/
annual *adj* /ˈænjʊəl/
antique shop *n* /ænˈtiːk ˌʃɒp/
athletics *pl n* /æθˈletɪks/
average *n* /ˈævərɪdʒ/
beat (of the heart) *v* /biːt/
brilliant (of sunshine) *adj* /ˈbrɪliənt/
bulb (of a flower) *n* /bʌlb/
can't bear sth *v* /ˌkɑːnt ˈbeə(r) .../
caravan *n* /ˈkærəvæn/
collect *v* /kəˈlekt/
common sense *n* /ˌkɒmən ˈsens/
complexion *n* /kəmˈplekʃn/
confess *v* /kənˈfes/
contented *adj* /kənˈtentɪd/
cookery book *n* /ˈkʊkəri ˌbʊk/
court (for tennis) *n* /kɔːt/
cruel *adj* /krʊəl/
daffodil *n* /ˈdæfədɪl/
decade *n* /ˈdekeɪd/
decorate *v* /ˈdekəreɪt/
delight *n* /dɪˈlaɪt/
delighted *adj* /dɪˈlaɪtɪd/
department store *n*
   /dɪˈpɑːtmənt ˌstɔː(r)/
designer *n* /dɪˈzaɪnə(r)/
detached *adj* /dɪˈtætʃt/
devote *v* /dɪˈvəʊt/
disaster *n* /dɪˈzɑːstə(r)/
dive *v* /daɪv/
earn *v* /ɜːn/
earthquake *n* /ˈɜːθkweɪk/
enthusiasm *n* /ɪnˈθjuːziæzəm/
equipment *n* /ɪˈkwɪpmənt/
exercises *pl n* /ˈeksəsaɪzɪz/
expiry date *n* /ɪkˈspaɪəri ˌdeɪt/
extremely *adv* /ɪkˈstriːmli/
fascinated *adj* /ˈfæsɪneɪtɪd/
figure (= number) *n* /ˈfɪgə(r)/
flight *n* /flaɪt/
football pitch *n* /ˈfʊtbɔːl ˌpɪtʃ/
generous *adj* /ˈdʒenərəs/
gloomy *adj* /ˈgluːmi/
goalkeeper *n* /ˈgəʊlkiːpə(r)/
goggles *pl n* /ˈgɒgəlz/
goods *pl n* /gʊdz/
grounds *pl n* /graʊndz/
hire *v* /ˈhaɪə(r)/
historian *n* /hɪˈstɔːriən/
improve *v* /ɪmˈpruːv/
increase *n, v* /ˈɪnkriːs, ɪnˈkriːs/
infect *v* /ɪnˈfekt/
inflation *n* /ɪnˈfleɪʃn/
instructress *n* /ɪnˈstrʌktrɪs/
joy *n* /dʒɔɪ/

keep-fit *n* /ˌkiːpˈfɪt/
kit *n* /kɪt/
knee pad *n* /ˈniː ˌpæd/
leotard *n* /ˈliːətɑːd/
luxurious *adj* /lʌkˈʒʊəriəs/
luxury *n* /ˈlʌkʃəri/
mean *adj* /miːn/
missing *adj* /ˈmɪsɪŋ/
mitten *n* /ˈmɪtn/
monastery *n* /ˈmɒnəstri/
nun *n* /nʌn/
opera *n* /ˈɒprə/
out of work /ˌaʊt əv ˈwɜːk/
particularly *adv* /pəˈtɪkjʊləli/
performance *n* /pəˈfɔːməns/
plain (of food) *adj* /pleɪn/
plainly (speak plainly) *adv* /ˈpleɪnli/
planet *n* /ˈplænɪt/
plant *n, v* /plɑːnt/
plumber *n* /ˈplʌmə(r)/
potter *v* /ˈpɒtə(r)/
prayer *n* /ˈpreə(r)/
protect *v* /prəˈtekt/
provide *v* /prəˈvaɪd/
quite *adv* /kwaɪt/
rather *adv* /ˈrɑːðə(r)/
referee *n* /ˌrefəˈriː/
relative (of a person) *n* /ˈrelətɪv/
relax *v* /rɪˈlæks/
remarkable *adj* /rɪˈmɑːkəbl/
resort (ski resort) *n* /rɪˈzɔːt/
respectable *adj* /rɪˈspektəbl/
ridiculous *adj* /rɪˈdɪkjʊləs/
rucksack *n* /ˈrʌksæk/
rude *adj* /ruːd/
run (run a business) *v* /rʌn/
rush *v* /rʌʃ/
sale *n* /seɪl/
seasonal *adj* /ˈsiːzənl/
semi-final *n* /ˌsemiˈfaɪnl/
series (on TV) *pl n* /ˈsɪəriːz/
severe *adj* /sɪˈvɪə(r)/
shorts *pl n* /ʃɔːts/
show (in a theatre) *n* /ʃəʊ/
silly *adj* /ˈsɪli/
smart *adj* /smɑːt/
solitude *n* /ˈsɒlɪtjuːd/
sore *adj* /sɔː(r)/
steady (of a job) *adj* /ˈstedi/
stuck (in a job) *pp* /stʌk/
stuffy *adj* /ˈstʌfi/
suburb *n* /ˈsʌbɜːb/
sweet (of a person) *adj* /swiːt/
tell a lie *v* /ˌtel ə ˈlaɪ/
tender (of meat) *n* /ˈtendə(r)/
throat *n* /θrəʊt/
tidy *adj, v* /ˈtaɪdi/

tolerant *adj* /ˈtɒlərənt/
tool *n* /tuːl/
top (clothing) *n* /tɒp/
tournament *n* /ˈtɔːnəmənt/
traffic warden *n* /ˈtræfɪk ˌwɔːdn/
train *v* /treɪn/
treasure *n* /ˈtreʒə(r)/
tulip *n* /ˈtjuːlɪp/
ugly *adj* /ˈʌgli/
unemployment *n* /ˌʌnɪmˈplɔɪmənt/
van *n* /væn/
volleyball *n* /ˈvɒlibɔːl/
weapon *n* /ˈwepən/
wedding anniversary *n*
   /ˈwedɪŋ ænɪˌvɜːsri/
wisdom *n* /ˈwɪzdəm/
work of art *n* /ˌwɜːk əv ˈɑːt/
wrinkled *adj* /ˈrɪŋkəld/

Unit 3

abandon *v* /ə'bændən/
absolutely *adv* /ˌæbsə'lu:tli/
accidentally *adv* /ˌæksɪ'dentli/
act (of a play) *n* /ækt/
affair *n* /ə'feə(r)/
amateur *adj, n* /'æmətə(r)/
amazement *n* /ə'meɪzmənt/
apologize *v* /ə'pɒlədʒaɪz/
archaeologist *n* /ˌɑ:kɪ'ɒlədʒɪst/
bald *adj* /bɔ:ld/
band (of musicians) *n* /bænd/
bandage *n* /'bændɪdʒ/
banjo *n* /'bændʒəʊ/
battered *adj* /'bætəd/
bent *adj* /bent/
biography *n* /baɪ'ɒgrəfi/
bitter (of feeling) *adj* /'bɪtə(r)/
blood *n* /blʌd/
blues (music) *n* /blu:z/
boarding school *n* /'bɔ:dɪŋ ˌsku:l/
branch (of a tree) *n* /brɑ:ntʃ/
break (rules) *v* /breɪk/
breathe *v* /bri:ð/
brush *n* /brʌʃ/
bugle *n* /'bju:gl/
bury *v* /'beri/
bustling *adj* /'bʌslɪŋ/
career *n* /kə'rɪə(r)/
castle *n* /'kɑ:sl/
chapter *n* /'tʃæptə(r)/
cheek (on your face) *n* /tʃi:k/
childhood *n* /'tʃaɪldhʊd/
chimney *n* /'tʃɪmni/
compose *v* /kəm'pəʊz/
composer *n* /kəm'pəʊzə(r)/
curly *adj* /'kɜ:li/
deposit *n* /dɪ'pɒzɪt/
desperately *adv* /'desprətli/
despite *prep* /dɪ'spaɪt/
determined *adj* /dɪ'tɜ:mɪnd/
diamond *n* /'daɪəmənd/
dig *v* /dɪg/
disappear *v* /ˌdɪsə'pɪə(r)/
disappoint *v* /ˌdɪsə'pɔɪnt/
dote on sb *v* /'dəʊt ɒn .../
draw (a picture) *v* /drɔ:/
drawing *n* /'drɔ:ɪŋ/
drive (in front of a building) *n* /draɪv/
driving test *n* /'draɪvɪŋ ˌtest/
elderly *adj* /'eldəli/
eventually *adv* /ɪ'ventʃʊəli/
excavation *n* /ˌekskə'veɪʃn/
exceptional *adj* /ɪk'sepʃənl/
fable *n* /'feɪbl/
feature (of a face) *n* /'fi:tʃə(r)/
fiction *n* /'fɪkʃn/
fist *n* /fɪst/

flow *v* /fləʊ/
foolish *adj* /'fu:lɪʃ/
forest *n* /'fɒrɪst/
fortune *n* /'fɔ:tʃu:n/
freezing *adj* /'fri:zɪŋ/
furious *adj* /'fjʊəriəs/
gambler *n* /'gæmblə(r)/
gangster *n* /'gæŋstə(r)/
genius *n* /'dʒi:niəs/
go hunting *v* /ˌgəʊ 'hʌntɪŋ/
go missing *v* /'gəʊ 'mɪsɪŋ/
grief-stricken *adj* /'gri:fˌstrɪkən/
heal *v* /hi:l/
heart failure *n* /'hɑ:t ˌfeɪljə(r)/
hit (= success) *n* /hɪt/
homesick *adj* /'həʊmsɪk/
horror movie *n* /'hɒrə ˌmu:vi/
hum *v* /hʌm/
hysterically *adv* /hɪ'sterɪkli/
in the distance /ˌɪn ðə 'dɪstəns/
influenza *n* /ˌɪnflu'enzə/
ironing *n* /'aɪənɪŋ/
knight *n* /naɪt/
laugh *v* /lɑ:f/
lead *v* /li:d/
lifelike *adj* /'laɪflaɪk/
limelight *n* /'laɪmlaɪt/
lord *n* /lɔ:d/
magnificent *adj* /mæg'nɪfɪsənt/
mansion *n* /'mænʃn/
masterpiece *n* /'mɑ:stəpi:s/
match (in sport) *n* /mætʃ/
merrily *adv* /'merəli/
moral *n* /'mɒrəl/
mysterious *adj* /mɪ'stɪəriəs/
necklace *n* /'nekləs/
negro *n* /'ni:grəʊ/
neighbourhood *n* /'neɪbəhʊd/
nervous breakdown *n*
  /ˌnɜ:vəs 'breɪkdaʊn/
oak tree *n* /'əʊk ˌtri:/
oil painting *n* /'ɔɪl ˌpeɪntɪŋ/
only (child) *adj* /'əʊnli/
onwards *adv* /'ɒnwədz/
orchestra *n* /'ɔ:kɪstrə/
outnumber *v* /aʊt'nʌmbə(r)/
painfully *adv* /'peɪnfəli/
part (in a play) *n* /pɑ:t/
peacefully *adj* /'pi:sfəli/
pianist *n* /'pɪənɪst/
pigeon *n* /'pɪdʒɪn/
poison *v, n* /'pɔɪzn/
pop group *n* /'pɒp ˌgru:p/
popularity *n* /ˌpɒpjʊ'lærəti/
portrait *n* /'pɔ:treɪt/
puncture *n* /'pʌnktʃə(r)/
record *v* /rɪ'kɔ:d/

refuse *v* /rɪ'fju:z/
release sb *v* /rɪ'li:s .../
report (in writing) *n* /rɪ'pɔ:t/
rough (area) *adj* /rʌf/
score (a goal) *v* /skɔ:(r)/
sculpture *n* /'skʌlptʃə(r)/
sensitive *adj* /'sensətɪv/
set off (on a journey) *v* /ˌset 'ɒf/
settle (a fight) *v* /'setl/
sketch *n* /sketʃ/
skill *n* /skɪl/
slave *n* /sleɪv/
spill *v* /spɪl/
spinster *n* /'spɪnstə(r)/
spoilt (child) *pp* /spɔɪlt/
spot (= see) *v* /spɒt/
star *v* /stɑ:(r)/
steamy *adj* /'sti:mi/
stink *n, v* /stɪŋk/
subsequent *adj* /'sʌbsɪkwənt/
suffer *v* /'sʌfə(r)/
sunbathe *v* /'sʌnbeɪð/
sway *v* /sweɪ/
talent *n* /'tælənt/
tap (your feet) *v* /tæp/
terrified *adj* /'terɪfaɪd/
thoroughly *adv* /'θʌrəli/
torn *adj* /tɔ:n/
tough (area) *adj* /tʌf/
treasure *n* /'treʒə(r)/
triangle *n* /'traɪæŋgl/
truly *adv* /'tru:li/
tune *n, v* /tʃu:n/
ultimately *n* /'ʌltɪmətli/
unbelievable *adj* /ˌʌnbɪ'li:vəbl/
undisputed *adj* /ˌʌndɪ'spju:tɪd/
unique *adj* /jʊ'ni:k/
unless *conj* /ʌn'les/
upset *adj* /ʌp'set/
vine *n* /vaɪn/
vineyard *n* /'vɪnjəd/
wake *v* /weɪk/
wave (in the sea) *n* /weɪv/
wealthy *adj* /'welθi/
wig *n* /wɪg/
wound *n* /wu:nd/
wrist *n* /rɪst/

Unit 4

admission *n* /əd'mɪʃn/
allow *v* /ə'laʊ/
anchovy *n* /'æntʃəvi/
arrange *v* /ə'reɪndʒ/
arrangement *n* /ə'reɪndʒmənt/
assume *v* /ə'sjuːm/
backpack *v* /'bækpæk/
bang on time /ˌbæŋ ɒn 'taɪm/
behave *v* /bɪ'heɪv/
blow your nose *v* /ˌbləʊ jə 'nəʊz/
bother *v* /'bɒðə(r)/
bow (of your body) *n, v* /baʊ/
browser *n* /'braʊzə(r)/
business card *n* /'bɪznəs ˌkɑːd/
campaign *n* /kæm'peɪn/
casual *adj* /'kæʒuəl/
casually *adv* /'kæʒuəli/
chalk *n* /tʃɔːk/
chew (gum) *v* /tʃuː/
choose *v* /tʃuːz/
clasp (hands) *v* /klɑːsp/
cleanliness *n* /'klenlɪnɪs/
cloth *n* /klɒθ/
code (of the phone) *n* /kəʊd/
colleague *n* /'kɒliːg/
confirm *v* /kən'fɜːm/
cool (of people) *adj* /kuːl/
corresponding *adj* /ˌkɒrɪ'spɒndɪŋ/
cry (= make a noise) *v* /kraɪ/
custom (= habit) *n* /'kʌstəm/
date of birth *n* /ˌdeɪt əv 'bɜːθ/
deal (in business) *n* /diːl/
deal with sb/sth *v* /'diːl wɪð .../
detention *n* /dɪ'tenʃn/
drop sb (somewhere) *v* /drɒp/
easy-going *adj* /ˌiːzi'gəʊɪŋ/
emotional *adj* /ɪ'məʊʃənl/
employee *n* /ˌemplɔɪ'iː/
employer *n* /ɪm'plɔɪə(r)/
engaged (on the phone) *adj*
 /ɪn'geɪdʒd/
entertain *v* /ˌentə'teɪn/
enthusiastic *adj* /ɪnˌθjuːzi'æstɪk/
essential *adj* /ɪ'senʃl/
establish *v* /ɪ'stæblɪʃ/
etiquette *n* /'etɪket/
exchange *v* /ɪks'tʃeɪndʒ/
executive *n* /ɪg'zekjʊtɪv/
expect *v* /ɪk'spekt/
extension (of a phone) *n* /ɪk'stenʃn/
fill in (a form) *v* /'fɪl ɪn .../
formal *adj* /'fɔːml/
fun-loving *adj* /'fʌnˌlʌvɪŋ/
gift-wrap *v* /'gɪftˌræp/
global *adj* /'gləʊbl/
greet sb *v* /griːt/
guidebook *n* /'gaɪdbʊk/

hand *v* /hænd/
hard-working *adj* /ˌhɑːd'wɜːkɪŋ/
have enough of sb/sth
 /ˌhæv ɪ'nʌf əv .../
headmaster *n* /hed'mɑːstə(r)/
heel *n* /hiːl/
height *n* /haɪt/
hold (= wait on the phone) *v* /həʊld/
hospitable *adj* /hɒ'spɪtəbl/
housework *n* /'haʊswɜːk/
humorous *adj* /'hjuːmərəs/
impersonal *adj* /ɪm'pɜːsənl/
income *n* /'ɪnkʌm/
insult *n, v* /'ɪnsʌlt, ɪn'sʌlt/
interrupt *v* /ˌɪntə'rʌpt/
knit *v* /nɪt/
lazy *adj* /'leɪzi/
length *n* /leŋθ/
lift (= ride in a car) *n* /lɪft/
light-hearted *adj* /ˌlaɪt'hɑːtɪd/
link *n* /lɪŋk/
loads of things (= lots of things) *n*
 /'ləʊdz əv ˌθɪŋz/
manners (= behaviour) *n* /'mænəz/
marital status *n* /ˌmærɪtl 'steɪtəs/
mark of respect *n*
 /ˌmɑːk əv rɪ'spekt/
matter (e.g. business matters) *n*
 /'mætə(r)/
modest *adj* /'mɒdɪst/
mussel *n* /'mʌsl/
nappy *n* /'næpɪ/
nationalistic *adj* /ˌnæʃnə'lɪstɪk/
note (of money) *n* /nəʊt/
notice-board *n* /'nəʊtɪsˌbɔːd/
occupation *n* /ˌɒkjʊ'peɪʃn/
offensive *adj* /ə'fensɪv/
outgoing *adj* /'aʊtgəʊɪŋ/
pint (of beer) *n* /paɪnt/
postcode *n* /'pəʊskəʊd/
pudding *n* /'pʊdɪŋ/
punctual *adj* /'pʌntʃuəl/
punishment *n* /'pʌnɪʃmənt/
put sb up (for the night) *v*
 /ˌpʊt ... 'ʌp/
rainy season *n* /'reɪni ˌsiːzn/
realize *v* /'riːəlaɪz/
register *v* /'redʒɪstə(r)/
regularly *adv* /'regjʊləli/
reserved *adj* /rɪ'zɜːvd/
respectful *adj* /rɪ'spektfl/
responsibility *n* /rɪˌspɒnsə'bɪləti/
retired *adj* /rɪ'taɪəd/
roll *v* /rəʊl/
romantic *adj* /rəʊ'mæntɪk/
rule *n* /ruːl/
rush *v* /rʌʃ/

search *n* /sɜːtʃ/
seat-belt *n* /'siːtbelt/
self-employed *adj* /ˌselfɪm'plɔɪd/
seniority *n* /ˌsiːni'ɒrəti/
serious *adj* /'sɪəriəs/
set (the table) *v* /set/
shake hands *v* /ˌʃeɪk 'hændz/
show off (= boast) *v* /ˌʃəʊ 'ɒf/
sign (your name) *v* /saɪn/
signal *v* /'sɪgnəl/
signature *n* /'sɪgnətʃə(r)/
skate-boarding *n* /'skeɪtˌbɔːdɪŋ/
slate *n* /sleɪt/
sleeve *n* /sliːv/
sociable *adj* /'səʊʃəbl/
sole (of your foot) *n* /səʊl/
sophisticated *adj* /sə'fɪstɪkeɪtɪd/
spray *n, v* /spreɪ/
status *n* /'steɪtəs/
stereotype *n* /'steriətaɪp/
strict *adj* /strɪkt/
stuff (= things in general) *n* /stʌf/
stuffy (of a room) *adj* /'stʌfi/
suncream *n* /'sʌnkriːm/
talkative *adj* /'tɔːkətɪv/
terrified *adj* /'terɪfaɪd/
thereafter *adv* /ðeə'rɑːftə(r)/
tidy *adj, v* /'taɪdi/
tip (= suggestion) *n* /tɪp/
tolerant *adj* /'tɒlərənt/
travellers' cheque *n* /'trævləz ˌtʃek/
universal *adj* /ˌjuːnɪ'vɜːsl/
valuable *n* /'væljʊəbl/
water (plants) *v* /'wɔːtə(r)/
welcome *v* /'welkəm/
well-dressed *adj* /ˌwel'drest/
widespread *adj* /'waɪdspred/
widowed *adj* /'wɪdəʊd/
wink *n, v* /wɪŋk/
yawn *n, v* /jɔːn/

Unit 5

accommodation *n* /əˌkɒməˈdeɪʃn/
agriculture *n* /ˈægrɪkʌltʃə(r)/
arable farm *n* /ˈærəbl ˌfɑːm/
arrange *v* /əˈreɪndʒ/
available *adj* /əˈveɪləbl/
avocado *n* /ˌævəˈkɑːdəʊ/
backbone *n* /ˈbækbəʊn/
baker's *n* /ˈbeɪkəz/
balcony *n* /ˈbælkəni/
boiling *adj* /ˈbɔɪlɪŋ/
cancel *v* /ˈkænsl/
caviar *n* /ˈkæviɑ.(ɪ)/
cereal *n* /ˈsɪəriəl/
chambermaid *n* /ˈtʃeɪmbəmeɪd/
characterize *v* /ˈkærɪktəraɪz/
chilly *adj* /ˈtʃɪli/
climate *n* /ˈklaɪmət/
cloud *n* /klaʊd/
cloudy *adj* /ˈklaʊdi/
coastline *n* /ˈkəʊstlaɪn/
collect *v* /kəˈlekt/
come across sb/sth (= find) *v*
  /ˈkʌm əˌkrɒs .../
confirm *v* /kənˈfɜːm/
consider *v* /kənˈsɪdə(r)/
crop *n* /krɒp/
crossing (in a boat) *n* /ˈkrɒsɪŋ/
crystal *n* /ˈkrɪstl/
cuckoo *n* /ˈkʊkuː/
dark *n* /dɑːk/
definitely *adv* /ˈdefɪnətli/
degree (of temperature) *n* /dɪˈgriː/
descent *n* /dɪˈsent/
dramatic *adj* /drəˈmætɪk/
edge *n* /edʒ/
effect *n* /ɪˈfekt/
en-suite (in a bedroom) *n* /ˌɑːnˈswiːt/
enquiry *n* /ɪnˈkwaɪəri/
exhausted *adj* /ɪgˈzɔːstɪd/
exhilarated *adj* /ɪgˈzɪləreɪtɪd/
experience *n* /ɪkˈspɪəriens/
face *v* /feɪs/
factory *n* /ˈfæktri/
fashion *n* /ˈfæʃn/
felt-tip pen *n* /ˌfeltɪp ˈpen/
ferry *n* /ˈferi/
field *n* /fiːld/
fog *n* /fɒg/
foggy *adj* /ˈfɒgi/
forecast *n* /ˈfɔːkɑːst/
fortnight *n* /ˈfɔːtnaɪt/
freezing *adj* /ˈfriːzɪŋ/
front (of weather) *n* /frʌnt/
frustrating *adj* /frʌˈstreɪtɪŋ/
gallery *n* /ˈgæləri/
gentle *adj* /ˈdʒentl/
goose bumps (USA) *n* /ˈguːs ˌbʌmps/

grateful *adj* /ˈgreɪtfl/
guest *n* /gest/
hair-cut *n* /ˈheəkʌt/
half way /ˌhɑːf ˈweɪ/
hang on (= wait) *v* /ˌhæŋ ˈɒn/
heavy (of rain) *adj* /ˈhevi/
heavy industry *n* /ˌhevi ˈɪndəstri/
hill *n* /hɪl/
honeymoon *n* /ˈhʌnimuːn/
hop in (a car) *v* /hɒp ˈɪn .../
hurry *v* /ˈhʌri/
include *v* /ɪnˈkluːd/
inhabit *v* /ɪnˈhæbɪt/
itinerary *n* /aɪˈtɪnəri/
joint (of meat) *n* /dʒɔɪnt/
lace *n* /leɪs/
land (a plane) *v* /lænd/
leather *n* /ˈleðə(r)/
left (there's no sugar left) *adv* /left/
lightning *n* /ˈlaɪtnɪŋ/
loaf *n* /ləʊf/
lowlands *pl n* /ˈləʊləndz/
mainly *n* /ˈmeɪnli/
materialistic *adj* /məˌtɪəriəˈlɪstɪk/
melon *n* /ˈmelən/
message *n* /ˈmesɪdʒ/
millionaire *n* /ˌmɪliəˈneə(r)/
mining *n* /ˈmaɪnɪŋ/
minus *prep* /ˈmaɪnəs/
mist *n* /mɪst/
misty *adj* /ˈmɪsti/
moor *n* /mɔː(r)/
navigate *v* /ˈnævɪgeɪt/
pack *v* /pæk/
penguin *n* /ˈpengwɪn/
petrol *n* /ˈpetrəl/
pleasure *n* /ˈpleʒə(r)/
pony *n* /ˈpəʊni/
poor *adj* /pʊə(r)/
populated *adj* /ˈpɒpjʊleɪtɪd/
preferably *adv* /ˈprefrəbli/
qualification *n* /ˌkwɒlɪfɪˈkeɪʃn/
range (of mountains) *n* /reɪndʒ/
recent *adj* /ˈriːsənt/
reception (after a marriage) *n* /rɪˈsepʃn/
recommend *v* /ˌrekəˈmend/
remind *v* /rɪˈmaɪnd/
removal man *n* /rɪˈmuːvl ˌmæn/
require *v* /rɪˈkwaɪə(r)/
revise *v* /rɪˈvaɪz/
revision *n* /rɪˈvɪʒn/
rough *adj* /rʌf/
shampoo *n* /ʃæmˈpuː/
shower *n* /ˈʃaʊə(r)/
showery *adj* /ˈʃaʊəri/
sidewalk (USA) *n* /ˈsaɪdwɔːk/

sightseeing *n* /ˈsaɪtsiːɪŋ/
situated (be situated) *v* /ˈsɪtjʊeɪtɪd/
smooth (sea) *adj* /smuːð/
souvenir *n* /ˌsuːvəˈnɪə(r)/
spot (= place) *n* /spɒt/
statue *n* /ˈstætʃuː/
storm *n* /stɔːm/
stormy *adj* /ˈstɔːmi/
straight away *adv* /ˌstreɪt əˈweɪ/
stress *n* /stres/
temperature *n* /ˈtemprətʃə(r)/
thunder *n* /ˈθʌndə(r)/
tip (= money) *n* /tɪp/
top *n* /tɒp/
towel *n* /ˈtaʊəl/
tower *n* /ˈtaʊə(r)/
twin room *n* /ˈtwɪn ˌrʊm/
vacation (USA) *n* /veɪˈkeɪʃn/
valley *n* /ˈvæli/
vast *adj* /vɑːst/
view *n* /vjuː/
wheat *n* /wiːt/
wild (animal) *adj* /waɪld/
wooden *adj* /ˈwʊdn/
wrap up (warm) *v* /ˌræp ˈʌp/
zoo *n* /zuː/

Unit 6

absorb *v* /əbˈzɔːb/
accent *n* /ˈæksənt/
accept *v* /əkˈsept/
agree *v* /əˈgriː/
agricultural *adj* /ˌægrɪˈkʌltʃərəl/
anonymous *adj* /əˈnɒnɪməs/
area *n* /ˈeəriə/
article *n* /ˈɑːtɪkl/
attitude *n* /ˈætɪtjuːd/
back door *n* /ˌbæk ˈdɔː(r)/
backwards *adv* /ˈbækwədz/
bank account *n* /ˈbæŋk əˌkaʊnt/
bizarre *adj* /bɪˈzɑː(r)/
boil (food) *v* /bɔɪl/
boom (succeed in business) *v* /buːm/
build (of a body) *n* /bɪld/
by the way /ˌbaɪ ðə ˈweɪ/
call in *v* /kɔːl ˈɪn/
can't stand sb/sth *v*
   /kɑːnt ˈstænd .../
charming *adj* /ˈtʃɑːmɪŋ/
comforting *adj* /ˈkʌmfətɪŋ/
common (in common) /ˈkɒmən/
compare *v* /kəmˈpeə(r)//
complicated *adj* /ˈkɒmplɪkeɪtɪd/
conclusion *n* /kənˈkluːʒn/
confidence *n* /ˈkɒnfɪdəns/
consist *v* /kənˈsɪst/
cosmopolitan *adj* /ˌkɒzməˈpɒlɪtən/
cough *n*, *v* /kɒf/
courgette *n* /kʊəˈʒet/
cross (= angry) *adj* /krɒs/
cry (have tears) *v* /kraɪ/
cute *adj* /kjuːt/
damage *v* /ˈdæmɪdʒ/
directly *adv* /dɪˈrektli/
disguise *v* /dɪsˈgaɪz/
disgusting *adj* /dɪsˈgʌstɪŋ/
dish *n* /dɪʃ/
display *v* /dɪˈspleɪ/
drive sb mad *v* /ˌdraɪv ... ˈmæd/
dry clean *v* /ˌdraɪ ˈkliːn/
enthusiastic *adj* /ˌɪnθjuːziˈæstɪk/
even *adv* /ˈiːvn/
event *n* /ɪˈvent/
except *prep* /ɪkˈsept/
exchange *n* /ɪksˈtʃeɪndʒ/
external *adj* /ɪkˈstɜːnl/
fan (= supporter) *n* /fæn/
fancy (not plain) *adj* /ˈfænsi/
fantastic *adj* /fænˈtæstɪk/
fast (food) *adj* /fɑːst/
fat *adj*, *n* /fæt/
fight *n*, *v* /faɪt/
floor (first, second, etc. floor) *n*
   /flɔː(r)/
flu *n* /fluː/

focal point *n* /ˈfəʊkl ˌpɔɪnt/
foreign trade *n* /ˌfɒrən ˈtreɪd/
fresh (food) *adj* /freʃ/
frozen *adj* /ˈfrəʊzn/
gastronomic *adj* /ˌgæstrəˈnɒmɪk/
get on (with sb) *v* /get ˈɒn (wɪð ...)/
get rid of sb/sth *v* /get ˈrɪd əv .../
gravitate *v* /ˈgrævɪteɪt/
health *n* /helθ/
historic *adj* /hɪˈstɒrɪk/
home-grown *adj* /ˌhəʊmˈgrəʊn/
horrendous *adj* /həˈrendəs/
hot (of curry) *adj* /hɒt/
human rights *pl n* /ˌhjuːmən ˈraɪts/
import *n*, *v* /ˈɪmpɔːt, ɪmˈpɔːt/
impression *n* /ɪmˈpreʃn/
incorporate *v* /ɪnˈkɔːpəreɪt/
increasingly *adv* /ɪnˈkriːsɪŋli/
industrial *adj* /ɪnˈdʌstriəl/
inferior *adj* /ɪnˈfɪəriə(r)/
influence *n* /ˈɪnfluəns/
ingredient *n* /ɪnˈgriːdiənt/
inquisitive *adj* /ɪnˈkwɪzətɪv/
inseparable *adj* /ɪnˈseprəbl/
instead of *prep* /ɪnˈsted əv/
invasion *n* /ɪnˈveɪʒn/
keen (of a supporter) *adj* /kiːn/
kettle *n* /ˈketl/
landscape *n* /ˈlændskeɪp/
legacy *n* /ˈlegəsi/
limitless *adj* /ˈlɪmɪtləs/
look forward (to sth) *v*
   /ˌlʊk ˈfɔːwəd .../
loss *n* /lɒs/
mad (about sth) *adj* /mæd/
major *adj* /ˈmeɪdʒə(r)/
manage *v* /ˈmænɪdʒ/
management *n* /ˈmænɪdʒmənt/
mashed (potatoes) *adj* /mæʃt/
ministry *n* /ˈmɪnəstri/
mug *n* /mʌg/
neither (of them) *det* /ˈnaɪðə(r)/
notice-board *n* /ˈnəʊtɪsˌbɔːd/
nowadays *adv* /ˈnaʊədeɪz/
obviously *adv* /ˈɒbviəsli/
occasion *n* /əˈkeɪʒən/
old-fashioned *adj* /ˌəʊldˈfæʃənd/
olive oil *n* /ˌɒlɪv ˈɔɪl/
overcrowded *adj* /ˌəʊvəˈkraʊdɪd/
owner *n* /ˈəʊnə(r)/
particularly *adv* /pəˈtɪkjʊləli/
passion *n* /ˈpæʃn/
path *n* /pɑːθ/
pie *n* /paɪ/
plain (food) *adj* /pleɪn/
plan (of a room) *n* /plæn/
plant (= flower) *n* /plɑːnt/

plenty (of time) *n* /ˈplenti/
polluted *adj* /pəˈluːtɪd/
preference *n* /ˈprefrəns/
produce *n*, *v* /ˈprɒdjuːs, prəˈdjuːs/
proud *adj* /praʊd/
pulley *n* /ˈpʊli/
queue *n*, *v* /kjuː/
rabbit *n* /ˈræbɪt/
race (= rush) *n*, *v* /reɪs/
ration *n*, *v* /ˈræʃn/
ray (of hope) *n* /reɪ/
recipe *n* /ˈresɪpi/
recover *v* /rɪˈkʌvə(r)/
rectangular *adj* /rekˈtæŋgjʊlə(r)/
replace *v* /rɪˈpleɪs/
reserved *adj* /rɪˈzɜːvd/
respect (in this respect) *n* /rɪˈspekt/
respected *adj* /rɪˈspektɪd/
rich (of food, soil) *adj* /rɪtʃ/
risk *n* /rɪsk/
row (= line) *n* /rəʊ/
rude *adj* /ruːd/
ruin *v* /ˈruːɪn/
rural *adj* /ˈrʊərəl/
sauce *n* /sɔːs/
search *n*, *v* /sɜːtʃ/
seaside *n* /ˈsiːsaɪd/
seldom *adv* /ˈseldəm/
shepherd *n* /ˈʃepəd/
sink *n* /sɪŋk/
size *n* /saɪz/
soil *n* /sɔɪl/
sophisticated *adj* /səˈfɪstɪkeɪtɪd/
spare *v* /speə(r)/
speak your mind *v* /ˌspiːk jɔː ˈmaɪnd/
spoil (food) *v* /spɔɪl/
spontaneous *adj* /spɒnˈteɪniəs/
starving *adj* /ˈstɑːvɪŋ/
steaming (of a hot drink) *adj*
   /ˈstiːmɪŋ/
stranger *n* /ˈstreɪndʒə(r)/
surely *adv* /ˈʃʊəli/
survive *v* /səˈvaɪv/
table manners *n* /ˈteɪbl ˌmænəz/
tasteful *adj* /ˈteɪstfl/
tasteless *adj* /ˈteɪstlɪs/
tasty *adj* /ˈteɪsti/
tie (piece of clothing) *n* /taɪ/
tie *v* /taɪ/
tragedy *n* /ˈtrædʒədi/
tremendously *adv* /trɪˈmendəsli/
troubled *adj* /ˈtrʌbəld/
unusable *adj* /ʌnˈjuːzəbl/
vacant *adj* /ˈveɪkənt/
waste (of time) *n* /weɪst/
whatever *det*, *pron* /wɒtˈevə(r)/

© Oxford University Press   Photocopiable

Unit 7

acceptable *adj* /æk'septəbl/
adore *v* /ə'dɔ:(r)/
advertisement *n* /əd'vɜ:tɪsmənt/
advice *n* /əd'vaɪs/
announce *v* /ə'naʊns/
answer phone *n* /'ɑ:nsə ˌfəʊn/
applicant *n* /'æplɪkənt/
application *n* /ˌæplɪ'keɪʃn/
apply (for a job) *v* /ə'plaɪ (fə ...)/
appreciate *v* /ə'pri:ʃieɪt/
approve *v* /ə'pru:v/
archaeology *n* /ˌɑ:ki'ɒlədʒi/
astronaut *n* /'æstrənɔ:t/
attendant *n* /ə'tendənt/
based (e.g. be based in Geneva) /beɪst/
blanket *n* /'blæŋkɪt/
bring up sth (= mention) *v*
  /ˌbrɪŋ ʌp '.../
bring up children *v* /ˌbrɪŋ ʌp '.../
brown (from the sun) *adj* /braʊn/
cell *n* /sel/
chaos *n* /'keɪɒs/
choice *n* /tʃɔɪs/
choir *n* /'kwaɪə(r)/
chuckle *v* /'tʃʌkl/
coach *n* /kəʊtʃ/
companion *n* /kəm'pænjən/
competition *n* /ˌkɒmpə'tɪʃn/
complain *v* /kəm'pleɪn/
convince (sb of sth) *v* /kən'vɪns .../
cookery *n* /'kʊkəri/
copy *n, v* /'kɒpi/
correspondent *n* /ˌkɒrɪ'spɒndənt/
cousin *n* /'kʌzn/
cover *v* /'kʌvə(r)/
creation *n* /kri'eɪʃn/
cruise *n, v* /kru:z/
CV (= curriculum vitae) *n* /ˌsi: 'vi:/
degree (from a university) *n* /dɪ'gri:/
delighted *adj* /dɪ'laɪtɪd/
disappointed *adj* /ˌdɪsə'pɔɪntɪd/
disaster *n* /dɪ'zɑ:stə(r)/
earthquake *n* /'ɜ:θkweɪk/
elect *v* /ɪ'lekt/
enclose *v* /ɪn'kləʊz/
excuse *n* /ɪk'skju:z/
explorer *n* /ɪk'splɔ:rə(r)/
extension (of a telephone) *n* /ɪk'stenʃn/
fashionable *adj* /'fæʃnəbl/
firmly *adv* /'fɜ:mli/
flood *n* /flʌd/
fluent *adj* /'flu:ənt/
footstep *n* /'fʊtstep/
force sb (to do sth) *v* /'fɔ:s .../
forgive *v* /fə'gɪv/
garden centre *n* /'gɑ:dn ˌsentə(r)/

get back to sb (on the phone) *v*
  /get 'bæk tə .../
get on with sb (e.g. your parents) *v*
  /get 'ɒn wɪð .../
get on with sth (e.g. your work) *v*
  /get ˌɒn wɪð '.../
get sth over (= communicate) *v*
  /ˌget ... 'əʊvə(r)/
get over sth (= recover) *v*
  /ˌget əʊvə(r) '.../
give up (= stop) *v* /gɪv 'ʌp/
go out with sb *v* /gəʊ 'aʊt wɪð .../
grow up *v* /grəʊ 'ʌp/
headline *n* /'hedlaɪn/
heavy (of rain) *adj* /'hevi/
hold (= wait) *v* /həʊld/
indeed *adv* /ɪn'di:d/
interpreter *n* /ɪn'tɜ:prɪtə(r)/
jockey *n* /'dʒɒki/
journalism *n* /'dʒɜ:nəlɪzəm/
judge *n* /dʒʌdʒ/
just in case /ˌdʒʌst ɪn 'keɪs/
kidnap *v* /'kɪdnæp/
lawyer *n* /'lɔ:jə(r)/
line (of a phone) *n* /laɪn/
look after sb/sth *v* /ˌlʊk ɑ:ftə(r) '.../
look like sb *v* /ˌlʊk laɪk '.../
look up (= improve) *v* /ˌlʊk 'ʌp/
look up sth (e.g. a phone number) *v*
  /ˌlʊk 'ʌp .../
make sb redundant *v*
  /ˌmeɪk ... rɪ'dʌndənt/
managing director *n*
  /ˌmænədʒɪŋ dɪ'rektə(r)/
manor *n* /'mænə(r)/
manual labour *n* /ˌmænjʊəl 'leɪbə(r)/
model (person) *n* /'mɒdl/
nanny *n* /'næni/
operation (medical) *n* /ˌɒpə'reɪʃn/
package holiday *n* /ˌpækɪdʒ 'hɒlədeɪ/
part-time *adj* /ˌpɑ:t'taɪm/
pat *n, v* /pæt/
personnel manager *n*
  /ˌpɜ:sə'nel ˌmænədʒə(r)/
persuade *v* /pə'sweɪd/
phase (= period) *n* /feɪz/
pick up (= get better) *v* /ˌpɪk 'ʌp/
pick sth up (= learn) *v* /ˌpɪk ... 'ʌp/
poet *n* /'pəʊɪt/
politics *n* /'pɒlətɪks/
post (= job) *n* /pəʊst/
pretend *v* /prɪ'tend/
priceless *adj* /'praɪsləs/
print (e.g. your name) *v* /prɪnt/
put sb through (on the phone) *v*
  /ˌpʊt ... 'θru:/

put up with sb/sth (= tolerate) *v*
  /ˌpʊt 'ʌp wɪð ... /
regret *n, v* /rɪ'gret/
resign *v* /rɪ'zaɪn/
resignation *n* /ˌrezɪg'neɪʃn/
retire *v* /rɪ'taɪə(r)/
retirement *n* /rɪ'taɪəmənt/
row (= argument) *n, v* /raʊ/
rubbish bin *n* /'rʌbɪʃ ˌbɪn/
run out of sth (e.g. sugar) *v*
  /ˌrʌn 'aʊt əv .../
safe (= well) *adj* /seɪf/
senior citizen *n* /ˌsi:niə 'sɪtəzən/
servant *n* /'sɜ:vənt/
standard *adj* /'stændəd/
successful *adj* /sək'sesfl/
suntan *n* /'sʌntæn/
surgeon *n* /'sɜ:dʒən/
surveyor *n* /sə'veɪə(r)/
take after sb (e.g. your mother) *v*
  /ˌteɪk ɑ:ftə(r) '.../
take off (= become successful) *v*
  /ˌteɪk 'ɒf/
take off (of a plane) *v* /teɪk 'ɒf/
take sth up (e.g. a sport) *v*
  /ˌteɪk ... 'ʌp/
taken aback *adj* /ˌteɪkn ə'bæk/
textile company *n* /'tekstaɪl
  ˌkʌmpəni/
tone (on a phone) *n* /təʊn/
training course *n* /'treɪnɪŋ ˌkɔ:s/
travel courier *n* /'trævl ˌkʊriə(r)/
twice *adv* /twaɪs/
twin *n* /twɪn/
van *n* /væn/
various *adj* /'veəriəs/
warning *n* /'wɔ:nɪŋ/
widely (travel widely) *adv* /'waɪdli/
widow *n* /'wɪdəʊ/
worldwide *adv* /ˌwɜ:ld'waɪd/
wrap *v* /ræp/

Unit 8

actually *adv* /ˈæktʃʊəli/
afford (can't afford) *v* /əˈfɔːd/
after all /ˌɑːftər ˈɔːl/
aid *n* /eɪd/
AIDS (= acquired immune deficiency
    syndrome) *n* /eɪdz/
amazed *adj* /əˈmeɪzd/
amnesty *n* /ˈæmnəsti/
amount *n, v* /əˈmaʊnt/
animal welfare *n* /ˌænɪml ˈwelfeə(r)/
anyway *adv* /ˈeniweɪ/
appreciate *v* /əˈpriːʃieɪt/
as soon as *conj* /əz ˈsuːn əz/
as well /əz ˈwel/
astonished *adj* /əˈstɒnɪʃt/
at least *adv* /ət ˈliːst/
badger *n* /ˈbædʒə(r)/
because of *prep* /bɪˈkɒz əv/
beg *v* /beg/
break the law *v* /ˌbreɪk ðə ˈlɔː/
broke (= having no money; *informal*)
    adj /brəʊk/
bunch (of flowers) *n* /bʌntʃ/
burglar *n* /ˈbɜːglə(r)/
calm *adj, n* /kɑːm/
camp *n* /kæmp/
carry on (= continue) *v* /ˌkæri ˈɒn/
charitable *adj* /ˈtʃærətəbl/
charity *n* /ˈtʃærəti/
circumstance *n* /ˈsɜːkəmstɑːns/
court (of law) *n* /kɔːt/
crop *n* /krɒp/
cruelty *n* /ˈkruːəlti/
delay *v* /dɪˈleɪ/
demand *v* /dɪˈmɑːnd/
deserving *adj* /dɪˈzɜːvɪŋ/
desperate *adj* /ˈdesprət/
diary *n* /ˈdaɪəri/
disease *n* /dɪˈziːz/
donation *n* /dəʊˈneɪʃn/
drought *n* /draʊt/
economic *adj* /ˌekəˈnɒmɪk/
effort *n* /ˈefət/
either (I don't, either) *adv* /ˈaɪðə(r)/
embassy *n* /ˈembəsi/
enormous *adj* /ɪˈnɔːməs/
envy *n, v* /ˈenvi/
especially *adv* /ɪˈspeʃli/
estimate *n, v* /ˈestɪmət, ˈestɪmeɪt/
evaporate *v* /ɪˈvæpəreɪt/
even (even Mary) *adv* /ˈiːvn/
exploit *v* /ɪkˈsplɔɪt/
fair (of a trial) *adj* /feə(r)/
fall in love *v* /ˌfɔːl ɪn ˈlʌv/
famine *n* /ˈfæmɪn/
fantasize *v* /ˈfæntəsaɪz/
fascinating *adj* /ˈfæsəneɪtɪŋ/

fee *n* /fiː/
filthy *adj* /ˈfɪlθi/
fix *v* /fɪks/
fluid *n* /ˈfluːɪd/
fond of sb/sth *adj* /ˈfɒnd əv .../
food poisoning *n* /ˈfuːd ˌpɔɪznɪŋ/
football pools *pl n* /ˈfʊtbɔːl ˌpuːlz/
for example /fər ɪgˈzɑːmpl/
fritter away *v* /ˌfrɪtər əˈweɪ/
game of cards *n* /ˌgeɪm əv ˈkɑːdz/
generally *adv* /ˈdʒenrəli/
generously *adv* /ˈdʒenrəsli/
get hold of sb (= contact) *v*
    /ˌget ˈhəʊld əv .../
get lost *v* /ˌget ˈlɒst/
groceries *pl n* /ˈgrəʊsəriz/
guard *n, v* /gɑːd/
handle *v* /ˈhændl/
hedgehog *n* /ˈhedʒhɒg/
hilarious *adj* /hɪˈleəriəs/
homeless *adj* /ˈhəʊmlɪs/
hospice *n* /ˈhɒspɪs/
humane *adj* /hjuːˈmeɪn/
improbable *adj* /ɪmˈprɒbəbl/
incurable *adj* /ɪnˈkjʊərəbl/
inherit *v* /ɪnˈherɪt/
insist *v* /ɪnˈsɪst/
intensive *adj* /ɪnˈtensɪv/
invest *v* /ɪnˈvest/
investigate *v* /ɪnˈvestɪgeɪt/
jigsaw *n* /ˈdʒɪgsɔː/
join *v* /dʒɔɪn/
kindness *n* /ˈkaɪndnɪs/
laboratory *n* /ləˈbɒrətri/
lawful *adj* /ˈlɔːfl/
leak *n, v* /liːk/
link *v* /lɪŋk/
loan *n* /ləʊn/
lottery *v* /ˈlɒtəri/
mate (= friend; *informal*) *n* /meɪt/
means (= methods) *pl n* /miːnz/
meanwhile *adv* /ˈmiːnwaɪl/
medical supply *n* /ˈmedɪkl səˌplaɪ/
misery *n* /ˈmɪzəri/
mugged (be mugged) *v* /ˈmʌgd/
nearly *adv* /ˈnɪəli/
of course /əv ˈkɔːs/
offer *v* /ˈɒfə(r)/
oil spill *n* /ˈɔɪl ˌspɪl/
on time /ˌɒn ˈtaɪm/
only *adv* /ˈəʊnli/
oppose *v* /əˈpəʊz/
penniless *adj* /ˈpenɪlɪs/
permission *n* /pəˈmɪʃn/
pick up sb/sth (= collect) *v*
    /ˌpɪk ˈʌp .../
possibility *n* /ˌpɒsəˈbɪləti/

pour *v* /pɔː(r)/
prevention *n* /prɪˈvenʃn/
prisoner of conscience *n*
    /ˌprɪznər əv ˈkɒnʃəns/
prize *n* /praɪz/
promote *v* /prəˈməʊt/
psychotherapist *n* /ˌsaɪkəˈθerəpɪst/
publicize *v* /ˈpʌblɪsaɪz/
purpose *n* /ˈpɜːpəs/
put pressure on sb *v*
    /ˌpʊt ˈpreʃər ɒn .../
racehorse *n* /ˈreɪshɔːs/
refugee *n* /ˌrefjʊˈdʒiː/
rehabilitate *v* /ˌriːhəˈbɪlɪteɪt/
release *v* /rɪˈliːs/
research *n, v* /rɪˈsɜːtʃ/
sanity *n* /ˈsænəti/
search *n* /sɜːtʃ/
secret *adj, n* /ˈsiːkrət/
smash *v* /smæʃ/
solve *v* /sɒlv/
spending spree *n* /ˈspendɪŋ ˌspriː/
sponsor *v* /ˈspɒnsə(r)/
sunburnt *adj* /ˈsʌnbɜːnt/
tempt *v* /tempt/
therefore *adv* /ˈðeəfɔː(r)/
treat *v* /triːt/
unfortunately *adv* /ʌnˈfɔːtʃənətli/
unpredictable *adj* /ˌʌnprɪˈdɪktəbl/
verse *n* /vɜːs/
visa *n* /ˈviːzə/
whale *n* /weɪl/
windfall *n* /ˈwɪndfɔːl/
winner *n* /ˈwɪnə(r)/
word processor *n*
    /ˌwɜːd ˈprəʊsesə(r)/
would rather (= prefer) *v*
    /ˌwʊd ˈrɑːðə(r)/

Unit 9

abandoned *v* /ə'bændənd/
acorn *n* /'eɪkɔːn/
air *n* /eə(r)/
ambition *n* /æm'bɪʃn/
ambitious *adj* /æm'bɪʃəs/
annoyed *adj* /ə'nɔɪd/
as a matter of fact
 /əz ə ˌmætər əv 'fækt/
au pair *n* /ˌəʊ 'peə(r)/
background *n* /'bækgraʊnd/
barren *adj* /'bærən/
breeze *n* /briːz/
cheat *n, v* /tʃiːt/
cheerful *adj* /'tʃɪəfl/
clear sth away (e.g. a mess) *v*
 /ˌklɪə(r) ... ə'weɪ/
clearly *adv* /'klɪəli/
coarse (of grass) *adj* /kɔːs/
colleague *n* /'kɒliːg/
colourless *adj* /'kʌləlɪs/
combine *v* /kəm'baɪn/
convince sb of sth *v*
 /kən'vɪns ... əv .../
crutch *n* /krʌtʃ/
curious (= wanting to know) *adj*
 /'kjʊəriəs/
daydream *n, v* /'deɪdriːm/
deal with sth *v* /'diːl wɪð .../
definite *adj* /'defɪnət/
depend on sb *v* /dɪ'pend ɒn .../
destruction *n* /dɪ'strʌkʃn/
discover *v* /dɪ'skʌvə(r)/
disturb *v* /dɪ'stɜːb/
drop (of water) *n* /drɒp/
drop *v* /drɒp/
easy-going *adj* /ˌiːzi'gəʊɪŋ/
effective *adj* /ɪ'fektɪv/
enormously *adv* /ɪ'nɔːməsli/
envy *v* /'envi/
exact *adj* /ɪg'zækt/
explore *v* /ɪk'splɔː(r)/
fade *v* /feɪd/
fertile *adj* /'fɜːtaɪl/
fire engine *n* /'faɪər ˌendʒɪn/
fizzy (of mineral water) *n* /'fɪzi/
forest *n* /'fɒrɪst/
fountain *n* /'faʊntɪn/
good-natured *adj* /ˌgʊd'neɪtʃəd/
grant *v* /grɑːnt/
hard-working *adj* /ˌhɑːd'wɜːkɪŋ/
harsh *adj* /hɑːʃ/
hire *v* /'haɪə(r)/
hopeless *adj* /'həʊplɪs/
housework *n* /'haʊswɜːk/
I bet! (= I'm sure) /ˌaɪ 'bet/
impatient *adj* /ɪm'peɪʃənt/
imperturbably *adv* /ˌɪmpə'tɜːbəbli/

impressive *adj* /ɪm'presɪv/
in spite of *prep* /ɪn 'spaɪt əv/
in the meantime /ˌɪn ðə 'miːntaɪm/
inclined to do sth *adj*
 /ɪnˌklaɪnd tə 'duː: .../
incredible *adj* /ɪn'kredəbl/
inhabitant *n* /ɪn'hæbɪtənt/
insistent *adj* /ɪn'sɪstənt/
inspect *v* /ɪn'spekt/
instead of *prep* /ɪn'sted əv/
keep an eye on sb/sth
 /ˌkiːp ən 'aɪ ɒn .../
laden *adj* /'leɪdn/
lavender *n* /'lævəndə(r)/
lazy *adj* /'leɪzi/
lifestyle *n* /'laɪfstaɪl/
literally *adv* /'lɪtrəli/
magnificent *adj* /mæg'nɪfɪsənt/
memory *n* /'meməri/
mess *n* /mes/
midday *n* /mɪd'deɪ/
mood *n* /muːd/
moody *adj* /'muːdi/
nettle *n* /'netl/
notice *v* /'nəʊtɪs/
nurse *n* /nɜːs/
ocean *n* /'əʊʃn/
only (child) *adj* /'əʊnli/
optimistic *adj* /ˌɒptɪ'mɪstɪk/
outweigh *v* /aʊt'weɪ/
oversleep *v* /ˌəʊvə'sliːp/
part *v* /pɑːt/
peace *n* /piːs/
peacefully *adv* /'piːsfəli/
perfect *adj* /'pɜːfɪkt/
pessimistic *adj* /ˌpesɪ'mɪstɪk/
philosopher *n* /fɪ'lɒsəfə(r)/
plain (= flat land) *n* /pleɪn/
plaster (on a broken leg) *n*
 /'plɑːstə(r)/
pool *n* /puːl/
put off doing sth (= postpone) *v*
 /ˌpʊt ɒf 'duːɪŋ .../
refill *v* /riː'fɪl/
regard *v* /rɪ'gɑːd/
regular *adj* /'regjʊlə(r)/
relationship *n* /rɪ'leɪʃnʃɪp/
reliable *adj* /rɪ'laɪəbl/
remainder *n* /rɪ'meɪndə(r)/
remains *pl n* /rɪ'meɪnz/
remarkable *adj* /rɪ'mɑːkəbl/
resentment *n* /rɪ'zentmənt/
reserved *adj* /rɪ'zɜːvd/
restore *v* /rɪ'stɔː(r)/
resume *v* /rɪ'zjuːm/
reverse *v* /rɪ'vɜːs/
rod *n* /rɒd/

role *n* /rəʊl/
row (in a boat) *v* /rəʊ/
scent *n* /sent/
sensitive *adj* /'sensətɪv/
shoestring (on a shoestring = with
 little or no money) *n* /'ʃuːstrɪŋ/
shy *adj* /ʃaɪ/
sick (= ill) *adj* /sɪk/
sihouette *n* /ˌsɪlʊ'et/
snore *v* /snɔː(r)/
sociable *adj* /'səʊʃəbl/
soldier *n* /'səʊldʒə(r)/
solitary *adj* /'sɒlətri/
soul *n* /səʊl/
spectacle (= sight) *n* /'spektəkl/
speechless *adj* /'spiːtʃlɪs/
sprout *v* /spraʊt/
stressful *adj* /'stresfl/
sunset *n* /'sʌnset/
suntan *n* /'sʌntæn/
talkative *adj* /'tɔːkətɪv/
threaten *v* /'θretn/
thrust *v* /θrʌst/
totally *adv* /'təʊtəli/
tough (= difficult) *adj* /tʌf/
tour operator *n* /'tʊər ˌɒpəreɪtə(r)/
tremendous *adj* /trɪ'mendəs/
trip *n* /trɪp/
turn up (= arrive) *v* /ˌtɜːn 'ʌp/
unemployed *adj* /ˌʌnɪm'plɔɪd/
unreasonable *adj* /ʌn'riːznəbl/
untidy *adj* /ʌn'taɪdi/
ups and downs *pl n* /ˌʌps ən 'daʊnz/
vain *adj* /veɪn/
vision *n* /'vɪʒn/
wasteland *n* /'weɪstlænd/
wilderness *n* /'wɪldənəs/
wish *n, v* /wɪʃ/

Unit 10

admire *v* /əd'maɪə(r)/
advertising *n* /'ædvətaɪzɪŋ/
aggressive *adj* /ə'gresɪv/
air-conditioning *n* /'eə kən,dɪʃnɪŋ/
airmail *n* /'eəmeɪl/
apart from *prep* /ə'pɑːt frəm/
ashtray *n* /'æʃtreɪ/
aspect *n* /æspekt/
attached (= fond of) *adj* /ə'tætʃt/
attack *n* /ə'tæk/
attic *n* /'ætɪk/
authority *n* /ɔː'θɒrəti/
autobiography *n* /,ɔːtəbaɪ'ɒgrəfi/
automatic car *n* /,ɔːtəmætɪk 'kɑː(r)/
award *n* /ə'wɔːd/
ban *v* /bæn/
birthday card *n* /'bɜːθdeɪ ,kɑːd/
bookcase *n* /'bʊkkeɪs/
brake *n* /breɪk/
brand (of cigarette) *n* /brænd/
brochure *n* /'brəʊʃə(r)/
bulk of sth (= majority) *n*
   /'bʌlk əv .../
candlestick *n* /'kændlstɪk/
celebrate *v* /'selɪbreɪt/
chain *n* /tʃeɪn/
chain smoker *n* /'tʃeɪn ,sməʊkə(r)/
chairman *n* /'tʃeəmən/
changing room *n* /'tʃeɪndʒɪŋ ,rʊm/
clutch *n* /klʌtʃ/
coffin *n* /'kɒfɪn/
collapse *v* /kə'læps/
collector *n* /kə'lektə(r)/
constraint *n* /kən'streɪnt/
contemporary *adj* /kən'tempəri/
convention *n* /kən'venʃn/
cool (= sophisticated) *adj* /kuːl/
coronation *n* /,kɒrə'neɪʃn/
credit card *n* /'kredɪt ,kɑːd/
current (= existing now) *adj* /'kʌrənt/
dedicated *adj* /'dedɪkeɪtɪd/
defiance *adj* /dɪ'faɪəns/
driving licence *n* /'draɪvɪŋ ,laɪsəns/
drown *v* /draʊn/
drug *n* /drʌg/
dust *n, v* /dʌst/
dustman *n* /'dʌsmən/
effect *n* /ɪ'fekt/
egg cup *n* /'eg ,kʌp/
encyclopaedia *n* /ɪn'saɪklə'piːdiə/
estate agent *n* /ɪ'steɪt ,eɪdʒənt/
even though *conj* /,iːvn 'ðəʊ/
expense *n* /ɪk'spens/
expose *v* /ɪk'spəʊz/
extend (a house) *v* /ɪk'stend/
fag (= cigarette; *informal*) *n* /fæg/
fault *n* /fɔːlt/

fire (a gun) *v* /'faɪə(r)/
fire engine *n* /'faɪər ,endʒɪn/
fireman *n* /'faɪəmən/
fireplace *n* /'faɪəpleɪs/
fireworks *n* /'faɪəwɜːks/
fondness *n* /'fɒndnɪs/
get-well card *n* /get'wel kɑːd/
giggly *adj* /'gɪgli/
graduate *n, v*
   /'grædʒʊət, 'grædʒʊeɪt/
grey (of hair) *adj* /greɪ/
hairbrush *n* /'heəbrʌʃ/
haircut *n* /'heəkʌt/
hairdresser *n* /'heədresə(r)/
hang-gliding *n* /'hæŋ,glaɪdɪŋ/
headphones *n* /'hedfəʊnz/
hedge *n* /hedʒ/
hypocrisy *n* /hɪ'pɒkrəsi/
illegal *adj* /ɪ'liːgl/
illustrate *v* /'ɪləstreɪt/
image *n* /'ɪmɪdʒ/
instructor *n* /ɪn'strʌktə(r)/
irritated *adj* /'ɪrɪteɪtɪd/
jumble sale *n* /'dʒʌmbl ,seɪl/
killjoy *n* /'kɪldʒɔɪ/
living (= job) *n* /'lɪvɪŋ/
loosely *adv* /'luːsli/
lung *n* /lʌŋ/
manufacture *v* /,mænjʊ'fæktʃə(r)/
market *v* /'mɑːkɪt/
memorabilia *n* /,memərə'biːliə/
merit *n* /'merɪt/
mesmerized *adj* /'mezməraɪzd/
misunderstand *v* /,mɪsʌndə'stænd/
motor racing *n* /'məʊtə ,reɪsɪŋ/
narrow *adj* /'nærəʊ/
network *n* /'netwɜːk/
nicotine *n* /'nɪkətiːn/
notebook *n* /'nəʊtbʊk/
order (= request for goods) *n*
   /'ɔːdə(r)/
packing *n* /'pækɪŋ/
panic *v* /'pænɪk/
postage *n* /'pəʊstɪdʒ/
poster *n* /'pəʊstə(r)/
pray *v* /preɪ/
prematurely *adv* /'premətʃəli/
press conference *n* /'pres ,kɒnfrəns/
proper *adj* /'prɒpə(r)/
prove *v* /pruːv/
puff *v* /pʌf/
puritan *n* /'pjʊərɪtən/
put sth out (e.g. a cigarette) *v*
   /,pʊt ... 'aʊt/
rare *adj* /reə(r)/
read (= study at university) *v* /riːd/
remind *v* /rɪ'maɪnd/

remote *adj* /rɪ'məʊt/
revise (for an exam) *v* /rɪ'vaɪz/
salty *adj* /'sɔːlti/
screen *n* /skriːn/
second-hand *adj* /'sekənd,hænd/
share *n* /ʃeə(r)/
shopping basket *n* /'ʃɒpɪŋ ,bɑːskɪt/
shopping centre *n* /'ʃɒpɪŋ ,sentə(r)/
skid (in a car) *v* /skɪd/
spare (time) *adj* /speə(r)/
specialist *n* /'speʃəlɪst/
split up (of a married couple) *v*
   /,splɪt 'ʌp/
sponsorship *n* /'spɒnsəʃɪp/
statement *n* /'steɪtmənt/
store *v* /stɔː(r)/
swap *v* /swɒp/
sympathy *n* /'sɪmpəθi/
tea-cloth *n* /'tiː,klɒθ/
teapot *n* /'tiːpɒt/
tear (in your eyes) *n* /tɪə(r)/
tear sth up *v* /,teə(r) ... 'ʌp/
tempt *v* /tempt/
toilet paper *n* /'tɔɪlət ,peɪpə(r)/
toothache *n* /'tuːθeɪk/
toothbrush *n* /'tuːθbrʌʃ/
toothpaste *n* /'tuːθpeɪst/
tractor *n* /'træktə(r)/
traffic warden *n* /'træfɪk ,wɔːdn/
trophy *n* /'trəʊfi/
tuition *n* /tjuː'ɪʃn/
vehicle *n* /'viːɪkl/
vending machine *n* /'vendɪŋ mə,ʃiːn/
wallpaper *n* /'wɔːl,peɪpə(r)/
warm *v* /wɔːm/
warning *n* /'wɔːnɪŋ/
wedding *n* /'wedɪŋ/
weigh *v* /weɪ/
weird *adj* /wɪəd/
wrapping paper *n* /'ræpɪŋ ,peɪpə(r)/

Unit 11

absent-minded *adj* /ˌæbsənt'maɪndɪd/
acid rain *n* /ˌæsɪd 'reɪn/
adopt *v* /ə'dɒpt/
appealing *adj* /ə'piːlɪŋ/
army *n* /'ɑːmi/
authoritative *adj* /ɔː'θɒrɪtətɪv/
balloon *n* /bə'luːn/
bench *n* /bentʃ/
bite *v* /baɪt/
blame *v* /bleɪm/
blow *v* /bləʊ/
bother *v* /'bɒðə(r)/
brain *n* /breɪn/
briefcase *n* /'briːfkeɪs/
bucket *n* /'bʌkɪt/
bustle *n* /'bʌsl/
century *n* /'sentʃəri/
chew *v* /tʃuː/
childbirth *n* /'tʃaɪldbɜːθ/
city-dweller *n* /'sɪti ˌdwelə(r)/
clap *v* /klæp/
colony *n* /'kɒləni/
concert *n* /'kɒnsət/
cope *v* /kəʊp/
corridor *n* /'kɒrɪdɔː(r)/
dental floss *n* /'dentl ˌflɒs/
desert *n* /'dezət/
diamond *n* /'daɪəmənd/
distressed *adj* /dɪ'strest/
dolphin *n* /'dɒlfɪn/
duck *n* /dʌk/
evidence *n* /'evɪdens/
evil *n* /'iːvl/
exchange rate *n* /ɪk'stʃeɪndʒ ˌreɪt/
explanation *n* /ˌeksplə'neɪʃn/
fluffy *adj* /'flʌfi/
forgetful *adj* /fə'getfl/
found *v* /faʊnd/
gallows *pl n* /'gæləʊz/
generation *n* /ˌdʒenə'reɪʃn/
give away (money) *v* /ˌgɪv ə'weɪ '.../
graze *n* /greɪz/
gun *n* /gʌn/
guy (= man; *informal*) *n* /gaɪ/
heavyweight champion *n*
   /ˌheviweɪt 'tʃæmpɪən/
hiccup *n* /'hɪkʌp/
historically *adv* /hɪ'stɒrɪkli/
hit *v* /hɪt/
hold *v* /həʊld/
horseshoe *n* /'hɔːsʃuː/
hug *v* /hʌg/
infancy *n* /'ɪnfənsi/
inspector *n* /ɪn'spektə(r)/
kick *v* /kɪk/
kneel *v* /niːl/
knot *n* /nɒt/

ladder *n* /'lædə(r)/
lecture *n* /'lektʃə(r)/
lick *v* /lɪk/
life expectancy *n* /ˌlaɪf ɪk'spektənsi/
lucky *adj* /'lʌki/
march *v* /mɑːtʃ/
monitor *v* /'mɒnɪtə(r)/
nail *n, v* /neɪl/
numerous *adj* /njuːmərəs/
officially *adv* /ə'fɪʃəli/
packed (= crowded) *adj* /pækt/
parcel *n* /'pɑːsl/
pat *v* /pæt/
permanently *adv* /'pɜːmənəntli/
pile (of books) *n* /paɪl/
point *v* /pɔɪnt/
population *n* /ˌpɒpjʊ'leɪʃn/
pros and cons *n* /ˌprəʊz ən 'kɒnz/
recognize *v* /'rekəgnaɪz/
rescue *v* /'reskjuː/
right-handed *adj* /ˌraɪt'hændɪd/
risky *adj* /'rɪski/
rope *n* /rəʊp/
rush hour *n* /'rʌʃ ˌaʊə(r)/
scratch *n, v* /skrætʃ/
shark *n* /ʃɑːk/
shuttle *n* /'ʃʌtl/
silver *n* /'sɪlvə(r)/
slippers *n* /'slɪpəz/
smart (= well-dressed) *adj* /smɑːt/
snail *n* /sneɪl/
space *n* /speɪs/
square *n* /skweə(r)/
stare *v* /steə(r)/
superstition *n* /ˌsuːpə'stɪʃn/
sword *n* /sɔːd/
take over sth (= conquer) *v*
   /ˌteɪk əʊvə(r) '.../
tie *n, v* /taɪ/
tiger *n* /'taɪgə(r)/
toffee *n* /'tɒfi/
tourist attraction *n* /'tɔːrɪst əˌtrækʃn/
tramp *n* /træmp/
trick *n* /trɪk/
tune *n* /tjuːn/
unlucky *adj* /ʌn'lʌki/
vase *n* /vɑːz/
wander *v* /'wɒndə(r)/
wavelength *n* /'weɪvleŋθ/
wax *n* /wæks/
whistle *n, v* /'wɪsl/
witch *n* /wɪtʃ/

Unit 12

accustomed (to sth) *adj* /əˈkʌstəmd (tə ...)/

admit *v* /ədˈmɪt/

advise *v* /ədˈvaɪz/

all-night party *n* /ˌɔːlnaɪt ˈpɑːti/

announcement *n* /əˈnaʊnsmənt/

argue *v* /ˈɑːgjuː/

babysit *v* /ˈbeɪbisɪt/

bang *v* /bæŋ/

best man *n* /ˌbes ˈmæn/

birth *n* /bɜːθ/

bone *n* /bəʊn/

bonnet *n* /ˈbɒnɪt/

bossy *adj* /ˈbɒsi/

bouquet *n* /buˈkeɪ/

bow (tie a bow) *n* /bəʊ/

bow (with your body) *n, v* /baʊ/

bridegroom *n* /ˈbraɪdgrʊm/

bridesmaid *n* /ˈbraɪdzmeɪd/

bury *v* /ˈberi/

cap *n* /kæp/

cemetery *n* /ˈsemətri/

christening *n* /ˈkrɪsnɪŋ/

contradict *v* /ˌkɒntrəˈdɪkt/

cool down *v* /ˌkuːl ˈdaʊn/

cot *n* /kɒt/

cotton *n* /ˈkɒtn/

creature *n* /ˈkriːtʃə(r)/

cut off (on the phone) *v* /ˌkʌt ˈɒf/

deny *v* /dɪˈnaɪ/

dismantle *v* /dɪsˈmæntl/

dotted (of a line) *n* /ˈdɒtɪd/

doubtful *adj* /ˈdaʊtfl/

dove *n* /dʌv/

drum *n* /drʌm/

edge *n* /edʒ/

eventful *adj* /ɪˈventfl/

exclaim *v* /ɪkˈskleɪm/

faintly *adv* /ˈfeɪntli/

falter *v* /ˈfɔːltə(r)/

flustered *adj* /ˈflʌstəd/

forceful *adj* /ˈfɔːsfl/

fortnight *n* /ˈfɔːtnaɪt/

frown *n, v* /fraʊn/

funeral *n* /ˈfjuːnərəl/

gamble *v* /ˈgæmbl/

gesture *n* /ˈdʒestʃə(r)/

get engaged *v* /ˌget ɪnˈgeɪdʒd/

give sb the sack *v* /ˌgɪv ... ðə ˈsæk/

godmother *n* /ˈgɒdmʌðə(r)/

grave *n* /greɪv/

greet *v* /griːt/

grief *n* /griːf/

hearing aid *n* /ˈhɪərɪŋ ˌeɪd/

honeymoon *n* /ˈhʌnimuːn/

humble *adj* /ˈhʌmbl/

indebted *adj* /ɪnˈdetɪd/

juicy *adj* /ˈdʒuːsi/

marriage guidance counsellor *n* /ˌmærɪdʒ ˈgaɪdəns ˌkaʊnsələ(r)/

maternity leave *n* /məˈtɜːnəti ˌliːv/

medium (of size) *adj* /ˈmiːdiəm/

meek *adj* /miːk/

mercy *n* /ˈmɜːsi/

miss (e.g. when hitting sb) *v* /mɪs/

moan *n, v* /məʊn/

mourner *n* /ˈmɔːnə(r)/

muffled *adj* /ˈmʌfəld/

nappy *n* /ˈnæpi/

noon *n* /nuːn/

obey *v* /əˈbeɪ/

objection *n* /əbˈdʒekʃn/

offer *n, v* /ˈɒfə(r)/

order sb to do sth *v* /ˈɔːdə(r) ... tə ˈduː .../

overhead *adv* /ˌəʊvəˈhed/

parlour *n* /ˈpɑːlə(r)/

posthumous *adj* /ˈpɒstʃʊməs/

pram *n* /præm/

pregnant *adj* /ˈpregnənt/

presentiment *n* /prɪˈzentɪmənt/

reception *n* /rɪˈsepʃn/

refuse *v* /rɪˈfjuːz/

ring (on your finger) *n* /rɪŋ/

scarf *n* /skɑːf/

scribble *v* /ˈskrɪbl/

selfish *adj* /ˈselfɪʃ/

severe *adj* /sɪˈvɪə(r)/

severity *n* /sɪˈverəti/

sob *v* /sɒb/

solicitor *n* /səˈlɪsɪtə(r)/

spring (i.e. the season) *n* /sprɪŋ/

sweep up *v* /ˌswiːp ˈʌp/

switchboard *n* /ˈswɪtʃbɔːd/

sympathy *n* /ˈsɪmpəθi/

tentatively *adv* /ˈtentətɪvli/

timid *adj* /ˈtɪmɪd/

tremble *n, v* /ˈtrembl/

unpack *v* /ʌnˈpæk/

vanish *v* /ˈvænɪʃ/

wedding *n* /ˈwedɪŋ/

widow *n* /ˈwɪdəʊ/

wreath *n* /riːθ/

© Oxford University Press Photocopiable

Index

An index of grammatical items and functional areas

(SB 1 = Student's Book Unit 1; WB 3 = Workbook Unit 3; p 2 = page 2)